"Ron Pernick and Clint Wilder's *Clean Tech Nation* dares to imagine a country in which bipartisanship reigns, green energy is our nation's greatest national resource, and our competitive edge in the global economy is restored. With their Seven-Point Action Plan for Repowering America, Pernick and Wilder show us *how*—now it's up to all Americans, across every sector, to follow through."
—**President Bill Clinton**

"While clean technology is not a panacea for all of the economic, energy, and environmental challenges that civilization faces in the early years of the new millennium, it comes close. *Clean Tech Nation* deftly illustrates how well placed and naturally advantaged the United States is in this race among nations, and offers a coherent and realistic seven-point action plan designed to secure that lasting advantage for the benefit of the American people."
—**David Crane,** president and CEO, NRG Energy

"Five years ago, Pernick and Wilder predicted a clean-energy revolution. Today that revolution is already under way—but without an aggressive energy strategy, America's leadership will falter. The action plan in this book is just what the country needs, and Pernick and Wilder are expert guides once again."
—**John Podesta**, chair and counselor, Center for American Progress

"*Clean Tech Nation* makes a compelling case not only for why the U.S. needs to focus on smart policies to drive clean-tech leadership, but how. The authors' action plan can help unleash America's innovative energy and ensure that we don't cede this trillion-dollar opportunity to other nations."
—**Rick Needham,** director, Energy and Sustainability, Google

"This book conveys an insightful insider's view of renewable energy and clean-tech markets, industry, finance, and policy in a way that will leave the reader with a deeper understanding of how this revolution happened and where it must go next."
—**Michael T. Eckhart,** managing director and global head of Environmental Finance, Citi Corporate and Investment Banking

"If the United States wants to maintain its status as the world's leading economy, it must put a stake in the ground for the clean-energy/clean-tech sector. In *Clean Tech Nation*, Ron Pernick and Clint Wilder describe both why and how the U.S. can seize this opportunity to lead, and in the process create jobs, produce more domestic clean energy, and be an innovation engine."
—**Bill Ritter,** director, Center for the New Energy Economy, and former governor of Colorado

"Too many are giving up on the U.S.'s critical role in building a clean-tech future. Against this backdrop, *Clean Tech Nation* makes an effective case for U.S. leadership and a path to get there."
—**Mark L. Vachon,** vice president, GE Ecomagination

"Ron Pernick and Clint Wilder have created a compelling vision for a Clean Tech Nation and a road map for creating it, even as they surprise and delight readers with a rich account of progress already achieved. I salute their unique combination of technical savvy, practical sense, and imperishable enthusiasm."
—**Ralph Cavanagh,** energy program co-director, Natural Resources Defense Council

"Clean tech is growing up. In *Clean Tech Nation*, Pernick and Wilder take an important look at the industry's challenging adolescent years and what it will take, in terms of both public and private action, to reach a successful adulthood—financially and societally."
—**Dan Reicher,** executive director, Steyer-Taylor Center for Energy Policy and Finance, Stanford University; former U.S. assistant secretary of Energy

"Pernick and Wilder present both practical and thought-provoking ideas for financing the clean-tech sector. Their book offers a compelling call to action, for investors, policymakers, and others, to fuel America's energy and economic future."
—**Puon Penn,** senior vice president and head of Global CleanTech Markets, Wells Fargo

CLEAN TECH
NATION

Also by Ron Pernick and Clint Wilder

THE CLEAN TECH REVOLUTION

CLEAN TECH
NATION

HOW THE U.S. CAN LEAD IN
THE NEW GLOBAL ECONOMY

RON PERNICK and **CLINT WILDER**
with *Trevor Winnie*

HARPER
BUSINESS

An Imprint of HarperCollins*Publishers*
www.harpercollins.com

CLEAN TECH NATION. Copyright © 2012 by Ron Pernick and Clint Wilder. All rights reserved. Printed in the United States of America. No part of this book may be used or reproduced in any manner whatsoever without written permission except in the case of brief quotations embodied in critical articles and reviews. For information, address HarperCollins Publishers, 10 East 53rd Street, New York, NY 10022.

HarperCollins books may be purchased for educational, business, or sales promotional use. For information, please write: Special Markets Department, HarperCollins Publishers, 10 East 53rd Street, New York, NY 10022.

FIRST EDITION

Library of Congress Cataloging-in-Publication Data has been applied for.

ISBN: 978-0-06-208844-4

12 13 14 15 16   OV/RRD   10 9 8 7 6 5 4 3 2 1

To our wives, Dena and Ellie, and to Jonah and Sanaa, whose wonderment, curiosity, and future are what this book is all about.

CONTENTS

INTRODUCTION
The Birth of Clean Tech   1

1   **THE GLOBAL LANDSCAPE**
    Current and Emerging Clean-Tech
    Leaders and the Competitive Threat   23

2   **VYING FOR LEADERSHIP**
    The Top Ten Clean-Tech States   53

3   **CENTERS OF INNOVATION**
    The Top 15 U.S. Cities for Clean Tech   111

4   **THE BIGGEST CLEAN-TECH DEVELOPMENTS
    RESHAPING THE WORLD**   147

5   **THE CLEAN-TECH IMPERATIVE**   201

6   **A SEVEN-POINT ACTION PLAN FOR
    REPOWERING AMERICA**   235

    Appendix: State Policy Checklist   275

    Acknowledgments   277

    Notes   281

    Index   287

CLEAN TECH
NATION

Introduction

THE BIRTH OF CLEAN TECH

Just west of Northern California's windswept Altamont Pass, where some of America's first clean-energy entrepreneurs installed wind turbines three decades ago, the seeds of a new energy revolution are taking root. Here in the Bay Area suburb of Livermore, at the sleek Silicon Valley–style headquarters of Bridgelux, engineers in sterile "bunny suits" are fabricating wafers that house the tiny components for light-emitting diode (LED) lighting technology, the world's most energy-efficient form of illumination. Bridgelux's proprietary process, known as metal-organic chemical vapor deposition (MOCVD), is accomplished by intricate state-of-the-art machines costing as much as $2.5 million each—and by the well-trained, highly skilled workers who run them.

LEDs, the next wave in mass-market energy-efficient lighting, use up to 90 percent less electricity and last 25 times longer than comparable incandescent bulbs. The Bridgelux facility in Livermore opened in 2009 and was the first new LED complete-fabrication facility opened in the United States in more than two decades. "There are 71 new LED factories in China, and none of them have the technology to do this yet," says Steve Lester, the company's chief technology officer and vice president of R&D, referring to the MOCVD process. "I don't want to move to China. I've been in the LED business for 24 years, and I'm really passionate about this. If we can find a way to keep making LEDs in the U.S., we will."

Bridgelux, a venture-capital-backed startup headed by top Silicon Valley executive Bill Watkins, is well-funded ($220 million raised by March 2012) and growing. In an industry sector that has 95 percent of its products made in Asia and Europe, Bridgelux employs 250 people in Livermore, and 140 of them are in highly skilled engineering and R&D jobs. The company has big plans for expansion and good prospects for market acceptance. But even if the company succeeds, will Bridgelux be part of a much broader trend that revitalizes the U.S. economy in the face of unprecedented world competition? Or will it just be a unique, feel-good story in a gloomier context of diminished American leadership in global business, innovation, and economic growth?

The answer to that question will depend heavily on critical decisions that the nation's policymakers, business leaders, and investors make in the next three to five years. We strongly believe that the U.S. has the brainpower, the business acumen, and the educational, financial, and natural resources to be the leading nation, with the most innovative and successful companies, in this new and emerging revolution. But we believe just as strongly that this will not occur if we continue on our present course. That is why we wrote this book.

CLEAN TECH AT THE FOREFRONT

As we forge ahead in the second decade of the 21st century, the U.S. economy is at a crossroads. It faces a frustratingly slow economic recovery from a devastating recession, record debt levels, high unemployment, a declining manufacturing base, rising income inequality, and a host of other challenges. At the same time, a dynamic, fast-growing, and potentially disruptive new industry, clean tech, has moved to the forefront as a central component of economic competitiveness among companies, cities, states, regions, and nations.

This did not happen overnight. Solar photovoltaic (PV) module technology, for example, is more than 50 years old—it was invented at AT&T's legendary Bell Labs in 1954, with an eye toward powering spacecraft with the sun. The first large-scale wind turbine in the U.S. debuted in 1941. But for several decades, solar power, wind energy, and other current clean-tech mainstays languished far from the mainstream, the province of research scientists and off-the-grid, back-to-the-land devotees of "alternative" lifestyles.

Over the past ten years, however, clean tech—any product, service, or process that harnesses renewable materials and energy sources, reduces the use of nonrenewable natural resources, and cuts or eliminates emissions and wastes—has unquestionably claimed its place as a large-scale global industry. Clean tech encompasses a wide range of technologies in the energy, transportation, materials, and water sectors, including solar and wind power, hybrid vehicles, green buildings, high-efficiency lighting, and water-filtration membranes. It is now embraced by many of the world's largest corporations and most influential investors, and by virtually all national governments in the industrialized world. Like the innovation-fueled technology revolutions that came before it in the late 20th century—computing, high-speed telecommunications, and the Internet—all led, it should be noted, by the U.S.—clean tech has enjoyed a very rapid growth trajectory as a global industry. From 2000 to 2010, the combined global market for solar PV and wind power grew more than twentyfold, from $6.5 billion to $131.6 billion. Add to that the $56.4 billion global biofuels industry and the "Big Three" clean-tech sectors accounted for $188.1 billion in 2010—larger than the market for all retail online sales in the U.S.—and are projected to grow to nearly $350 billion by 2020.

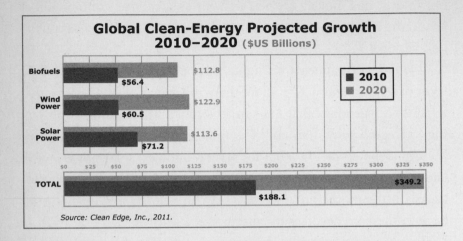

Source: Clean Edge, Inc., 2011.

Clean-tech-related products and services have become a major component of business strategy, investment, and revenue for many of the world's largest industrial giants, among them General Electric, Siemens, ABB, and Samsung. The biggest names in high tech, notably IBM, Google, Intel, and Microsoft, have embraced smart-grid technologies and other aspects of clean tech as a major new business opportunity.

In the arena of entrepreneurs and venture capital, clean tech has grown in the past decade from a tiny sliver of VC investments in the U.S. to nearly a quarter of total VC dollars in 2010, according to annual tracking by the Cleantech Group research firm. That puts clean tech right up there among traditional VC-attracting sectors such as software, telecommunications, biotech, medical devices, and Internet technology.

Clean-Tech Venture Capital Investments in U.S.-Based Companies as Percent of Total 2001–2010

Year	Total Venture Investments ($Millions)	Clean-Tech Venture Investments ($Millions)	Clean-Tech Percentage of Venture Total
2001	$37,624	$458	1.2%
2002	$20,737	$651	3.1%
2003	$18,789	$807	4.3%
2004	$21,699	$760	3.5%
2005	$22,535	$1,158	5.1%
2006	$26,010	$2,685	10.3%
2007	$29,901	$3,761	12.6%
2008	$28,105	$6,120	21.8%
2009	$18,276	$3,553	19.4%
2010	$21,823	$5,055	23.2%

Source: Cleantech Group, 2011, with Clean Edge analysis. Clean-tech venture investment includes seed funding and follow-on rounds prior to private equity activity related to stake acquisitions or buyouts. Investment categories include agriculture, air & environment, energy efficiency, energy generation, energy infrastructure, energy storage, materials, manufacturing/industrial, recycling & waste, transportation, and water & wastewater.

DEEPLY IN THE MAINSTREAM

In terms of deployment, clean tech has become a key, growing, and increasingly mainstream component of energy supply and daily life in many places around the world. Consider the following:

- The states of Iowa, North Dakota, and California each generate more than 10 percent of their electricity supply from wind, solar, and/or geothermal power.

- U.S. renewable energy reached a major milestone in the first quarter of 2011, surpassing energy production from nuclear power. Renewable energy sources (biomass/biofuels, geothermal, solar, hydroelectric, wind) provided 2.245 quadrillion BTUs of energy, or 11.73 percent of total U.S. energy production, in the first quarter of 2011, beating out nuclear power's 2.125 quadrillion BTUs. While nuclear power's contribution has remained relatively unchanged in recent years, the contribution of renewable energy has shown steady double-digit annual growth.

- In Denmark, Portugal, and Spain, wind power contributes more than 15 percent of the electricity supply nationwide. During March of 2011, wind became Spain's leading source of electricity for the first time—covering 21 percent of the country's demand for the month and beating out other sources like nuclear (19 percent) and hydroelectric (17 percent).

- Just a few years ago, residential solar power installation in the U.S. was a highly fragmented, mom-and-pop service. Now, Americans in many states can get solar price quotes and sign up for installation on a Saturday afternoon visit to Home Depot or Lowe's; both home improvement giants are partners with nationwide solar installer/lessor companies like SolarCity, Sungevity, and SunRun. Speaking of mainstream, there are even solar panels on the Infineon Raceway NASCAR track, in Sonoma, California, supplying 41 percent of the speedway's electricity needs.

- In 2000, fewer than 10,000 hybrid electric vehicles were being driven on U.S. roads, and only two models, the Honda Insight and the original Toyota Prius, were available worldwide. In 2010, more than 1.4 million U.S. motorists drove hybrids, and 30 models, from carmakers in Asia, the U.S., and Europe, were on the world auto market. Ford, the number-two automaker in the U.S., has predicted that by 2020, one of every four cars it sells will have electric power, either as a hybrid or as a 100 percent electric vehicle (EV).

- Only three commercial buildings in the world in 2000 were certified as green with the LEED (Leadership in Energy and Environmental Design) designation from the U.S. Green Building Council. By the end of 2010, more than 8,100 commercial structures had been LEED certified globally.

- In the five years from 2006 through 2010, Walmart and Sam's Club stores sold more than 460 million energy-saving compact fluorescent (CFL) lightbulbs. CFLs and LEDs together accounted for more than 20 percent of lightbulb sales worldwide in 2010.

THE COMPETITIVE IMPERATIVE

Every day, new examples highlight the growing mainstreaming of clean tech. But clean tech's business growth and increasing ubiquity are only part of the story. As we will outline in this book, clean tech has become the most critical industry of the 21st century—an essential component to global economic success for all developed countries, and increasingly for developing nations as well.

To some, that may seem like a bold statement. And let's be honest: In terms of current annual revenue, even the giants of clean tech pale in comparison with oil behemoths like ExxonMobil, Shell, BP, Chevron, and ConocoPhillips. But consider that in the first half of this century, the move to cleaner, more efficient, less carbon-intensive energy will hugely impact, if not completely transform, many of the largest industries on earth, including electric power utilities, suppliers of transportation fuel, residential and commercial construction companies, and automotive and aerospace manufacturers. This transformation is well under way from Shanghai to Stuttgart, from San Francisco to Seoul.

"The low-carbon economy will absolutely survive the recession," John Fernandez, the U.S. assistant secretary of commerce for economic development, told a nationwide convention of economic development officials in June 2011. "China, Germany, Brazil, and other countries are making new bets on technology that will be critical to manufacturing and moving all industries forward. There is only one path forward for the U.S.—to invest in clean technologies and energy efficiency to drive global economies."

Fernandez has plenty of company. An increasingly loud chorus of influential voices—among them German chancellor Angela Merkel, GE chairman and CEO Jeffrey Immelt, and renowned Harvard Business School professor Michael Porter—have begun pointing to clean tech as the key driver of technology innovation, high-skills job creation, and global economic competitiveness in the years and decades ahead.

PROGRESS REPORT: THE SIX C'S

In our 2007 book *The Clean Tech Revolution*, we identified six global forces driving the rapid growth of clean energy, transportation, and related technologies around the world: Costs, Capital, Competition, China, Consumers, and Climate. All are still critical factors, but five years later, in the context of a dynamic and rapidly changing industry, we've made some modifications. With China having emerged as the key competitor to watch in the global clean-tech industry, we've combined China and Competition into one "C" and added a new one— Connectivity—reflecting the strong influence of today's high-speed, ubiquitous communications technology and culture on the growth of clean tech.

Here's a small snapshot of what's happened in the realm of each of the Six C's since the publication of *The Clean Tech Revolution*:

Costs. The basic premise here—that the costs of clean technologies will fall over time, as they do in the high-tech industry—has absolutely been borne out in recent years. Solar PV prices have been the most striking example. The cost of solar power worldwide (including both traditional crystalline silicon and newer thin-film technologies), which ranged from 25 to 41 cents per kilowatt-hour in 2007, dropped to between 17 and 28 cents per kilowatt-hour by 2010. This continued the dramatic ten-year cost decline of solar energy. In terms of installation cost, the price per peak watt of power generated fell by nearly half in ten years, from an average of $9 in 2000 to $4.82 in 2010. By 2011, global installed pricing for solar PV systems dropped even further, to around $3.50. As in so many other industries, large-scale low-cost manufacturing in China and other Asian nations, combined with technology breakthroughs in the West and elsewhere, is accelerating this trend.

PV INSTALLED COST AND COST PER KWH: 2007–2020				
	C-SI		THIN FILM	
Year	Global Average Installed Cost ($/W)	LCOE (cents/kWh)	Global Average Installed Cost ($/W)	LCOE (cents/kWh)
2007	$7.20	33 – 41	$5.50	25 – 32
2008	$7.00	32 – 40	$5.10	25 – 30
2009	$5.35	25 – 31	$4.00	19 – 24
2010	$4.82	22 – 28	$3.60	17 – 21
2011e	$4.24	20 – 25	$3.19	15 – 19
2012e	$3.64	17 – 21	$2.92	14 – 18
2013e	$3.28	15 – 20	$2.68	13 – 16
2014e	$2.95	14 – 18	$2.47	12 – 15
2015e	$2.69	13 – 16	$2.27	11 – 14
2016e	$2.44	12 – 15	$2.09	10 – 13
2017e	$2.22	11 – 14	$1.92	9 – 12
2018e	$2.02	10 – 13	$1.77	9 – 11
2019e	$1.84	9 – 12	$1.63	8 – 10
2020e	$1.68	8 – 11	$1.50	8 – 10

Source: Clean Edge, Inc., 2011.

The director of GE's global research unit and the former head of its Power Systems group, Mark Little, predicted in a May 2011 interview with Bloomberg that solar may be cost-competitive with fossil fuel– and nuclear-generated power in three to five years. By 2020, Clean Edge, our clean-tech research and advisory firm, projects that solar prices will drop even more, making the cost of solar power about the same as or even lower than projected residential electric rates in more than 20 U.S. states. Innovative financing models, such as the no-money-down solar lease from SolarCity and other nationwide solar installers, have also helped make solar energy much more affordable for consumers and businesses.

Wind power is already considered the cheapest source of new generation in some regions of the U.S., averaging roughly 5 to 8 cents per kilowatt-hour nationwide in 2010, according to Clean Edge. All-electric vehicles, once prohibitively expensive (like the Tesla Motors Roadster, which debuted in 2007 with a sticker price of about $100,000), where available, are seeing the positive effect of increased competition. The Mitsubishi i, on the U.S. market in early 2012, listed for $27,990—more than $5,000 below the Nissan LEAF and just $20,240 after a buyer's federal tax credit. Falling prices are clearly key to the rapid adoption of all clean technologies, and we see every sign that these trends will continue.

"It's just like every other technology industry," says Alan Salzman, CEO and managing director of VantagePoint Capital Partners, a leading clean-tech VC firm in San Bruno, California, whose portfolio includes Bridgelux, Tesla, and utility-scale solar plant developer BrightSource Energy. "First you do it, and it's very expensive; the technology and the manufacturing economies of scale aren't idealized at all. Then the market develops, competitors come in, and prices fall. Three years after the Tesla, we had the Nissan LEAF at less than $35,000. Three years from now, we'll probably have Taiwanese all-electric cars on the market at fifteen grand."

The next force at play here is **Capital**. The growth in venture capital, as noted above, and other investment in clean tech have rebounded well since the 2008–09 global financial crisis. In 2011 alone, corporate and government global investment in and financing of clean energy was a record $260 billion—a nearly 40 percent increase from 2009, according to Bloomberg New Energy Finance (BNEF), a London- and New York–based financial research firm. Perhaps even more striking, the 2011 figure represents a fivefold increase in just seven years, from $52 billion in 2004.

But the biggest story of clean-tech capital in the past five years has been unprecedented levels of investment by national governments around the world. The U.S. played its part, with a roughly $90 billion injection in federal stimulus dollars (cash grants, loan guarantees, and other financing mechanisms) directed to domestic clean-energy companies and projects from 2009 through 2011.

As we will analyze in greater detail in the next chapter, however, the U.S. is just one part of a massive global influx of public money into the sector, including both stimulus and other programs. These include China (with up to $660 billion in government spending on clean energy in the next ten years), South Korea ($4 billion in 2011 alone, in a much smaller economy), Germany ($41.2 billion in 2010), and many other nations that have made clean tech a centerpiece of their present and future economic plans. This influx of private and public money is driving clean-energy growth around the world and rewriting the competitive rules of the global economy—the phenomenon that inspired us to write this book.

The third force is **Competition**. In the spring of 2006, we attended the first-ever Renewable Energy Finance Forum–China conference in Beijing. At the time, Chinese officials were just beginning to discuss their ambitious plans for clean-tech growth. In just six years, the nation's rise to the top of the industry has rendered moot our earlier distinction of China and Competition as separate global forces moving clean tech ahead. China is the world's number-one manufacturer of solar PV cells, the number-one market for wind power, and the largest producer and user of lithium-ion batteries (used in EVs and other clean-tech products), and it is at or close to the top in many other sectors. Although a wide range of nations in Europe, Asia, and North and South America have emerged as formidable competitors in different clean-tech sectors, China is quite clearly at the top of everyone's list.

As we will detail throughout the book, Competition refers not only to the battle for economic success among nations but to that among companies as well. In the U.S. clean-tech industry, China is on the minds of entrepreneurs, corporate executives, and financiers on a daily basis. And China's competitive challenge goes far beyond its attractive labor costs and strong government incentives for companies to locate there. It has become a fast-growing center of clean-tech R&D activity and innovation breakthroughs as well. In posing the all-important question of who will own the key technologies of the future, this last point may be the most critical factor in China's competitive favor.

It's not just China that's playing a central competitive role. As we'll explore in chapter 1, "The Global Landscape," a range of nations spanning four continents are all making clean tech a key focus of their global economic competitiveness. Competition also continues to drive clean-tech growth among regions, states, and cities. That is the focus of chapters 2 and 3, on the leading U.S. clean-tech states and cities, respectively.

As we noted in *The Clean Tech Revolution*, Competition also includes the increasingly critical factor of energy security. Given the interconnected global industry of oil in particular, the oft-cited target of true "energy independence" may be unrealistic for any country, and certainly for the U.S., in the foreseeable future. But the goal of reducing dependence on energy supplies that come from less-than-friendly nations such as Iran, Libya, and Venezuela is certainly attainable, and it's a goal that the U.S., Germany, and dozens of other energy-hungry countries share.

Equally important in the U.S., the concept of energy security as a competitive driver of clean tech enjoys support among legislators and citizens of all political stripes. As we'll discuss in the climate section below, not all drivers of clean tech can make that claim. To attain the bipartisan support that will be necessary for making the policy changes that can turn the U.S. into a global clean-tech leader, the framing of clean energy as a matter of national security needs to be at the forefront of any conversation.

Next is **Consumers**. In the past five years, a wide range of clean-tech products and services have caught on with a broad swath of consumers worldwide. CFL bulbs (and, increasingly, LED lights) and other energy-efficient products populate the aisles and shelves of mainstream retailers like Walmart, Lowe's, and Home Depot. In January 2011, IKEA stopped selling incandescent bulbs at all of its stores in the U.S. and Canada. Viewers of San Francisco Giants baseball telecasts in Northern California see regular ads for local solar PV installer the Solar Company, with popular team broadcaster Duane Kuiper as the featured customer. And in a nice twist of irony, actor Larry Hagman, who portrayed one of America's most iconic (albeit fictional) oil barons, J. R. Ewing of the classic TV series *Dallas*, is now the official spokesman in the U.S. for German solar PV manufacturer SolarWorld.

Hagman lives in a fully solar-powered home in Southern California, but clean tech's consumer reach in the U.S. extends far beyond the traditional environmentally minded, early-adoption markets of the Pacific Coast and the Northeast. Arizona and North Dakota, for example, ranked in the top five states for most four-wheel passenger EVs registered per capita in 2010, and Virginia ranked number five in hybrids per capita. South Carolina, one of the nation's most politically conservative states, ranked number four in public EV-charging stations per capita as of March 2011. Texas, New Mexico, Wisconsin, and Utah are among the top ten states for the highest percentage of utility customers who choose to pay a small optional rate premium for a greener mix of electricity.

In the 21st century, however, the U.S. consumer market represents literally a tiny fraction of the overall picture. International commerce experts know, but many people are shocked to learn, that at least 95 percent of the world's consumers live outside the U.S. Not surprisingly, the meteoric rise of China's middle class leads the way. Credit Suisse predicts that China's consumer market will reach $16 trillion by 2020, surpassing the U.S. as the world's largest—with a projected 700 percent growth in per capita income from 2000 levels. To a somewhat less dramatic extent, this same expanding-consumer-class trend is playing out across India, Brazil, Indonesia, Vietnam, and many other rapidly developing nations. This global phenomenon, the so-called Base of the Pyramid market opportunity, has profound implications for the growth of the global clean-tech industry.

Over the next decade, these trends mean millions of new buyers of middle-class goods such as vehicles, homes, and appliances. In order to prevent massive increases in greenhouse-gas (GHG) emissions and other detrimental environmental impacts from this increased economic activity, those products will need to use significantly less energy than their historical predecessors in North America and Western Europe. Although this is admittedly a huge challenge, the market opportunity for global providers of energy-efficient products is enormous.

In the clean-transportation sector, for example, a Boston Consulting Group (BCG) study in July 2011 predicted that China will be the world's largest market for EVs by 2020, surpassing Europe and the U.S. The study found that about 13 percent of consumers in China say they are willing to pay a premium of $4,500 to $6,000 for a green vehicle (EV or hybrid), compared with 9 percent of Europeans and just 6 percent of U.S. car buyers. BCG projects sales of five million EVs in China in 2020, up from just 2,000 in 2010. In India, pioneering EV manufacturer Mahindra Reva has opened more than 20 sales outlets for its small two-door, four-seat EV, considered the world's lowest-priced electric car, at $12,000. So while the U.S. consumer market remains critically important, clean-tech providers in the U.S. and elsewhere have great growth potential to tap the millions of current and new middle-class buyers living outside America's borders.

Next we have **Climate**. Although we believe that the evidence of increasing global climate change due to human activity is irrefutable, the political dynamics around the issue have changed dramatically since the publication of *The Clean Tech Revolution* in 2007. The earth's climate may be warming, but the political climate for a global agreement on reducing CO_2 emissions has definitely chilled. The list of setbacks includes the so-called Climategate controversy of 2009; very mixed results from carbon cap-and-trade systems in the European Union and elsewhere; the failure to reach meaningful global agreements at the United Nations international climate talks in Copenhagen in 2009, Cancún in 2010, and Durban in 2011; and, above all, the failure of the U.S. Congress to pass comprehensive climate legislation.

Quite frankly, we had an internal debate about whether Climate is still a significant driver of the global clean-tech industry in 2012. After considerable discussion, we concluded that the answer is yes—particularly outside the U.S. and in the private sector. The Kyoto Protocol, despite the absence of the top two greenhouse-gas-emitting nations (China and the U.S.) as signatories and Canada's withdrawal from the pact in late 2011, still requires nearly 40 of the world's largest industrial nations around the world to reduce their carbon emissions by the end of 2012.

Perhaps more important, the vast majority of the world's largest corporations, for a variety of reasons, care about carbon. In 2010, 409 of the S&P Global 500—and more than 3,000 companies overall—responded to the annual CO_2 emissions tracking survey of the Carbon Disclosure Project (CDP), a British nonprofit advised by PricewaterhouseCoopers. More than 550 institutional investors worldwide, managing more than $70 trillion in assets, use the CDP's data to help shape their investment decisions. And the fastest-growing area of CDP tracking is the GHG impact of corporate supply chains. Led by the pioneering work of Walmart and others in mandating sustainability initiatives among suppliers, the number of Global 500 companies reporting on their supply chains' carbon footprints doubled in just two years, to nearly 50 percent in 2010.

Those efforts drive the clean-tech industry forward in a myriad of ways, from McGraw-Hill's 14.1-megawatt solar power plant—the largest privately owned solar array in the Western Hemisphere—at its East Windsor, New Jersey, campus, to GE's plans to purchase 25,000 EVs for corporate fleet use by 2015. Despite political rhetoric and U.S. federal legislative inaction to the contrary, corporate efforts to reduce carbon emissions around the world are alive and well.

In terms of framing the political discussion, we find the debate moving beyond climate change per se to a much broader environmental impetus that embraces clean air, clean water, public health, and, of course, the main focus of this book: economic competitiveness and prosperity. If the moral imperative of "we must fight global warming" has become a political nonstarter, so be it. "Believe in climate change. Or don't. It doesn't matter," wrote renowned corporate sustainability consultant L. Hunter Lovins in her recent book with Boyd Cohen, *Climate Capitalism: Capitalism in the Age of Climate Change.* "But you'd better understand this: the best route to rebuilding our economy, our cities, and our job markets, as well as assuring national security, is doing precisely what you would do if you were scared to death about climate change."

We will delve more deeply into the political realities facing U.S.

federal, state, and local policymakers in chapter 5. But suffice it to say that the reduction of carbon emissions, whether by companies or countries, brings a huge range of desirable results that people across the political spectrum—and countries across the industrialized-nation/developing-nation divide at international climate talks—can agree on. Cleaner air for your children to breathe, cleaner water for your grandchildren to drink, a national energy supply that relies less on imports and creates more jobs at home—not even extremist politicians would argue against those benefits.

The final factor is **Connectivity**. History has seen many energy revolutions over the centuries, with the world moving from wood (and, for a time, whale oil) to coal, oil, natural gas, hydroelectric, and nuclear power as primary energy sources. But clean tech, which did not begin to coalesce as a high-profile global industry until the early 2000s, is the first energy revolution—and one of the first major nondigital industries—to grow up in the Internet era. Having seen this play out since the publication of our last book five years ago, we decided to add Connectivity (and the collaboration that it enables) as our sixth "C" driving clean-energy growth.

Some of the impacts of Connectivity on clean tech are obvious. The entire concept of the smart grid, for example, relies on high-speed and often wireless networks of information sharing to maximize efficiencies in the generation, distribution, and usage of electricity. Small wonder that so many giants of the high-tech and Internet industries, such as Cisco, Google, and IBM, are major players in smart grid (and have so many ex-employees starting and/or running smart-grid startups like Comverge, Silver Spring Networks, and Tendril). It's not unlike the large degree of cross-pollination between the semiconductor-chip and solar PV industries witnessed over the past decade.

But Connectivity as a driver of clean tech encompasses much more than just technologies and skill sets common to both industries. The capability of instantaneous collaboration across the globe—whether by a Chicago-to-Guangzhou conference call on Skype, a new global market niche created by a Facebook page, or a computer-aided design updated simultaneously on four continents—is helping clean tech to grow on a daily basis. Clean-energy entrepreneurs out of MIT and Stanford are starting U.S.-based companies whose first customers are in India or Israel. Other startups like RelayRides (whose investors include Google Ventures) and Getaround essentially use Internet connectivity as their business model, connecting car owners and renters through a web page or iPhone/iPad app.

Collaborating with partners outside a company or organization is nothing new, of course, but many key players in clean tech are using today's high-speed-connectivity tools to bring inter-organizational collaboration to unprecedented new levels. Through the Open Architecture Network, created by San Francisco–based nonprofit Architecture for Humanity (AFH), more than 30,000 designers worldwide use tools like Autodesk's Freewheel to share 2-D and 3-D designs and ideas for low-cost, durable, energy-efficient homes and buildings in developing nations and disaster recovery areas. Launched in 2007 and renamed Worldchanging in 2011 after an AFH acquisition, the network had 6,500 projects in the design phase and more than 80 projects completed as of June 2011. "The Internet has created an incredible democratization of the architecture industry," AFH cofounder and CEO Cameron Sinclair said in a March 2011 interview with *The Atlantic*. "The realm of the pre-determined geniuses of the profession is no longer dictated by the number of inches in a broadsheet, an appearance on Charlie Rose, or the weight of a coffee table book. The Web has allowed us to act locally and act globally simultaneously."

But the most dramatic example of online, outside-the-company collaboration—true "crowdsourcing"—comes from GE's Ecomagination clean-tech initiative. Launched in July 2010, GE's $200 million Open Innovation Challenge invited companies, individuals—anyone—to submit ideas for business ventures in smart-grid technologies. Working with four leading clean-tech venture capital firms, GE has funded the best ideas and, in some cases, acquired the company outright, as it did with Ireland-based power-line-monitoring company FMC-Tech in May 2011. More than 90,000 people have participated in the Open Innovation Challenge—the largest corporate crowdsourcing effort in history. So far.

This trend will only accelerate. As members of the connected generation (so-called Generation Z) grow up, never knowing a world without instant global connectivity in the palm of their hand, online collaboration among companies, customers, partners, and even competitors will become the natural order of 21st-century business. Young people are generally much more comfortable sharing data, whether it's time-of-day electricity usage with their utility or ride-sharing plans with strangers—leading to greater efficiency, energy savings, and scores of clean-tech business ideas that no one has thought of yet.

The digital age of Connectivity will cause the transition to clean energy to occur much faster than the multiple decades or even centuries required by previous energy revolutions. It's a good thing, too, because due to resource constraints, climate concerns, population growth, and a range of other global challenges, the world can't wait that long. And in global competition, the need for speed by industries that traditionally have moved very slowly—notably energy, utilities, and automotive—has never been greater.

Not that these and other large global industries, with their massive physical infrastructures, regulatory constraints, and often well-entrenched business processes, will ever move or change at cyberspeed. And the new world of Connectivity also brings new security challenges. More sophisticated online applications seem to bring ever more sophisticated cyber-attacks, such as the Stuxnet computer worm that infected computers at an Iranian nuclear power plant in 2010. Global energy transitions are not seamless; plenty of old and new obstacles stand in the way. But we still believe that Connectivity, along with the other five C's, will make the transition to clean energy occur faster than the energy revolutions of the past.

THE CHALLENGE AHEAD

As the 21st century moves through its second decade, these six powerful global forces will continue to accelerate clean-tech development, deployment, and growth around the world—and make clean tech the most vital competitive industry of our time. The U.S. can play a leading role in this industry—as it did in the earlier technology revolutions of computing, telecommunications, and the Internet—but currently, it is falling behind.

What can and should be done? In this book, we'll show that while the challenge is great, the U.S. can absolutely meet it. We also recognize that in today's interconnected global economy, competition among nations is not a zero-sum game. In many cases, collaborative approaches that create clean-tech jobs and grow businesses in both Ohio and China, say, are the best strategy to pursue. What we don't want to see is the U.S. falling behind a large contingent of other nations in the race to own the key technologies of this century and to, in President Obama's words, "win the future." Yet that is precisely what we see happening without the important policy and business-strategy corrections that we'll detail in the rest of this book.

First, in chapter 1, on the global landscape, we'll discuss the major developments and commitments to date that have made nations such as China, Germany, Japan, and Brazil formidable competitors and/or leaders in various aspects of clean tech. In the next two chapters we'll return to the U.S., showing why—so far—certain American states and cities have been where the clean-tech action is in our nation. Chapter 2 will spotlight the top ten U.S. states for clean-energy technology, policy, and capital, as ranked by Clean Edge's *State Clean Energy Leadership Index*, extracting the most important lessons for growing a clean-energy economy at the state level. Going beyond public policy, this chapter will also list the top five clean-tech companies to watch in each leading state.

Chapter 3 will present the top 15 U.S. cities for clean-tech jobs, from building-energy-efficiency specialists in New York City to solar-cell-manufacturing technicians in Portland, Oregon. This chapter draws on the latest research from Clean Edge and other globally recognized sources of data and analysis from this rapidly emerging jobs sector. As with the states, we'll examine the mix of assets in technology, policy, and both financial and human/intellectual capital that makes these cities leaders in clean-tech employment and economic growth.

In chapter 4 we'll return to a global view, identifying the four biggest clean-tech developments reshaping the world's power-grid, transportation, and energy systems. That will lay the groundwork for chapter 5, "The Clean Tech Imperative," where we take a hard look at the new rules of global economic competition in the 21st century—and drive home the case that the clean-tech industry is vital to our economic future. We'll also examine the political realities of Capitol Hill, K Street, and elsewhere that present formidable—but not insurmountable—hurdles to enacting key federal clean-energy policies. We'll take a look back at history to show how America has successfully met such transformational challenges in the past: with its manufacturing effort in World War II, the development of ARPANET (the precursor to today's Internet), and the Apollo space program. And we'll briefly profile 20 American leaders we call the Transformers: the top business, political, educational, and other luminaries—including many who have moved into clean tech from other fields—who are striving to make the U.S. clean-tech industry competitive with any in the world.

The book's concluding chapter is a Seven-Point Action Plan—covering both the public and private sectors—which presents a blueprint for U.S. leadership in the global clean-tech industry. Ambitious but realistic, the plan includes recommendations for government policy, business strategy, financial investment, education, and other areas to supercharge our efforts in clean energy, clean transportation, energy efficiency, smart grid, green building, and other critical clean-tech sectors.

Many experts and participants in the clean-tech industry are saying that the race for global supremacy is already over, with China sure to expand its overall lead, Germany to continue as the world's largest solar energy market, and a future certain to erode America's competitive standing in clean tech in the same way it has been damaged in other industries. We do not agree. We believe that the U.S. can leverage its unparalleled assets—among them great research universities, the world's best entrepreneurs, a culture of innovation, a robust network of venture capital, and strong patent-protection laws—to lead this dynamic, game-changing industry. We do not minimize the scope of that challenge. But with some new directions in policy, business, and above all, thinking, we are absolutely convinced that the U.S. of the 21st century can be the world's leading Clean Tech Nation.

1

THE GLOBAL LANDSCAPE

Current and Emerging Clean-Tech Leaders and the Competitive Threat

Jiangsu Province, in eastern China, is home to 63 million people and more than 600 solar PV and supply-chain-related companies, including the world's largest manufacturer of crystalline-silicon solar modules, Suntech Power. The province's self-proclaimed "solar cities" of Wuxi and Changzhou produce approximately 60 percent of China's solar PV output, according to the Jiangsu PV Industry Association. That's an impressive feat, considering that Chinese manufacturers produced about half of the world's total solar PV output in 2010. Not surprisingly, the air throughout much of the province is sullied and gray with the stench of industry excess, reflecting the Chinese dichotomy of clean-tech pursuits paired with unbridled growth. Jiangsu, admittedly, is not just a center for solar production but also home to a host of industries such as high-tech, chemical, and automobile manufacturing. But it's a clear message from China's master economic planners and its entrepreneurial leaders: We will lead the manufacturing of clean-tech industries at whatever cost.

Indeed, in less than a decade, China has gone from a clean-energy neophyte to the number-one global clean-tech force to be reckoned with. From LED streetlights on the teeming streets of Beijing and Shanghai to wind farms on the barren steppes of Inner Mongolia, clean tech is now one of the major cornerstones of China's aggressive economic development plans. "Chinese entrepreneurs are not just focused on saving the earth," says Suntech Power chief commercial officer Andrew Beebe. "They are driven, perhaps more than many of their Western counterparts, by the pure capitalist goal of making money."

And it's not only in manufacturing that China is flexing its entrepreneurial spirit. The nation is increasingly leading the world in the deployment of clean-energy technologies, and setting its sights on becoming a technology intellectual-property (IP) powerhouse as well. In 2010, the country installed more new wind turbines and solar water heaters than any other nation, and China is now home to an increasing number of public and private clean-tech-focused research labs and academic institutions. "There's a misconception that China is stealing technology and not innovating," adds Beebe, "but that's not an accurate view of modern China, where skilled engineering and an innovation mind-set is firmly taking hold."

The rapid rise of an entrepreneurially motivated China has many U.S. clean-tech participants on edge. In a survey of Clean Edge subscribers, we asked the question "Which three nations pose the greatest competitive threat to the U.S. in clean tech?" China led the responses by a significant margin, followed by Germany, India, Brazil, and Japan. On the flip side, many respondents also felt these same countries offered some of the best opportunities for international clean-tech collaboration. As in countless other industries, clean tech is increasingly blurring the lines between competition and cooperation in an interconnected global marketplace.

NODES AROUND THE WORLD

Clean technology is sprouting from dozens of nodes across the globe. As we highlighted in our first book, clean technology represents a broad set of industries and is a highly dispersed movement. For those seeking to gain a foothold in the clean-tech market, there's a silver lining in all this hypercompetition and activity: No single nation can, or will, lead in all clean-tech sectors.

At Clean Edge, we divide the overall clean-tech industry into four major buckets: clean energy, clean transportation, clean water, and advanced materials. This encompasses diverse industries ranging from solar PV and green building to all-electric vehicles and water filtration. In many ways, clean tech is more akin to biotech than high tech, in the sheer diversity of sectors covered. Whereas high tech focuses primarily on computers, handheld devices, and communication networks, biotech encompasses applications in pharmaceuticals, agriculture, manufacturing, energy, the environment, and many other areas. Similarly, clean tech covers a wide umbrella of sectors and activities, as highlighted in Clean Edge's sector breakdown below.

CLEAN-TECHNOLOGY TAXONOMY

CLEAN ENERGY

Renewable Energy
Biomass/Waste to Energy
Geothermal
Marine Power (Wave, Tidal, Ocean Thermal)
Small-Scale Hydropower
Solar PV (Thin-Film, Crystalline)
Solar Thermal (Hot Water Heating, CSP)
Wind

Smart Grid
Advanced Metering Infrastructure
Grid Monitoring and Controls
Smart Appliances
Smart Meters
Transmission and Distribution
Vehicle to Grid

Energy Efficiency
Building Automation
Combined Heat and Power
Demand Side Management
Efficient HVAC
Efficient Lighting (CFLs, LEDs, OLEDs, Ballasts and Controls)
Green Buildings

Energy Storage
Advanced Batteries
Capacitors
Compressed Air
Flywheels
Fuel Cells
Thermal Storage

Renewable Fuels
Algal-Based Fuels
Biobutanol
Biodiesel
Ethanol
Next-Generation Ethanol

CLEAN TRANSPORTATION

All-Electric Vehicles
EV Charging Infrastructure
Electric Rail
Energy Storage/Advanced Batteries
Emissions Controls
Fuel-Efficient Transport (Air, Land, Marine)
Hybrid-Electric Vehicles
Plug-In Hybrid Electric Vehicles

CLEAN WATER

Desalination
Filtration and Purification
Recovery and Capture
Smart Irrigation
Water Metering, Controls, and Management

ADVANCED MATERIALS

Bio-Based Materials and Products
Green Building Materials
Green Chemistry
Membranes
Natural Resources/Restoration
Recycling and Waste Management

Source: Clean Edge, Inc., 2012.

The clean-tech industry, perhaps because of the richness of the sectors covered, is also very diverse geographically. Japan, China, and the U.S. currently lead the world in the development and manufacturing of electric vehicles. The U.S. and Brazil lead, by a wide margin, in ethanol refining, representing more than 80 percent of the global market. China, Germany, Japan, and the U.S. lead in solar PV manufacturing, while Germany, Italy, the Czech Republic, Japan, and the U.S. lead in new grid-connected solar PV installations. In wind deployment, the front-runners include China, the U.S., Spain, India, and Germany. The lists go on and on.

This is welcome news for those competing in the clean-tech sector. Too often, hotheaded and misguided rhetoric leads to country bashing and fearmongering. People exclaim that one country will dominate and crush all others, often demonizing the perceived front-runner in the process. But it's important to remain levelheaded in this conversation. First of all, healthy competition, as long as the playing field is level (and that can be a big "if"), is important to the innovation-and-scaling process. Second, the economic, environmental, and energy-security challenges facing humanity are so great that we need to have as many individual, corporate, and governmental hands on deck as possible. As noted earlier, this isn't a zero-sum game we're talking about. In other words, both established and emerging economies need to be on board.

As New York–based clean-tech investor and former Generation Investment Management venture capitalist David Yeh points out, to meet today's challenges, "You have to focus on China and India. In the U.S. and Europe, you're working on the margins." This doesn't mean that the U.S. and Europe can't and won't play a central role in innovation, IP, manufacturing, development, and deployment, but you have to tackle the issue head-on in the world's rapidly emerging economies in order to make a real dent in addressing global energy and environmental issues. "In China, the urgency isn't values-based; it's a reality," adds Yeh. "You can't breathe the air in Beijing. [The Chinese] have impressive goals, but they are going to have to do a lot more."

THE THREE PILLARS OF BUSINESS
ACTIVITY AND JOB CREATION

To understand the most relevant clean-tech opportunities for a given nation or region, it's helpful to divide business opportunities into three major categories: manufacturing, technology deployment, and IP development. While some companies are able to capture all three of these opportunities, more often organizations need to focus on one or two of these areas and play to their core strengths. Companies that do compete in all three areas often acquire capabilities via mergers-and-acquisitions activity in a later stage of their development. When U.S.-based thin-film-solar powerhouse First Solar, which had both strong IP and manufacturing capabilities, wanted to get into the deployment/installation game, for example, the Tempe, Arizona–based company acquired solar-project pipelines from developers such as OptiSolar. Japan-based Sharp, a global leader and early pioneer in advanced solar PV manufacturing, similarly garnered development expertise with its 2010 acquisition of California-based Recurrent Energy. The same is happening in a host of other clean-tech sectors. Swiss electric power infrastructure giant ABB acquired software company Ventyx in 2010. Energy-efficiency-and-building-controls company Johnson Controls bought demand-response service provider EnergyConnect in 2011.

Here's a closer look at clean-tech business opportunities in—and regional strengths for—manufacturing, deployment, and IP development.

Centers of Commoditized Manufacturing. Manufacturing is scattered globally for many clean-tech sectors, with China, the U.S., Japan, Germany, Denmark, Spain, Taiwan, South Korea, India, and others playing a key role. Manufacturing depends on a skilled, well-trained, readily available workforce plus managerial and industrial infrastructure and know-how. Nations like China have been gaining increasing dominance in the clean-tech sector, with manufacturing of commoditized, undifferentiated products increasingly going to the lower-cost manufacturing centers of Asia.

Can't Outsource Deployment. Whereas commoditized manufacturing will continue to chase the lowest-cost markets globally, deployment is another matter entirely. Jobs installing solar PV systems, wind turbines, triple-paned windows, smart meters, and other clean-tech products and services simply cannot be outsourced overseas. These installation jobs, because they often integrate with the larger power grid and require engineering expertise, generally pay quite a bit more than overseas manufacturing jobs in the same industry.

The Battle for Intellectual Property. Another area of expertise is the development of unique IP. Whereas some companies might focus on a conventional, readily accessible technology, others might be in the vanguard, developing new types of electric vehicles, like California-based Tesla Motors, or completely new ways of casting silicon wafers for the solar industry, like Massachusetts-based 1366 Technologies. These companies tend to closely guard their innovations and often reserve their manufacturing for countries that support strong IP protection. Intel provides a great example of this strategy in the more mature high-tech industry. Although it operates commodity-type semiconductor facilities in several locations in Asia, Intel continues to manufacture its most advanced chips at factories in Arizona and Oregon.

TOP TEN CLEAN-TECH COUNTRY LEADERS

Based on an analysis of investment activity, renewables deployment, patent activity, and other key indicators from such organizations as Bloomberg New Energy Finance (BNEF), Ernst & Young, the Pew Charitable Trusts, the United Nations Environment Programme (UNEP), and our own internal Clean Edge research and editorial review, we've narrowed the list of key national players down to ten global market leaders. They are:

1. China
2. United States
3. Germany
4. Japan
5. Italy
6. India
7. United Kingdom

8. France
9. Brazil
10. South Korea

There are, of course, dozens of other national and regional players that are having a significant impact on the clean-tech market, among them Australia, Canada, Denmark, Israel, Spain, and Singapore. And one can find important pockets of notable clean-tech development and leadership in the Czech Republic, Iceland, Mexico, Morocco, the Philippines, Portugal, New Zealand, South Africa, Taiwan, Turkey, the United Arab Emirates (particularly Abu Dhabi) and elsewhere. The market landscape is changing on practically a daily basis, meaning that any rankings can change dramatically in a year, or even in a quarter. But these ten nations came to the top of our benchmarking analysis and editorial review and reflect a diversity that spans Asia, Europe, and North and South America.

Below is an overview of key market activities in each of our top ten nations, and how the clean-tech industry is unfolding across these unique and increasingly interconnected boundaries.

1. CHINA

On just about every measure, China is becoming the clean-energy leader to watch and, in many cases, emulate. The world's most populous nation is now its largest manufacturer of solar PV modules and wind turbines and is investing more money than almost any other nation on its clean-energy activities, including a record $54.4 billion investment in 2010, according to BNEF. China surpassed the U.S. in 2010 on a number of other critical clean-tech and broader economic measures. These include China's status as the largest installer of wind turbines globally, with its record 17 gigawatts of new wind power capacity in the ground in 2010, surpassing the U.S. for the title of most cumulative wind installed. (The U.S. still led in total grid-connected wind power capacity, as approximately a third of China's wind power was not yet connected to the grid at the end of 2010.)

Outside of clean tech, China became the world's leading consumer of energy in 2010, according to the International Energy Agency (IEA), and, for the first time, beat out the U.S. in total manufacturing output. According to a report from Englewood, Colorado–based research-and-advisory firm IHS Global Insight, China accounted for 19.8 percent of global production in 2010 in terms of total dollars, slightly higher than the 19.4 percent of the U.S. This is admittedly just one measure, but even so, it marked the first time in more than 100 years that the U.S. did not lead the world in manufacturing output based on total dollars. But as the report points out, much of China's manufacturing is driven by U.S.-headquartered companies and technologies (think Apple's iPad and iPhone, to name just two examples), and the U.S. does remain a far more efficient manufacturer. The study found that the U.S. manufacturing sector produced roughly the same amount of output in total dollars with 11.5 million workers, as opposed to China's approximately 100 million workers.

But for China, manufacturing efficiency isn't necessarily the point. The country, with more than 1.3 billion people and a burgeoning middle class, needs to create as many new jobs as possible, and clean tech is clearly playing a role in that push. In a Clean Edge review of the world's largest publicly traded pure-play clean-tech employers, Chinese-headquartered companies now represent seven of the top ten employers. While many of these Chinese companies also have manufacturing outside of their home country, most of their facilities are in China. These results show the benefit of relatively cheap labor, government incentives to create jobs, and strategic decision making around how to invest money in a rapidly changing industry. In solar, for example, some claim it's easier and cheaper to train workers in new processes than to replace expensive automated machinery. Chinese solar manufacturers alone make up six of the top seven global pure-play clean-tech employers.

Top 10 Clean-Tech Employers (Publicly Traded Pure Plays)

Rank	Company	Headquarters	Sector/Activity	Employees
1	Vestas Wind Systems	Randers, Denmark	Wind	23,200
2	LDK Solar	Xinyu, China	Solar	22,400
3	Suntech Power	Wuxi, China	Solar	20,200
4	Trina Solar	Changzhou, China	Solar	12,800
5	Yingli Green Energy	Baoding, China	Solar	11,400
6	JA Solar	Shanghai, China	Solar	10,700
7	Hanwha Solarfun	Shanghai, China	Solar	10,200
8	Neo-Neon Holdings	Hong Kong	LED Lighting	10,000
9	Itron	Liberty Lake, Washington, USA	Smart Grid	9,500
10	Canadian Solar	Kitchener, Ontario, Canada	Solar	8,700

Source: Clean Edge, Inc., 2011. Job figures accurate as of December 31, 2010.

How has China risen so rapidly to this level of clean-tech prominence? In 2006, the country issued its 11th five-year plan (FYP), the first FYP to include extensive support for the development and deployment of clean-energy and environmental initiatives. The FYP, which has been a fundamental part of Chinese policy and investment direction for more than 50 years, is a key part of China's economic development strategy. The 12th and most recent FYP, voted in by the National People's Congress in early 2011, is even more ambitious than its predecessor, with approximately a third of its targets relating to clean-energy and environmental issues. The current plan calls for primary energy generated by non–fossil fuels to rise to 11.3 percent by 2015, including at least 70 gigawatts of new wind power and 5 gigawatts of new solar power.

Clearly, the ability of China's national government to guide, shape, and dictate policy, technology, and capital in lockstep provides a great competitive advantage in the global clean-tech marketplace. As noted earlier, this isn't so much about saving the earth as it is about meeting the needs of the fastest-growing nation on the planet without outstripping its capacity to provide services and avoid environmental disaster.

The environmental issues facing China far outpace anything seen in the rest of the world, and aren't related to climate-change forecasts as much as to day-to-day reality. The country is now home to 16 of the 20 most polluted cities on the planet, according to the World Bank. In the past decade, cancer rates and other modern ailments related to water and air pollution have exploded. Cancer is now the nation's biggest killer, responsible for nearly one in four deaths. The World Health Organization reports that cancer rates in China are now higher than in industrialized countries like the U.S. and the U.K., with the nation having experienced a dramatic rise in cancer cases over the past 30 years during the country's dramatic economic expansion.

What do these environmental concerns have to do with clean tech in China? First, however unlikely for a country that keeps a tight lid on popular dissent, we could see citizen-based uprisings in China demanding significant improvements, not unlike earlier movements in the U.S., Japan, and Europe. When children are sickened by melamine-laden milk or factory emissions from Mommy's or Daddy's place of work, strange things can happen. And it means we'll continue to see some of the most aggressive programs on the planet as China's government continues to support the growth of clean-tech manufacturing, deployment, and innovation.

But these same issues will face clean technologies in China as concerns around quality and safety impact not only toys and milk, but also clean-tech products like solar cells, wind turbines, and high-speed rail. China's aggressive embrace of rapid development over quality assurance has many observers concerned. As any builder or project developer knows, speed is not always a good thing, as infrastructure deployment requires planning, quality control, and failproof processes. Indeed, moving too fast in deploying technologies and products and building out infrastructure can cause serious and unforeseen problems.

In China's clean-tech industry, this can be seen in wind turbines sitting idle because of a lack of a utility grid to carry the electrons to population centers, and in fast-tracked high-speed-rail plans that are now being scrutinized because of corruption and alleged corner cutting. In February 2011, the high-speed-rail program's minister was accused of taking bribes amounting to $152 million, and in March auditors reported that $28 million had been embezzled in the Beijing–Shanghai line alone. The minister of the once lauded high-speed-rail system was sacked, but that wasn't enough to avert a pending disaster. In July 2011, a major high-speed-rail crash involving two brand-new trains proved many people's worst fears, leaving at least 40 people dead, nearly 200 injured, and everyone demanding answers. If not put in check, China's breakneck pace of growth and greed may scare off future customers, especially in international markets, if it sacrifices quality, integrity, and safety.

China will also continue to live in a seemingly contradictory reality, with its rapacious need for new energy from fossil fuels being one of its greatest Achilles' heels. As the U.S, Germany, and Japan move ahead on learning how to build out their energy futures without the need for new coal-fired and nuclear plants, China will not be so lucky. It will have one foot boldly stepping into a clean-tech future and one foot solidly planted in the energy past.

One other rising area of strength and opportunity for China could involve moving beyond being the manufacturer for the world, and becoming a true innovator. While the U.S. remains the global patent leader (for all types of patents, clean tech and otherwise) by a wide margin, followed by Japan and Germany, China has rapidly risen to fourth place, ahead of South Korea, France, and the U.K., according to the UN World Intellectual Property Organization's review of 2010 global patent applications (which does not include national-level patents). In recent years, multinationals like Dow Chemical, GE, IBM, and Denmark-based Vestas Wind Systems, along with domestic Chinese firms and the Chinese national government, have set up dozens of R&D centers in China that focus on clean-tech initiatives.

2. UNITED STATES

The United States, perhaps in spite of itself, has been able to retain a central role in clean tech. States like California, Massachusetts, Oregon, New York, and Colorado have demonstrated focused leadership in the sector with technology, policy, and capital investments that demonstrate the old axiom that "all energy is local." And the federal government's stimulus expenditures, part of the American Recovery and Reinvestment Act of 2009, provided much-needed additional support. But the lack of a national U.S. energy plan, with strong renewables and efficiency commitments akin to those of China and Germany, have put U.S. clean-tech leadership at serious risk.

The country's technology prowess, demonstrated by the sheer amount of patent activity and new-company entrants, has historically been supported by world-class capital markets and unprecedented IP protections. In 2010, U.S. venture capital represented 40 percent of total global clean-tech venture activity, according to data provided by the Cleantech Group. Between 1988 and 2007 (the most recent data period available), the U.S. ranked second, behind only Japan, in clean-energy patents granted, according to research conducted by UNEP.

And while China's clean-energy dominance is being heralded in the headlines and in boardrooms, the U.S. is still a dominant force. China is huge, and as it grows, of course it's going to be a behemoth. But that doesn't mean it's leading in all clean-tech indicators, and it's critical to put some of the China-U.S. comparative figures in perspective. Take clean-energy investments. The 2010 edition of the respected annual Pew Charitable Trusts and BNEF report *Who's Winning the Clean Energy Race?* noted that China led all nations, with $54.4 billion in private clean-energy investment, outpacing the $34 billion in total investment in the U.S. in 2010. But if you look at the data on a per capita basis, the U.S. is investing $110 per man, woman, and child, whereas China is investing $41 per person.

Despite all the political hand-wringing, missed opportunities, and lack of federal leadership and focus, the U.S. maintains a unique early-adopter position in the world of clean tech. The solar PV cell was invented at Bell Labs in New Jersey in the 1950s, the first major modern wind farms and concentrating-solar-power (CSP) thermal plants were deployed in California in the 1980s, the world's leading green-building standards were developed here in the late 1990s, and smart grid, energy storage, advanced lighting, and other core clean technologies all have strong roots and continued support in the U.S.

And the U.S. isn't just a technology innovator; it's also innovating in areas like project finance. The Solar Energy Industries Association (SEIA) estimates that the U.S. could become the largest market in the world for solar (PV and CSP) installations by 2014, outgunning Germany and Japan. That's partly because, as solar prices decline, a host of innovative companies, such as fast-growing multistate solar installers SolarCity, SunRun, and Sungevity, are packaging residential and commercial PV systems with no money down and customer savings embedded from the very beginning. And industrial and utility-scale solar deployment and financing schemes continue to gain traction as well. There's still extensive innovation that needs to occur on the financing front as cities, states, and the federal government face unprecedented budget constraints, but green banks, power purchase agreements (PPAs), and other financing innovations are being pursued and designed across the U.S. and could provide the country with a unique competitive advantage.

One thing's for sure, though: The U.S. can't rest on its clean-tech laurels. "If you look at the numbers—if you look at VC in particular—innovation is happening here," says Nancy Floyd, founder and managing director of San Francisco–based pioneering clean-tech VC firm Nth Power and a speaker at the 2008 Democratic convention. "But we don't have any comprehensive national framework." And, she asks quite soberly, "if it's not front and center for the Obama administration, who is it going to be front and center for?"

3. GERMANY

In many ways, China, the U.S., and Germany represent the perfect clean-tech trifecta. Spanning Asia, North America, and Europe, these three countries are playing the top three leadership roles in the build-out of the clean-tech markets, each in a unique way. Germany, an early clean-energy supporter via policy and capital frameworks, not to mention its world-class technology and intellectual-capital infrastructure, upped the ante in July 2011 by becoming the first nation with nuclear power to approve the complete planned phaseout of its nuclear-generation plants by 2022.

Germany's new goal, forwarded by Chancellor Angela Merkel in a surprise U-turn policy stance in the aftermath of the Fukushima nuclear disaster in Japan, further positions the country as a clean-tech leader. But before we take a closer look at this post-Fukushima policy jolt, let's look at Germany's past. In 2000, the country passed the Erneuerbare-Energien-Gesetz (EEG), also known as the Renewable Energy Sources Act, which resulted in the increase of renewables from 10 percent to 17 percent of total electricity generation between 2000 and 2010. This law, more than anything else, has powered Germany to the forefront of clean tech. The government now estimates that more than 350,000 Germans work in renewable-energy industries, at such companies as SolarWorld, Schott Solar, and Enercon, up from just 30,000 in 1998.

Chief among Germany's policy pursuits has been the aggressive application of feed-in tariffs (FITs). FITs have been a largely successful policy mechanism used to encourage renewable-energy installations by guaranteeing long-term power purchase agreements at an agreed-upon price. While FITs have been a successful tool, accounting for up to 75 percent of all solar deployment and 45 percent of all wind deployment globally, according to some industry analyses, they have also been criticized for being too expensive and slow to reflect declining technology costs. (The less it costs to install solar or wind, the less it should cost to purchase the energy produced over a long-term contract.) With recent budget constraints and some political backlash, Germany has had to reduce its solar FIT and restructure the program multiple times. While there's no doubt that FITs provide a great incentive and do work very effectively in building markets, the counter-question is often "at what cost?"

Germany invested more money in clean energy than the U.S. did in 2010, coming in second behind China, with more than $41 billion, according to BNEF. On a per capita basis, Germany beat out both the U.S. and China. The majority of Germany's 2010 investments went into solar, with the next-biggest contribution going to wind power. In 2010, the nation added more new grid-connected solar PV and produced more biodiesel than any other country, while placing in the top five for wind-capacity additions. And Germany's investments in clean tech are only likely to increase.

Italy, Switzerland, and other European countries have announced aggressive plans to reduce their nuclear power holdings, but no other nation has gone as far as Germany. The government's policy objective is to be a clean-energy leader while ensuring "that energy supplies will not be interrupted, that the cost of power does not become prohibitive, that Germany remains an attractive place to do business, and that we meet our climate change mitigation targets," according to official papers released by Germany's lower house of parliament, the Bundestag.

Germany has positioned itself as one of the key clean-tech nations to watch. The country's upper chamber of parliament, the Bundesrat, approved the latest version of Germany's pioneering EEG on July 8, 2011, after earlier approval by the Bundestag. The new version of the law, which offers higher incentives for offshore wind, biofuels, and geothermal power and retains commitments to solar PV deployment, went into effect January 1, 2012. Under the new plan, the government is committed to shuttering all of its nuclear power plants by 2022 and replacing them with a massive buildout of renewables and aggressive energy- and building-efficiency improvements, with targets of 35 percent renewables by 2020 (up from less than 20 percent today) and at least 80 percent by 2050.

Cognizant of the magnitude of this goal, and perhaps the audacity of it, the government has stated that "the change-over will be a mammoth task." And some critics have expressed concern that Germany will need to rely on more coal- and gas-fired power plants to meet its energy requirements. But the government sees the opportunity for Germany to act as a living laboratory, to ensure the nation a significant share of clean-tech-driven exports, jobs, and growth, and to play a historic role in the shift from polluting, costly, and volatile foreign fossil fuels. "Germany has the chance to become the first major industrialized country to have a highly efficient energy system, based on the use of renewables," says an official 2011 German cabinet resolution. "We can become a pioneer and an example for the rest of the world, demonstrating how a sustainable shift to renewables can be managed while remaining economically successful." As a developed global industrial power with a democratic government, Germany has a political infrastructure far more akin to that of the U.S. than China's—and its national policies continue to show what's possible in clean-tech leadership even without a centralized authoritarian regime.

4. JAPAN

In the late 1980s, Japan's economy was seemingly unstoppable. The nation was viewed by many business and policy observers as the next great global force, with predictions that it would grow from the world's second-largest economy at the time into the largest and most powerful, leading the world into a new Japan-propelled Asian era. Its economy was strong, its people confident, and its companies innovating new products and services at a rapid pace.

Japan, however, did not end up reaching such lofty heights, instead going into two decades of devastating deflation and ceding its status as the world's second-largest economy (behind the number-one U.S.) to China in 2010. Even so, the country has continued to play a critical role in a host of technology-driven industries, including as a central actor in the buildout of many facets of the clean-tech sector. Japan was the first in the world to have a long-term sustained commitment to solar power, with the Sunshine Program, launched in 1974, providing policy and financial commitment to the solar industry for more than two decades. Perhaps more than in any other country, Japan's largest corporations have been at the vanguard of eco-innovation, with Toyota, Sharp, Honda, and others committing significant human and financial capital to developing green products and services.

Japan was granted more clean-tech patents than any other nation between 1988 and 2007. Toyota exemplifies this Japanese push for product innovation and manufacturing prowess, introducing the world's first hybrid electric vehicle, the Prius, back in 1997. By 2009 the Prius had become Toyota's best-selling vehicle in Japan, and it is on target to reach similar status elsewhere in the world. Sharp led the world in PV manufacturing between 2000 and 2006, with other key

Japanese solar players like Sanyo, Mitsubishi, and Kyocera also carving out significant market shares.

One thing many of these Japanese firms have in common is their commitment to long-term thinking, with corporate strategic plans that can span decades. But extreme competition, product commoditization, and better regulatory supports and incentives in other countries have left many of these manufacturers hurting. Japanese firms in the solar industry, for example, represented less than 10 percent of total manufacturing output for solar PV in 2010. Quite a change of fortune, considering that just a decade earlier, Sharp alone represented nearly 20 percent of total solar PV manufacturing output worldwide.

Perhaps even more disconcerting for the nation's planners is how far Japan has fallen behind in renewables deployment. In 2010, the once mighty solar-deployment leader ranked third in total installed solar PV capacity, behind Germany and Spain. It ranked fourth, behind China, Turkey, and Germany, for cumulative installed solar water-heating capacity, with very few new additions in recent years. Add in other renewables, like wind and geothermal, and Japan's rankings drop significantly, with all renewables, including hydro, contributing only around 8 percent of the nation's electricity needs in 2010.

But it appears that things could be changing dramatically. In the aftermath of the Fukushima disaster in 2011, the Japanese populace has turned increasingly against nuclear power as an option moving forward. And all but three of Japan's 54 nuclear power plants remained shut down for safety tests by the end of 2011, with the possibility that all of its nuclear facilities would be shuttered by the end of 2012. (Before the Fukushima disaster, nuclear supplied 30 percent of Japan's electric power, with government plans to increase it to 50 percent of electricity generation by 2030.) A growing chorus of politicians, especially at the prefecture level, have called for a moratorium on new nuclear power plants and for the country to rely instead on renewables, energy efficiency, and other non-nuclear options. This could prove particularly positive news for Japan's solar industry, which, as noted earlier, has been hit hard by a highly valued yen and the global commoditization of solar. Existing players like Sharp and newcomers like Solar Frontier, which is backed by the oil company Showa Shell Sekiyu and which in 2011 opened one of the world's largest thin-film solar plants in Miyazaki, could be well served by a new national focus on renewables.

With a deep history of eco-innovation, corporate and financial tentacles that span the globe, and the ability and expertise to pursue localized assembly and/or manufacturing of products, Japan could once again be a rising star in the world of clean-tech manufacturing, deployment, and finance.

5. ITALY

Shortly after Japan's Fukushima nuclear disaster, the Italian people, by a stunning 94 percent majority vote in June 2011, went against pro-nuke prime minister Silvio Berlusconi and passed a referendum rejecting any new nuclear plants. (Italy, by the way, is also highly susceptible to earthquakes.) "We shall probably have to say goodbye to nuclear," conceded Berlusconi, who had sought to revive an Italian nuclear industry that had been dormant since the world's last major reactor disaster, Chernobyl, in the 1980s.

That leaves big renewables like wind, solar, and geothermal as the carbon-free pillars of Italy's energy future, and in recent years the nation has rather quietly become one of the world's largest and fastest-growing markets for solar power. In 2011, the land of the celebrated Tuscan sun installed more solar PV energy (7 gigawatts) than any other country except Germany. Italy's solar growth was also a big reason why in 2011 nearly half of all new electricity-generating capacity in Europe came from solar PV.

Its solar surge propelled Italy to fourth in the world in most new clean energy installed overall in 2010, behind China, Germany, and the U.S. In some parts of southern Italy, solar power is already at grid parity, meaning its cost is comparable to standard retail electricity rates.

Italy is home to the world's second-largest solar PV power array, the 84.2-megawatt ground-mounted Montalto di Castro plant on the Tyrrhenian coast northwest of Rome. The plant is owned by Sun-Power, the U.S.-based company that's majority-owned by French oil giant Total—thanks to its 2010 acquisition of European project developer SunRay Renewable. Italy boasts a robust market in small-scale rooftop solar PV as well.

At the end of 2011, Italy ranked second in the world, behind only Germany, in total installed PV capacity—well ahead of the fifth-place U.S., a country more than 30 times larger; in square miles, Italy is roughly the size of Arizona. Italy is also fifth in the world in total geothermal power capacity and sixth in wind energy.

As in Germany, Spain, parts of Canada, and other nations, Italy's solar growth has been spurred by government policy, particularly a generous feed-in tariff. This policy, called Conto Energia, has been adjusted and modified several times since its inception in 2006, and it is generally considered highly successful in catalyzing Italy's global solar leadership. But as with most FIT policies, Italy's is an often controversial delicate balance between supporting clean-energy deployment and managing government budget outlays. Most analysts expect Italy to reduce its FIT levels in coming years, slowing growth rates from the boom years of 2010–11. But Italy should still remain one of the world's best markets for solar.

Not surprisingly, Enel Green Power (EGP), the clean-energy unit of Italy's formerly state-owned utility Enel, has emerged as one of the world's largest and most aggressive players in renewable energy. EGP is particularly active in wind power, which represents about 80 percent of its energy mix, but also plays in solar (both PV and CSP), geothermal, biomass, and traditional large-scale hydro. EGP plans to invest $9.2 billion by 2015 to increase its capacity of renewable energy (including hydro) by two-thirds, to 10.4 gigawatts worldwide. About 40 percent of that development will be in Italy, Spain, and Portugal.

EGP's parent, Enel, is also considered the world's first mover in the wide-scale deployment of smart meters. By the end of 2006, virtually every Enel customer had received a smart meter—more than 30 million total meters installed in just five years—representing one of the world's most aggressive rollouts to date.

So far, Italy's clean-tech leadership has been much more on the deployment side than the manufacturing side. Local solar cell production, for example, trails far behind the likes of China, Germany, and Japan. But EGP is moving on that front as well, through joint ventures with Japan's Sharp and Switzerland-based STMicroelectronics. In July 2011, their joint venture 3Sun opened Italy's largest solar PV production plant, a 160-megawatt facility in Catania, Sicily. The site initially employed 280 workers and has the potential to triple in size.

6. INDIA

Among developing nations, China gets all the clean-tech headlines, with its deep financial war chest and aggressive manufacturing incentives and programs. India, on the other hand, has been experiencing a much quieter and slower clean-tech buildout for a nation with so much pent-up energy demand. The country is certainly a key player, and is moving up in its clean-tech rankings, but it has significant room for improvement if it is going to become one of the top emerging nations to grow and expand its domestic markets and be a key exporter of clean-tech products. India is currently investing less than one-tenth as much as China in its clean-energy buildout.

Infrastructure shortcomings present India with both a unique opportunity and a significant obstacle. The nation is riddled with energy, water, road, and other infrastructure constraints that leave it seriously compromised. Among India's greatest infrastructure challenges is the lack of a reliable grid. Power outages are a fact of daily life in both cities and rural areas. And not only is the grid unreliable in most places, but it lacks a unified national inter-connection system to provide redundancy and the ability to ship electrons across the country. This provides a certain level of oppor-tunity for distributed renewables like rooftop and ground-mounted solar PV that can provide power at or near the point of use. But it leaves the country with a big disadvantage in its pursuit to add the massive new generation capacity it requires, whether from fossil fuels, nuclear, or renewables.

Among its strong suits, India is particularly well positioned in the area of human capital. The nation now produces approximately 400,000 engineering grads a year, among the highest outputs in the world, and millions more in related technical fields that are being attracted to clean-tech jobs at such companies as Suzlon, Tata, and Moser Baer. In March 2011, the country launched a new tradable-renewable-energy-certificates scheme that could bolster investment in new projects nationwide. And with more than 18 gigawatts of installed renewables, India currently ranks seventh among nations for total renewables-capacity deployment.

But not unlike China, India will likely need to pursue an "all of the above" energy strategy to meet the needs of its growing population. And whereas China is poised to see a general decline in population over the next several decades (once it peaks, at approximately 1.4 bil-lion, by around 2025) and faces an increasingly aging populace and workforce, the opposite is true for India, with projections for signifi-cant population growth that would make it the world's most populous country by 2030. But whatever decisions it makes moving forward with regard to its deployment of nuclear power and fossil fuels, India will have to aggressively pursue renewables, efficiency, advanced transportation, and other clean-tech products and services to meet the needs of both its rural and urban populations and to ensure its global economic export competitiveness.

7. UNITED KINGDOM

Seven miles off the scenic coast of Kent, in southeastern England, and 80 meters above the waves, the blades of 100 Vestas V90 offshore wind turbines harness the breezes of the North Sea into electricity that powers up to 240,000 homes. Operated by Swedish energy giant Vattenfall, the 300-megawatt Thanet Offshore Wind Farm is one of the world's two largest, along with the Walney Wind Farm off Britain's west coast. Both fittingly symbolize the U.K.'s status as the world's number-one generator of offshore wind power. The nation surpassed Denmark for that crown in 2008, and actually generates more power from offshore wind farms than the rest of the world combined.

And it could be just the beginning. A 2009 British government report assessed the nation's potential offshore wind capacity at 33 gigawatts—enough to power every home in the country and create up to 70,000 jobs in the process. It won't all be constructed, of course, but as much as 8 gigawatts of offshore capacity is currently operational or under development. It's a sobering (or, we would hope, inspirational) reminder about the potential of offshore wind technology for the U.S., where not a single kilowatt of offshore wind power had come online by the end of 2011. The U.K. also ranks eighth in the world in total wind energy capacity (offshore and onshore combined), with more than 6.5 gigawatts installed through 2011.

Perhaps mindful of the environmental and public health damage of its coal-fired industrial heritage, the U.K. has long been a world leader in policies to reduce carbon and transition to a cleaner energy mix. As early as 1990, the U.K. had a nationwide mandate, the Non–Fossil Fuel Obligation (NFFO), to change its energy mix, although "non–fossil fuels" at that time included nuclear power. But in 2002 (when only a handful of U.S. states had an RPS, or renewable portfolio standard, in place), the U.K. replaced that original mandate with a Renewables Obligation (RO), for which nuclear was not eligible. The RO initially required British utilities to generate a modest 3 percent of their electricity from renewable sources, but the requirement for England, Scotland, and Wales had risen to 11.1 percent by 2011 and will hit 15.4 percent by 2016. For Northern Ireland, it was 4 percent by 2011 and will be 6.3 percent by 2016.

The RO has not been a completely smooth ride. British Gas, one of the U.K.'s "Big Six" energy firms, was assessed more than £4 million ($6.4 million) in fines and repayments in July 2011 for under-reporting its total energy production, resulting in a smaller amount of required clean energy. And Conservative prime minister David Cameron's coalition government is currently assessing potential changes to the RO, which may or may not make it weaker. Nonetheless, it has shown the impact of a national renewable energy standard in spurring developers and entrepreneurs to tap a country's available energy resources.

The British Isles have never been famous for sunshine, yet, surprisingly, the U.K. is the fastest-growing solar PV market in Europe and one of the fastest in the world, albeit starting from a small base. PV installations in the U.K. grew from less than 25 megawatts in early 2010 to 750 megawatts at the end of 2011. But as in European solar powerhouses Germany, Italy, and Spain, uncertainty over FIT levels may dampen that robust growth. The government's Department of Energy and Climate Change announced in June 2011 that FIT funds would be shifted from large-scale solar PV projects to support smaller rooftop installations. The nation's two largest solar PV power plants—the 1-megawatt Fen Farm installation, in Lincolnshire, and the 1.4-megawatt Wheal Jane solar park, on the site of a former tin mine in Cornwall—both came online in July 2011 to beat the funding cut taking effect in August.

8. FRANCE

France, which leads the world in percentage of electricity coming from nuclear power (around 75 percent), might seem like a strange member of this renewables- and efficiency-driven clean-tech list. But the country does well enough on a range of indicators to make it into our top ten list. While it doesn't lead in any single category, it racks up favorably in overall ethanol and biodiesel production (both in the top five) and is number nine in total dollars invested in clean energy among G20 nations.

Even more than its government policy, however, France's corporate titans seem to be leading the charge. A host of French companies are increasingly betting at least part of their future success and growth on the development and deployment of clean tech. In 2011, French oil-and-gas giant Total (the world's sixth-largest oil company by gross revenues) acquired a 60 percent stake in San Jose, California–based solar PV company SunPower for nearly $1.4 billion. The company, for now, plans to leave the SunPower brand and corporate staff in place as it expands into the solar business.

Other French corporate players with similar forays into clean tech include Schneider Electric, which has acquired multiple smart-grid and grid-infrastructure companies, such as Spain-based Telvent and India-based Luminous; industrial giant Saint-Gobain, which invested $80 million in Faribault, Minnesota–based energy-efficient-window company SAGE Electrochromics in 2011; Veolia Environnement, which is aggressively buying up water companies and waste management firms; and Nissan-Renault, one of the top manufacturers of EVs, which is leading the charge with the release of the world's first mass-marketed EV, the Nissan LEAF. Even nuclear power behemoth AREVA has gotten into the clean-tech act, buying up U.S.-and-Australia-based utility-scale solar thermal company Ausra in early 2010.

There's no doubt that France, with considerable nuclear holdings, will take a very different path than other industrialized nations such as Germany and Japan. But clearly, the French pursuit of clean technology, especially in the corporate domain, will ensure the nation's leadership role in the near to mid-term, and potentially much longer.

9. BRAZIL

Among emerging nations, Brazil ranks just behind China in clean-tech investments. In 2010, Brazil invested nearly $8 billion in its clean-energy buildout. And it's not just a biofuels story. In addition to allocating 40 percent of those investments to biofuels (mostly sugarcane-based bioethanol), Brazil also contributed 31 percent to wind and 28 percent to other renewable energy sources such as biomass and small-scale hydro, according to BNEF. In 2010, the nation received approximately 14 gigawatts of its energy capacity from renewables.

A new national ten-year plan from Brazil in 2011 showed that the country plans to significantly increase its deployment of renewable resources, doubling it to around 27 gigawatts installed by 2020. The country, which gets nearly 75 percent of its electricity from large and small hydro and approximately 7 percent from non-hydro renewables, is already one of the most clean-energy-intensive nations on the planet. All of this is complemented by Brazil's extensive push into sugarcane-based ethanol, which accounts for more than 40 percent of the nation's transportation fuel supply and has made Brazil one of the top two nations in the world, alongside the U.S., for the production of biofuels.

Brazil's clean-energy industry faces a host of challenges, including an uncertain regulatory environment, uneven taxes, and commodity shortages, but recent developments point to the continued growth of its clean-tech sector. The nation is investing heavily in the buildout of wind power, with plans to increase total wind power installations from around 1.5 gigawatts in 2011 to 14 gigawatts by 2020. And in 2011, Brazil's state-run oil company Petrobras announced plans to increase its share of ethanol production from 5 percent in 2011 to 15 percent of total output in Brazil by 2015. The company has also been on an acquisition spree. If successful, Petrobras could become the largest producer of ethanol in Brazil and potentially the world.

International players are also betting on the Brazilian clean-tech sector, with Dow Chemical and Japan-based investment firm Mitsui investing in a renewable-biopolymers facility in Santa Vitória, in the state of Minas Gerais. Once completed, the companies claim it will be the world's largest integrated facility for the production of biopolymers from sugarcane ethanol. Other companies, like GE, are investing in Brazil-based research capabilities and betting they can capture a growing share of the nation's wind power buildout.

10. SOUTH KOREA

South Korea's government embarked on one of the most aggressive stimulus packages for clean energy in 2009. Coined the Green New Deal, the stimulus package will provide approximately $38 billion over five years to spur clean-energy job growth and initiatives. But as in France, the greatest push is coming from the private sector.

Samsung, one of South Korea's marquee brands and largest conglomerates, announced in 2010 that it would transform itself to become a global leader in clean tech. It's been compared to GE's game-changing Ecomagination announcement and strategy a few years earlier, but only time will tell if Samsung is able to reinvent itself like GE has done. The company plans to invest $21 billion over a ten-year period, focusing on such sectors as solar cells, rechargeable batteries for hybrid cars, wind turbines, and energy-saving LED lighting technology. Samsung is already a player in solar and wind, and won a massive and controversial $7 billion contract in early 2010 to create a clean-energy cluster in Ontario, Canada, to produce and deploy wind turbines and solar modules throughout the province and create an estimated 16,000 jobs. But Samsung's ability to leverage its corporate know-how and manufacturing heft to become a clean-energy giant still remains a question mark, as does the strength of its deal in Ontario.

Other South Korean behemoths, like state-owned Korea Electric Power and LG (including its subsidiaries LG Electronics and LG Chem), are investing billions of their own to become key players in clean tech. LG Chem in particular is aggressively pursuing the development of next-generation lithium-ion batteries, including inking a licensing deal with Argonne National Laboratory, in DuPage County, Illinois, to manufacture advanced batteries for GM's Chevy Volt and other vehicles.

There's no doubt that South Korea has a dual need to prop up export-oriented industries and to provide cleaner air, water, and green spaces to its citizens, all while ensuring the jobs of the future. The pursuit of clean tech fills both of these needs and fits South Korea's technology-driven roots (think electronics and cars). And for South Korea, things may be warming up just in time for the 2018 Winter Olympics in Pyeongchang. The country, which was awarded that year's Games over Munich, Germany, and Annecy, France—joining Japan and China as the only Asian nations to host an Olympics—is certain to use the occasion as an opportunity to showcase its clean-tech cred to the world.

WHAT GLOBAL COMPETITION MEANS TO THE U.S.

Whereas America's Silicon Valley ruled high tech for decades, the clean-tech industry is growing up with a wealth of corporate and governmental competitors representing a geographic and sectoral diversity that makes such centralized leadership neither possible nor desirable. While this distributed competition is both healthy and productive, it also creates an urgent call to action for the U.S. If America's business, government, academic, technology, financial, and other leaders don't get increasingly serious about making clean tech a cornerstone of the nation's economic development plans, the U.S. risks falling dramatically behind other, more committed and active nations.

The review of the global competitive landscape highlighted in this chapter provides a clarion call to America's leaders and citizens. The nation's future economic and technology prowess rests on moving the country from century-old industries to the business and technology engines of the future—those that ensure true economic, environmental, and energy security.

Clean Edge subscribers, in replying to a 2011 survey about what they viewed as the U.S.'s greatest assets in the battle for clean-tech leadership, responded overwhelmingly that the U.S.'s competitive advantage lies in its culture of innovation and world-class research and financial infrastructures. As they pointed out: What other nation has such a diversity of nationalities and freedom of views? What other country has the same high caliber of academic research institutions and labs across the engineering and industrial landscape? And what other country currently matches America's three-pronged corporate, venture capital, and entrepreneurial spirit of innovation?

But, we ask, will this predilection toward disruptive creation be enough to ensure the U.S. a leading role in the next industrial revolution? What steps must the nation take to ensure that its cities, states, businesses, and other institutions not only survive but thrive in this rapidly changing environment as other nations claim a larger share of the clean-tech innovation-and-leadership pie?

2

VYING FOR LEADERSHIP

The Top Ten Clean-Tech States

On a Monday morning in March 2010, the offices of Denver-based solar installer SolSource became the front line of Colorado's battle to build a clean-energy future. That's where then-governor Bill Ritter signed into law the state's latest RPS (renewable portfolio standard) legislation, mandating that 30 percent of Colorado's electricity come from renewable sources by 2020. For a state where oil and gas has been and continues to be the largest industry, such a commitment to clean energy might come as a surprise. But in recent years, the Centennial State has been a leading supporter of efforts to move the U.S. beyond an economy dependent on fossil fuels.

In November 2004, Colorado became the first state to establish a renewable energy standard by ballot initiative. On the same day that Colorado voters delivered the state's nine electoral votes to President George W. Bush by about 5 percentage points—and despite heavy campaigning against the ballot measure by top utility Xcel Energy and others—they passed the RPS initiative by a convincing 54 to 46 percent tally. Although the 2004 RPS iteration called for only a 10 percent renewables target, the policy has since been strengthened on two occasions and now, at 30 percent, is one of the strongest state renewable targets in the country.

Ritter, recognizing Colorado's potential to capitalize on its energy industry leadership, directed the state toward establishment of a "new energy economy" focused on aggressive development of clean energy as well as environmentally responsible use of the state's vast natural gas resources. During his term as governor, he oversaw the state's evolution into a bona fide clean-tech powerhouse. From the unveiling of Colorado's Climate Action Plan in 2007 to the signing of the state's Clean Air Clean Jobs Act in 2010, Ritter's gubernatorial tenure— supported by the state legislature—was a display of committed clean-energy support. When Ritter left office in early 2011 after deciding not to seek a second term, Colorado had expanded its total wind capacity to nearly 1,300 megawatts, and solidified its solar leadership, becoming the nation's third-largest market for deployed PV, with 117 megawatts of installed capacity at the end of 2010. In the 2011 *State Clean Energy Leadership Index*, a comprehensive ranking of all 50 states developed by our firm, Clean Edge, Colorado placed fifth, ahead of states with notable green reputations such as Washington, Vermont, and Wisconsin.

While surging to the top tier of states in clean energy, Colorado continues to be a major player in the U.S. fossil-fuel industry. The state ranks in the top ten for crude oil production, is fifth in the U.S. for natural gas production, and in 2009 ranked fifth nationally for the total number of workers in fossil-fuel sectors. But clean tech is quickly becoming integral to the Colorado economy as well. By 2010, there were more than 400 solar companies doing business in Colorado, up from only 40 just five years earlier. At the 2011 Renewable Energy Finance Forum–Wall Street conference in New York, Ritter—now director of Colorado State University's Center for the

New Energy Economy—said that under his reign, "clean energy became the best growth sector in the Colorado economy."

WHY STATES ARE DRIVING CLEAN TECH IN THE U.S.

In the absence of a comprehensive federal energy plan, stories like Colorado's have come to define the evolution of clean energy in America. Whether through rooftop solar installations, deployment of smart-grid technologies, or EV adoption, it is states and cities that have forged ahead in clean-tech economic development. And for a variety of regulatory, political, financial, and environmental reasons, states will continue to find themselves at the forefront of America's clean-energy-economy development.

Historically, the highly regulated business of energy delivery has been organized on a state-by-state basis rather than at the federal level. Even as deregulation and interstate activity enhance the federal government's role, state utility commissions maintain the capacity to stand in the way of interconnection standards, transmission coordination rules, revenue decoupling, and other reforms that can accelerate the deployment of renewable-energy and energy-efficiency technologies. From a political standpoint, the lack of a federal mandate to advance clean energy leaves the most effective industry-supporting policies—such as renewable portfolio standards and building codes—in the hands of state legislators, regulators, and governors.

In addition to these factors, the most significant reason for states' leadership in clean-energy development is the extreme diversity of natural resource availability across the U.S. The blazing Southwest sun cannot be harvested in the same fashion as gusting winds in the Great Plains. Powerful Northwest waterways cannot be managed in the same way as the vast geothermal reserves beneath Nevada's deserts. Each region's unique environment necessitates a one-of-a-kind strategy in order to best develop local energy resources.

BENCHMARKING STATE CLEAN ENERGY LEADERSHIP

In recent years, clean energy has become somewhat of a public relations darling, with images of wind turbines and solar panels dominating utility and energy department marketing materials. After being greeted with a breathtaking aerial view of a Texas wind farm, a visitor to Exelon's website, for example, might be surprised to learn that the Chicago-based electricity giant is America's largest owner and operator of nuclear power plants. Although more than 90 percent of Exelon's generating capacity comes from nuclear sources, the company is exceedingly eager to play up its renewable-energy activities.

Positive association with clean energy is an encouraging sign for the industry, but this type of prominence can easily obstruct the public's understanding of clean energy in the U.S. Opponents of clean energy argue that renewables will never make up more than a sliver of our energy supply—and seeing that non-hydro renewable sources still made up only 5 percent of U.S. electricity generation in 2011, the casual observer might be quick to believe this claim. But stand-alone data points such as these do not tell the entire story. In fact, when you look at America's total energy consumption—including transportation energy use along with electricity demand—the first quarter of 2011 saw renewables (including hydro) move past nuclear power, becoming the nation's second-largest source of energy behind fossil fuels.

Recognizing the lack of comprehensive, data-driven analysis of states' clean-energy activities, our company, Clean Edge, set out to investigate beyond conflicting anecdotes and claims of leadership to use tangible data in evaluating state clean-energy performance. Our *State Clean Energy Leadership Index* is an annual ranking of all 50 states based on a set of more than 70 individual clean-energy-related indicators. By aggregating industry statistics from a wide variety of sources—and adjusting them for state size to avoid skewed results in favor of large states—we established a quantitative process by which to measure state-level clean-energy activity. Our ultimate goal is to let the data speak for itself.

STATE CLEAN ENERGY LEADERSHIP INDEX

TECHNOLOGY

Clean Electricity	Clean Transportation	Energy Intelligence & Green Building
(9 Indicators)	*(7 Indicators)*	*(10 Indicators)*

POLICY

Regulations & Mandates	Incentives
(15 Indicators)	*(14 Indicators)*

CAPITAL

Financial Capital	Human & Intellectual Capital
(9 Indicators)	*(6 Indicators)*

Source: Clean Edge, Inc., 2011.

The index is broken down into three main categories of technology, policy, and capital—with individual indicators further separated into several subcategories—providing a comprehensive look at clean-energy activity in the U.S. The graphic on page 58 shows overall state rankings for the 2011 edition of the index. And even with this very top-line look, some basic regional demographics are revealed.

2011 STATE CLEAN ENERGY LEADERSHIP INDEX

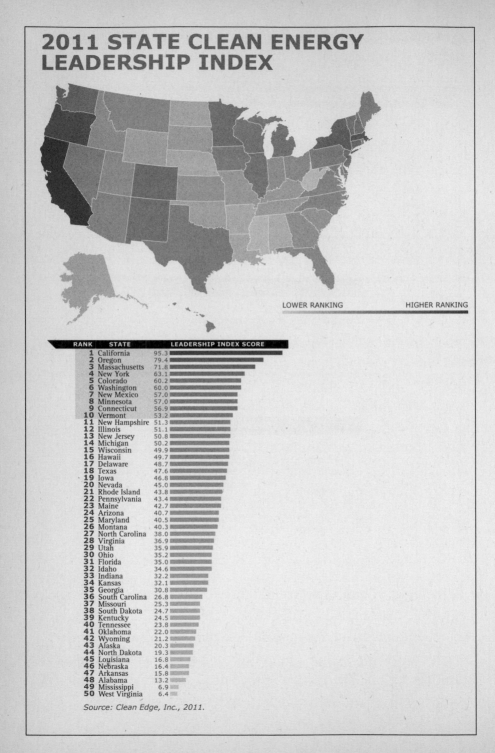

LOWER RANKING   HIGHER RANKING

RANK	STATE	LEADERSHIP INDEX SCORE
1	California	95.3
2	Oregon	79.4
3	Massachusetts	71.8
4	New York	63.1
5	Colorado	60.2
6	Washington	60.0
7	New Mexico	57.0
8	Minnesota	57.0
9	Connecticut	56.9
10	Vermont	53.2
11	New Hampshire	51.3
12	Illinois	51.1
13	New Jersey	50.8
14	Michigan	50.2
15	Wisconsin	49.9
16	Hawaii	49.7
17	Delaware	48.7
18	Texas	47.6
19	Iowa	46.8
20	Nevada	45.0
21	Rhode Island	43.8
22	Pennsylvania	43.4
23	Maine	42.7
24	Arizona	40.7
25	Maryland	40.5
26	Montana	40.3
27	North Carolina	38.0
28	Virginia	36.9
29	Utah	35.9
30	Ohio	35.2
31	Florida	35.0
32	Idaho	34.6
33	Indiana	32.2
34	Kansas	32.1
35	Georgia	30.8
36	South Carolina	26.8
37	Missouri	25.3
38	South Dakota	24.7
39	Kentucky	24.5
40	Tennessee	23.8
41	Oklahoma	22.0
42	Wyoming	21.2
43	Alaska	20.3
44	North Dakota	19.3
45	Louisiana	16.8
46	Nebraska	16.4
47	Arkansas	15.8
48	Alabama	13.2
49	Mississippi	6.9
50	West Virginia	6.4

Source: Clean Edge, Inc., 2011.

The West, home to five of the top seven states, reigns supreme in clean-energy leadership. The combination of advantageous natural resources and sustained policy support has allowed California, Oregon, Colorado, Washington, and New Mexico to cement themselves among clean-energy front-runners.

Four of the top ten states are located in the Northeast: Massachusetts, New York, Connecticut, and Vermont. Even without ideal conditions for large-scale clean electricity production, the Northeast has established leadership almost on par with the West. The Boston metro area has become the East Coast equivalent of the San Francisco Bay Area (albeit on a smaller scale) as a hub of clean-tech innovation and venture capital activity, and states across the Northeast have adopted broad policies supporting advancement of clean energy.

The Midwest has only one state in the top ten, Minnesota, but it places five in the top 20 (Minnesota, Illinois, Michigan, Wisconsin, and Iowa). The South brings up the rear—six of the ten lowest-ranked states are in the South, and no Deep South state makes the top 25. Texas, at number 18, comes the closest geographically. But it's important to view this underperforming region through the lens of "room for improvement," because for clean-energy entrepreneurs, investors, and climate-change activists alike, this region may be home to the most productive opportunities.

THE PURSUIT OF CLEAN ELECTRONS

The world's electricity admittedly still comes mostly from nonrenewable energy sources like coal, natural gas, and nuclear power. But a transition is definitely under way. The year 2010 marked the first time that global generating capacity from renewable sources excluding hydro—wind, solar, geothermal, and biomass—exceeded the world's nuclear capacity. Even in the U.S., where federal heel-dragging has tempered clean-energy growth, renewables' share of *new* generating capacity additions exploded from just 2 percent in 2004 to 55 percent in 2009. Around the world, we are witnessing a fast-paced shift to clean, low-carbon energy sources that will diminish air and water pollution, ease future resource constraints, and help prepare populations for climate adaptation.

The absence of strong federal leadership over the years in the U.S. has created a fragmented clean-energy narrative, with some states pushing hard to advance renewable energy and others opting to ignore the emerging clean-energy economy almost entirely. In 2010, three states—Iowa, North Dakota, and California—achieved more than 10 percent of their in-state, utility-scale generation from non-hydro clean sources, mainly wind in Iowa and North Dakota and a mix of solar, wind, and geothermal in California. But these states were exceptions, not the rule. For roughly half of all states, clean energy is still essentially a rounding error, with renewable sources adding up to less than 1 percent of total electricity generation. Eleven states generated less than 1,000 megawatt-hours from clean sources, registering a statistical zero percent in this category.

WIND POWER

The rise of the U.S. wind market in the past decade has been staggering, growing from 2.5 gigawatts of the nation's installed capacity in 2000 to 47 gigawatts by the end of 2011, representing an astounding compound annual growth rate of more than 30 percent, with utility-scale projects now located in 38 states. During 2010, electricity from wind accounted for 2.3 percent of all U.S. electricity generation, a seemingly small portion but enough to power nearly nine million American households for the entire year. And the future for American wind energy looks promising. A widely cited 2008 U.S. Department of Energy (DOE) report estimated that wind could provide 20 percent of U.S. electricity by 2030.

2010 UTILITY-SCALE CLEAN ELECTRICITY GENERATION: WIND, SOLAR, GEOTHERMAL

State	Rank	% of Total Generation, 2010	Thousand MWh, 2010
Iowa	1	15.40%	8,799
North Dakota	2	11.99%	4,175
California	3	10.06%	20,395
Minnesota	4	9.70%	5,231
South Dakota	5	8.34%	849
Kansas	6	7.14%	3,456
Oregon	7	7.12%	3,919
Nevada	8	6.72%	2,362
Wyoming	9	6.72%	3,197
Colorado	10	6.70%	3,463
Texas	11	6.38%	26,134
Oklahoma	12	5.12%	3,701
New Mexico	13	5.04%	1,830
Idaho	14	4.76%	579
Washington	15	4.59%	4,652
Hawaii	16	3.91%	409
Montana	17	3.14%	935
Maine	18	2.89%	486
Indiana	19	2.36%	2,930
Illinois	20	2.24%	4,512
New York	21	2.01%	2,750
Utah	22	1.72%	727
Missouri	26	1.00%	927
Pennsylvania	27	0.80%	1,854
Michigan	28	0.31%	352
New Hampshire	29	0.28%	63
Vermont	30	0.21%	14
Alaska	31	0.19%	13
Arizona	32	0.12%	136
New Jersey	33	0.07%	49
Tennessee	34	0.05%	41
Florida	35	0.04%	99
Massachusetts	36	0.04%	17
Ohio	37	0.03%	42
North Carolina	38	0.01%	13
Maryland	39	0.00%	1
Alabama	40	0.00%	0
Arkansas	40	0.00%	0
Connecticut	40	0.00%	0
Delaware	40	0.00%	0
Georgia	40	0.00%	0
Kentucky	40	0.00%	0
Louisiana	40	0.00%	0
Mississippi	40	0.00%	0
Rhode Island	40	0.00%	0
South Carolina	40	0.00%	0
Virginia	40	0.00%	0

Source: Clean Edge, Inc., 2011. EIA data with Clean Edge analysis.

Texas, better known for its iconic oil tycoons than its environmental advocates, plays a major role in the U.S. wind energy industry. The Lone Star State is by far the number-one U.S. market for wind capacity, with more than 10 gigawatts installed—nearly triple the capacity of Iowa, the second-ranking wind state. Iowa's position makes a great "amaze your friends" clean-energy factoid. Thanks in part to state policies that have focused on both building wind farms and attracting wind industry manufacturers to the Hawkeye State, Iowa has surged past wind power pioneer and number-one overall clean-energy leader California to become the nation's second-largest generator of wind energy.

Texas's wind leadership stems from a variety of factors. When 1999 state legislation deregulated the Texas energy market, making electricity rates more vulnerable to volatile natural gas prices, wind's promise of fixed, predictable costs became increasingly attractive. This legislation—signed into law by then-governor George W. Bush— also introduced a small renewable generation requirement that, while modest, was an early example of a state having mandated renewable energy production. Texas also benefits from an electricity industry that operates almost exclusively within the state, expediting transmission and grid integration matters that can seriously delay projects dealing with interstate energy markets. Finally, the state's bountiful wind resources and plentiful open land on which to develop make Texas a natural fit for the industry. Local farmers looking for fresh revenue streams can lease land to wind developers, sometimes earning up to $10,000 a year for each turbine sited on their land.

Texas governor and former presidential candidate Rick Perry has never claimed to be a protector of the environment, going so far as to sue the EPA in 2010 over its regulation of greenhouse gases. But even Perry recognizes the importance of wind energy in Texas. "One of the greatest economic generators for the Panhandle and all of West Texas is Mother Nature—not only farming and ranching, but energy, too," Perry once said. "And that is increasingly true when it comes to wind energy."

As a percentage of total electricity generation, however, a number of smaller states outperform Texas in wind power. The leader by this measure is Iowa, with wind accounting for an impressive 15 percent of its in-state electricity generation in 2010. And given that the Iowa Wind Energy Association is aiming to reach 10,000 megawatts of capacity by 2020 and 20,000 megawatts by 2030, it's safe to assume that this number will quickly be on the rise. One other state, North Dakota, also passed the 10 percent mark in 2010, albeit with a much smaller generation total.

2010 INSTALLED WIND CAPACITY - TOP 10 STATES			
State	Rank	% of Peak Capacity, 2010	Cumulative Capacity (MW)
Iowa	1	25.17%	3,675
North Dakota	2	21.99%	1,424
South Dakota	3	20.26%	709
Wyoming	4	17.62%	1,412
Minnesota	5	14.78%	2,192
Oregon	6	14.74%	2,104
Colorado	7	9.48%	1,299
Texas	8	9.41%	10,085
Idaho	9	8.96%	353
New Mexico	10	8.72%	700

Source: Clean Edge, Inc., 2011. EIA and AWEA data with Clean Edge analysis.

Wind power is also making headlines elsewhere across the nation. With a $100 million investment from Google and a $1.3 billion loan guarantee from the DOE, the 845-megawatt Shepherds Flat Wind Farm being constructed in eastern Oregon—the number-six state in wind as a percentage of total generation—has already contracted the sale of its electricity to Southern California Edison through a 20-year fixed-price purchase agreement. North of Los Angeles, the Alta

Wind Energy Center—another wind development to receive more than $100 million from Google—is a collection of wind farms that, when completed, are expected to have a capacity exceeding 1,000 megawatts. And although the U.S. offshore wind industry has not yet taken off, the Obama administration is working to streamline permitting procedures in hopes of catalyzing offshore development. The Department of the Interior has even designated "wind energy areas" along the Atlantic coast, where an estimated 1,000 gigawatts of offshore wind capacity resides.

But for wind to become a dominant source of energy in the United States, shedding its "alternative" energy label, it will have to overcome several major challenges. First and foremost, wind's intermittent nature needs to be addressed. Some look to grid energy storage as the immediate solution, but storing electricity is expensive and complex, especially on a large scale. Intermittent output also raises technical issues as wind energy reaches a higher percentage of grid capacity. Management of a grid with large amounts of intermittent energy sources will present a new breed of conflicts, as was showcased in 2011 when energy companies filed a complaint with the Federal Energy Regulatory Commission (FERC) against the Bonneville Power Administration (BPA), grid operator in the Pacific Northwest, for its preferential treatment of BPA-owned hydro sources over private wind projects during times of oversupply. In December 2011, the FERC ruled that BPA's action—curtailing wind generation when record snowmelt caused a surge in available hydropower—was "discriminatory" and that the grid operator must revise its operating policy to avoid future conflict. While the full impact of this ruling remains to be seen, it was undeniably a victory for the wind industry.

In the U.S. specifically, the lack of long-term certainty over federal policy incentives continues to present an enormous roadblock to wind project development. Since 1992, the federal government has offered a production tax credit (PTC) for owners of renewable energy projects, but the PTC has generally been a short-term incentive that's had to be extended several times in the past—often with an extension vote coming not long before incentives were set to expire. Therein lies the problem: While federal support can usually be guaranteed for only a few years at a time, wind installations produce a steady, predictable amount of electricity over several decades. For wind power and other renewable energy technologies facing similar challenges, development is severely hindered by this stop-and-start incentive structure. But even with its challenges, wind power will be an integral source of energy in the 21st century. The upside potential is too large for it not to be.

SOLAR POWER

The sun can be used to generate electricity in two ways. Solar photovoltaic (PV) technology converts sunlight directly into electricity using cells made of conductive materials, while solar thermal systems (also called concentrating solar power, or CSP) focus the sun's rays to heat liquid and create steam. The potential for harnessing energy from the sun is immense. A favorite statistic of solar energy enthusiasts is that enough sun hits the earth each hour to power the planet for an entire year.

With its massive resource potential, solar is arguably the most promising weapon in America's clean-energy arsenal. But the age of solar in the U.S. is not yet upon us. The 1.8 gigawatts of new PV capacity installed in the U.S. during 2011 represented a more than doubling from the previous year's additions. However, even with this immense growth, the U.S. market remains behind markets in Germany, Italy, and China, which installed roughly 7.5, 7, and 2.5 gigawatts of PV respectively in 2011. Germany, despite having solar resource conditions similar to Alaska's, has used lucrative government incentives to establish itself as the world's preeminent solar market, with more than 24.8 gigawatts installed by the end of 2011. In the U.S., however, where political realities make such strong nationwide incentives all but impossible, solar activity has been limited to those states willing to take proactive steps to create a local market.

With the aid of committed government support, California has capitalized on its rich natural resources and solar-supporting citizens to become the nation's unmistakable solar leader—at the beginning of 2011, roughly half of all U.S. solar capacity could be found in the state. California's solar incentive programs, known collectively as the Go Solar California campaign, are part of a state goal to install 3 gigawatts of solar projects on homes and businesses by the end of 2016. (The campaign is an evolution of former governor Arnold Schwarzenegger's Million Solar Roofs vision.) With reliable incentives in place, California has seen an explosion of distributed solar capacity, and the number of solar installations has grown from fewer than 2,000 in 2002 to more than 87,000 in 2011.

While California's early solar market growth came almost entirely from small rooftop installations, the key driver of the future will be utility-scale projects with capacities of 1 megawatt or larger. By mid-2011, more than 900 megawatts of utility-scale projects were under construction in the Golden State, with another 16 gigawatts in earlier stages of development, according to the Solar Energy Industries Association. But even with this sizable pipeline, California's influence over the U.S. solar market is diminishing as other states become active in the sector. California's 30 percent share of the U.S. market in 2010 is a far cry from the 80 percent share the state enjoyed just five years earlier.

One state to emerge as a surprising star of America's solar story is New Jersey. As the second-largest solar market in the country, the Garden State's 573 megawatts of solar capacity at the end of 2011 (more than double the state's 260 megawatts in 2010) was more than the combined capacities of third- and fourth-ranked Colorado and Arizona. In some aspects, New Jersey is even besting California. When 9 megawatts of SunPower panels were installed on the massive roof of a marine terminal warehouse next to the Walt Whitman Bridge, in Gloucester City, New Jersey, in 2011, the project became the largest solar rooftop installation in the U.S. It bested a 4.26-megawatt installation that had been commissioned only a few months earlier. The location of this now-second-largest rooftop installation in the U.S. is a commercial office building in Edison, New Jersey.

While not home to a particularly sunny climate, New Jersey's solar rise can be attributed to a variety of factors. The state is home to some of the country's highest electricity rates, making it easier for solar to be cost-competitive. Its RPS legislation—mandating 20 percent electricity from renewables by 2020—requires that a certain amount of power, in what's known as a carve-out, be generated by solar. And since 2004, the New Jersey Board of Public Utilities has offered solar renewable energy certificates (SRECs), performance-based incentives that valued each solar-generated megawatt-hour of electricity at about $400 in 2011 (with lower pricing now). Due to these and other market dynamics, community solar financier One Block Off the Grid identified New Jersey as the region with the shortest payback time for solar installations in the U.S.—approximately four years for a typical residential project.

Solar is also becoming an increasingly popular clean-energy option elsewhere in the U.S. In Hawaii, the nation's highest electricity rates have already made solar an economically wise choice, even without incentives (a feat known fondly in the clean-energy industry as grid parity). By the end of 2010, 1.7 percent of Hawaii's in-state generating capacity was solar power, more than any other state. In Arizona, 350 megawatts of utility-scale solar was under construction by mid-2011—enough to more than triple the size of that state's solar market. And in Nevada, the open desert has become an increasingly popular source for California's future clean electrons. In early 2011, Southern California Edison announced a deal to buy electricity from a 250-megawatt First Solar project to be built on Nevadan land in the northern Mojave Desert.

2010 INSTALLED SOLAR PV CAPACITY - TOP 10 STATES			
State	Rank	% of Peak Capacity, 2010	Cumulative Capacity (MW)
Hawaii	1	1.72%	44.70
California	2	1.52%	1,021.50
New Jersey	3	1.40%	259.90
Nevada	4	0.89%	102.00
Colorado	5	0.86%	117.40
New Mexico	6	0.54%	43.30
Arizona	7	0.40%	104.90
Massachusetts	8	0.27%	37.50
Connecticut	9	0.27%	22.30
Vermont	10	0.26%	2.90

Source: Clean Edge, Inc., 2011. EIA and IREC data with Clean Edge analysis.

This is all exciting, but for solar to ever contribute more than a percent or two to U.S. electricity supply, technology costs must come down. The good news is that solar costs, specifically for PV, have already fallen significantly over the years—from roughly $9 per peak watt globally in 2000 to less than $4 per watt in 2011. And this trend shows little sign of slowing down: PV prices dropped by more than 50 percent from 2008 to 2011.

In the next few years, PV's price decline will begin hitting critical market-driving points as it becomes cost-competitive with grid electricity. Clean Edge research shows that by 2015, power from distributed solar PV systems will be equal to or less than retail electricity rates in at least six states. By 2020, cost parity is likely to have been reached in roughly half of all states. And with DOE-led efforts to accelerate the drop in PV costs, these projections, if anything, are conservative.

Cost-competitive PV and deployment of massive utility-scale plants will transform the U.S. energy landscape. Solar will also serve as a valuable job engine for the U.S. economy. By the end of 2010, the solar industry in the U.S. already accounted for 100,000 direct and indirect jobs, according to the SEIA—more than the number of Americans working in steel production. And just as U.S. steel helped catalyze 20th-century economic growth, solar has the potential to play an important role in driving economic growth in the 21st century.

GEOTHERMAL POWER

Maybe the most underappreciated source of clean energy is geothermal—the use of heat from beneath the earth's surface to create steam, which is then used to drive a turbine and generate electricity. The biggest appeal of geothermal power is that the heat is always there. With a constant source of steam, geothermal projects can provide baseload electricity production—a major challenge for intermittent renewables like wind and solar. And geothermal resources are vast. Veteran global energy and environment expert Lester Brown, in his book *World on the Edge,* notes that "the heat in the upper six miles of the earth's crust contains 50,000 times as much energy as found in all of the world's oil and gas reserves combined—a startling statistic." Startling indeed. But with today's technology, large-scale geothermal plants can be located only in volcanic zones, restricting this energy resource in the U.S. to states west of the Great Plains. At the end of 2010, only nine states were home to operating geothermal power projects, and U.S. geothermal capacity was only 3,100 megawatts.

But the geothermal market is heating up. By mid-2011, more than 5,000 megawatts of new capacity were in development across 15 states, according to the Geothermal Energy Association. Nevada alone has more than 60 projects in development, worth more than 2,250 megawatts of new geothermal capacity. California, already the nation's capacity leader and home to the world's largest geothermal project—the 850-megawatt Geysers complex, north of Napa Valley—has more than 1,500 megawatts of geothermal capacity under development.

Idaho, Oregon, Utah, and Alaska are among other states working to commission new geothermal plants. Although geothermal projects take years to bring online, with today's heightened development activity, geothermal will soon be an important source of clean energy for America.

2010 INSTALLED GEOTHERMAL CAPACITY - TOP 9 STATES			
State	Rank	% of Peak Capacity, 2010	Cumulative Capacity (MW)
Nevada	1	3.86%	441.80
California	2	3.82%	2,565.50
Hawaii	3	1.35%	35.00
Utah	4	0.56%	42.00
Idaho	5	0.40%	15.80
Alaska	6	0.04%	0.73
Wyoming	7	0.003%	0.25
New Mexico	8	0.003%	0.24
Oregon	9	0.002%	0.28
n/a	10	n/a	n/a

Source: Clean Edge, Inc., 2011. EIA and GEA data with Clean Edge analysis.

BIOMASS AND HYDROELECTRIC POWER

Biomass power and hydropower are two other key sources of renewable, low-carbon electricity. Both of these sectors are essential to the U.S.'s ability to combat climate change and limit dependency on fossil fuels, but each has caveats deserving of attention.

Hydroelectric dams, while capable of delivering carbon-free, gigawatt-scale baseload power, can hardly be considered environmentally neutral structures. Construction of the massive Three Gorges Dam along the Yangtze River in China, for example, created a new 400-mile-long lake upriver and in the process displaced a staggering 1.3 million Chinese residents. In the U.S., hydro projects generate roughly 6 percent of all electricity. The West, with an abundance of powerful rivers carving through the region's landscapes, is home to America's hydropower leaders. More than 20,000 megawatts of hydro capacity is online in Washington, another 10,000 megawatts exists in California, and about 8,000 megawatts can be found in Oregon. In total, the U.S. has nearly 80,000 megawatts of hydropower-generating capacity.

Biomass power incorporates a variety of technologies, from landfill gas plants capturing methane emissions to direct-combustion facilities, which do little more than burn woody biomass to generate steam. Not all biomass is created equal, and while some biopower technologies deliver efficient, cost-effective clean electrons, others can actually cause harm. In a briefing on biomass power on its website, the Union of Concerned Scientists outlines the risks clearly. "If not managed carefully, biomass for energy can be harvested at unsustainable rates, damage ecosystems, produce harmful air pollution, consume large amounts of water, and produce net greenhouse emissions." Still, the potential benefits from biomass power in the U.S. are significant, especially with a wealth of waste streams readily available to be converted into clean energy. By the end of 2010, biomass accounted for nearly 1.5 percent of electricity generation in America, with the states of Pennsylvania, Florida, California, and Maine leading the way.

21ST-CENTURY INFRASTRUCTURE: GREEN BUILDINGS, SMART GRIDS, AND MORE

Clean electricity consistently dominates discussion of the U.S. clean-energy economy, but limiting attention to this scope misses the far-reaching realities of the nation's energy landscape. Many overlook the fact that the built environment—residential and commercial buildings, along with buildings and power used for industry—is responsible for nearly half of all U.S. energy usage and roughly three-quarters of electricity demand. So while cleaning up our electricity supply is indeed of utmost importance, improvement to the processes of delivering, consuming, and conserving energy may offer the most immediate steps to begin addressing 21st-century energy challenges.

Since its launch in 2000, the Leadership in Energy and Environmental Design (LEED) rating system, administered by the U.S. Green Building Council (USGBC), has done much to boost awareness of and support for sustainable building methods—by 2010, LEED-certified green building projects covered more than 1 billion square feet worldwide. While California, with more than 1,000 certified buildings, is home to the most LEED projects, Oregon is number one in the nation in terms of LEED projects per capita: Oregon's 60 projects per million people is more than double California's 29 projects per million people. Other front-runners in LEED project deployment include Vermont, Colorado, and Washington, all with more than 50 projects per million people by the end of 2010.

2010 LEED BUILDING DEPLOYMENT

State	Rank	LEED Certified Projects Per 1M People	Total LEED Certified Projects	Platinum Projects	Gold Projects	Silver Projects
Oregon	1	59.9	231	29	116	53
Vermont	2	56.2	35	2	11	12
Colorado	3	51.8	264	10	118	92
Washington	4	51.0	344	12	150	125
Massachusetts	5	43.9	291	14	109	91
Maine	6	35.0	46	1	12	21
Maryland	7	32.4	186	10	77	64
Virginia	8	30.8	245	7	84	95
Illinois	9	30.1	390	24	166	125
New Mexico	10	30.0	61	3	28	21

Source: Clean Edge, Inc., 2011. USGBC data with Clean Edge analysis.

The EPA's Energy Star program also offers certification for buildings, but with more of a focus on energy than on overall sustainability. To earn Energy Star certification, a facility must earn a score of 75 or higher on the EPA's 1–100 energy performance scale, meaning that it is performing more efficiently than at least 75 percent of similar buildings nationwide. Today, more than 15,000 certified Energy Star buildings exist in the U.S., saving a combined $1.9 billion in energy costs every year when compared to average building energy performance. California again leads all states for the most total Energy Star–certified buildings, with Colorado leading in terms of projects per capita. Also performing well in Energy Star building certification are North Carolina, Virginia, and Wisconsin, three states that generally do not come to mind when thinking of clean-tech deployment—each of these states had more Energy Star–certified buildings per capita than California by the end of 2010.

Driving much of the push for efficiency in newly constructed and renovated buildings are energy codes that set minimum standards for materials, equipment, and energy-use performance. Because it's up to states and local jurisdictions to adopt building energy codes, the strictness of standards varies widely across the U.S. In general, states on the coasts have chosen to adopt stronger energy codes than inland states, although there are exceptions to this trend. More than 25 states have adopted the strongest commercial-building energy codes, while approximately 20 states have adopted the strongest energy codes for residential buildings.

Energy codes establishing minimum standards are only the beginning, though. Net-zero energy communities—developments that produce as much power as they use—are quickly becoming a reality in America. Forty miles north of St. Louis, in the small farm town of Jerseyville, Illinois, the 32-home LEED Platinum-certified Lexington Farm Estates community offers its residents the opportunity to live an energy-efficient lifestyle with monthly electric bills of zero.

Houses use efficient lighting, ground-source heat pumps, solar PV installations, and even garage-mounted vertical-axis wind turbines to achieve net-zero living for residents. And because it was financed largely by American Recovery and Reinvestment Act stimulus funds, federal tax credits, and state grants, Lexington Farm Estates exists as an affordable housing community targeted at rural families earning less than $41,000 per year. Michael Morrissey, vice president of Morrissey Construction, the project's developer, spelled out the appeal to a local newspaper, saying people can rent "a brand-new house with three bedrooms and an attached two-car garage and no utility bills for $590 per month."

Taking the ultra-efficient theme beyond just residential developments, the city of Fort Collins, Colorado, is pursuing what's known as a net-zero energy district. The goal is to completely power a major section of the city from renewable energy sources within a 50-mile radius of the district, renewable and conventional distributed sources within the district, and demand reduction and response within the district. Known as FortZED, the initiative launched in January 2011 and covers downtown Fort Collins and the campus of Colorado State University. At this scale, FortZED begins addressing very important concerns about the efficient delivery and monitoring of electricity, activities at the heart of developing a 21st-century smart grid.

"Smart grid" is an umbrella term used to describe the range of technologies and services aimed at improving the efficiency, control, and intelligence of electric infrastructure. Smart grid encompasses everything from smart meters and grid monitoring to advanced transmission infrastructure and the integration of distributed renewable-energy projects. The first wave of smart-grid development in the U.S has been the deployment of smart meters, which allow utilities to better monitor and control their customers' electricity consumption. By the end of 2010, U.S. smart-meter deployment had reached about 13 million homes and businesses, representing approximately 9 percent of the nation's electric meters. Arizona's 29 percent smart-meter penetration was number one in the nation, with four other states—Oregon, Idaho, Pennsylvania, and Wisconsin—also achieving more than 20 percent smart-meter deployment.

2010 SMART METER MARKET PENETRATION			
State	Rank	% of Total Meters	Total Smart Meters
Arizona	1	29.1%	847,177
Oregon	2	25.2%	478,897
Idaho	3	24.7%	198,370
Pennsylvania	4	24.3%	1,493,201
Wisconsin	5	22.2%	757,688
California	6	16.7%	2,475,896
Missouri	7	16.5%	506,416
South Carolina	8	12.8%	312,894
Georgia	9	11.7%	514,403
Texas	10	11.7%	1,284,179

Source: Clean Edge, Inc., 2011. FERC data with Clean Edge analysis.

To date, however, smart-grid project performance has been a mixed bag. On the plus side, in Oklahoma, a study of the first phase of Oklahoma Gas & Electric's $366 million system-wide smart grid has returned some promising results. Residential customers with smart thermostats were shown to have reduced demand by up to 57 percent during peak times, compared with customers without them. And for customers participating in variable peak pricing, average energy consumption dropped as much as one-third during the highest-priced periods. However, in Boulder, Colorado, Xcel Energy's much-touted SmartGridCity project has not seen the same success. While not massive in scale, the SmartGridCity project was pitched as a model for a fully functional, citywide smart grid that would utilize a variety of technologies and services beyond simple smart meters. The utility, which did not deliver any sort of cost-benefit analysis before embarking on the project, quickly began facing significant cost overruns. Original capital costs for SmartGridCity were targeted at slightly more than $15 million, but costs exceeded $40 million even before the project was completed. A major mismanagement like this, especially in a highly publicized pilot project, has the potential to hamstring momentum for the entire sector.

But the need to upgrade the U.S. electric grid is too great to be derailed by short-term mishaps. If America is to move beyond its dependence on fossil fuels, it will need to improve the efficiency with which the country consumes and delivers energy.

CLEAN TRANSPORTATION CHARGES AHEAD

Transportation is the third leg of America's energy story, making up roughly a third of all U.S. energy consumption. With petroleum representing more than 90 percent of the sector's supply source, changing the energy source we use to commute, travel, and deliver goods is the only way we'll ever alleviate our addiction to oil. In a quest to move beyond petroleum, everything from ethanol and biodiesel to natural gas and hydrogen has been touted—with equal enthusiasm—as the fuel of tomorrow. These fuel alternatives will play significant roles, but we firmly believe that the evolution of transportation in the 21st century will be a tale of vehicle electrification.

By 2010, the Everyman's EV had not yet arrived. The realm of electric-powered personal transportation in America remained limited to golf carts, goofy-looking neighborhood vehicles, and the über-flashy Tesla Roadster—which, at a price of more than $100,000, is just as quick to empty your bank account as it is to make the jump from zero to 60. But after December 2010, with the widespread release of the plug-in hybrid electric (PHEV) Chevrolet Volt and the all-electric

Nissan LEAF, things began to change. In the first six months, Chevy had delivered 2,510 Volts and Nissan had delivered 2,186 LEAFs—not insignificant numbers, considering that at the end of 2010 only 33,000 plug-in EVs were on the road in the U.S. Now, with President Obama aiming (some say quite ambitiously and perhaps unrealistically) for one million plug-in EVs on U.S. roads by 2015, consulting firm Roland Berger is estimating that more than 10 percent of new U.S. vehicles will be electric by 2020.

But growing pains remain. In March 2012, sluggish sales of the Volt caused GM to halt all production for five weeks, temporarily idling 1,300 workers at company's Detroit-Hamtramck production line in order to sell off excess inventory. GM, looking to sell 10,000 Volts in 2011, ended up selling only 7,671 for the year. Sales troubles continued into 2012 as the National Highway Transportation Safety Agency investigated the Volt over safety concerns related to the possibility of post-crash battery fires. Although the investigation was closed in late January 2012, ultimately finding no evidence of safety issues, it was the source of some reputation-damaging publicity.

Are the Volt's early setbacks a sign that high price tags, plug-in requirements, and new generations of traditional hybrids (like Toyota's new Prius C) impeding widespread customer acceptance of EVs? Possibly. But there are also signs that EVs are taking the first small step toward a greater market share. While GM tempers sales targets to avoid overproduction, Nissan is doing all it can to boost LEAF manufacturing. Nissan CEO Carlos Ghosn sees the 9,764 LEAFs sold in the U.S. during 2011 as only the beginning. "The only reason we couldn't sell more is because we couldn't build more," he said at the North American International Auto Show in January 2012. "We're expecting in 2012 to double that number." How accurate Ghosn's lofty expectations are remains to be seen.

While first-year EV sales were cause for some skepticism, they tended to follow a pattern akin to early hybrid-electric vehicle

sales—and it was hybrids that truly launched the electrification revolution. Using an internal combustion engine in cooperation with
a battery-powered electric motor to improve efficiency, hybrids are
typically 20 to 30 percent more fuel-efficient than standard gasoline vehicles. By 2010, there were more than 1.7 million hybrids on
the road in America. The most successful hybrid to date has clearly
been Toyota's Prius. Toyota first introduced it to the U.S. market in
2000, selling 5,562 units its first year. By 2011, Toyota had sold its
millionth Prius in the U.S. (The Prius is even more popular in Japan,
where it was the best-selling car in both 2009 and 2010.) In the U.S.,
the West Coast has led the way, with California, Oregon, and Washington accounting for three of the top four states in hybrids per
capita. Vermont also performs very strongly on a per capita basis,
just behind California. Because the consumer appeal for EVs is generally the same as for hybrids, identifying these leading markets for
hybrid sales is a good indicator of where EVs are likely to take off in
the future.

HYBRID ELECTRIC VEHICLES IN USE (REGISTERED VEHICLES, 2010)			
State	Rank	HEVs Per 1M People	Total HEVs
California	1	11,748.2	437,814
Vermont	2	10,365.8	6,452
Oregon	3	9,639.9	37,167
Washington	4	8,657.3	58,404
Virginia	5	8,402.5	66,818
Massachusetts	6	8,186.7	54,288
Maryland	7	7,835.4	44,954
New Hampshire	8	7,686.3	10,173
Connecticut	9	7,518.1	26,516
Hawaii	10	7,337.2	9,539

Source: Clean Edge, Inc., 2011. R. L. Polk data with Clean Edge analysis.

ELECTRIC VEHICLES IN USE (REGISTERED VEHICLES, 2010)			
State	Rank	EVs Per 1M People	Total EVs
California	1	494.7	18,435
Arizona	2	331.5	2,213
New York	3	217.1	4,251
North Dakota	4	191.2	125
Oklahoma	5	180.4	672
Vermont	6	152.6	95
Hawaii	7	145.4	189
Florida	8	131.8	2,461
Michigan	9	52.5	521
New Hampshire	10	52.1	69

Source: Clean Edge, Inc., 2011. R. L. Polk data with Clean Edge analysis.

As America gears up for the biggest transformation of personal transportation in generations—possibly since the Model T displaced the Stanley Steamer nearly a century ago—states and cities are competing to become test beds for the first wave of EVs. Some regions got a head start, with inaugural deliveries of Chevy's Volt limited to California, Washington, D.C., Austin, and the New York City metropolitan area. For the Nissan LEAF, primary markets included California, Arizona, Oregon, Seattle, and Tennessee. But because EVs require frequent charging, vehicle sales are only half the battle. Establishing a robust network of charging infrastructure will likely prove to be the ultimate asset in developing a viable EV hub.

The work to deploy America's EV-charging infrastructure is well under way. Non-residential charging stations totaled fewer than 600 in 2010 and were located almost entirely in California, but by early 2012 this number had multiplied to nearly 7,000, led by California (1,692 charging stations), Washington (576), Texas (570), Florida (464), Michigan (456), and Oregon (379). This growth will only accelerate as a combination of local initiatives and nationwide campaigns hit full stride. The EV Project, America's largest charging-infrastructure-deployment effort, intends to install more than 14,000 chargers across California, Oregon, Washington, Arizona, Texas, Tennessee, and Washington, D.C.

Much government activity to support EVs will come from the city level, given that urban environments will see a majority of the EV adoption. But states also have an important role to play, whether through purchasing incentives, permitting processes, or state fleet adoption requirements. In addition to the $7,500 EV-purchasing incentive offered by the federal government, several state-level incentives also exist. Colorado's $6,000 incentive tops the field, and California, Oregon, and Georgia trail close behind, with incentives of up to $5,000. Other lucrative incentives can be found in Hawaii, Illinois, New Jersey, Louisiana, and Maryland. In total, 20 states were offering purchasing incentives for high-efficiency vehicles by the end of 2010.

With an opportunity to breathe life back into the long-struggling American auto industry, manufacturing will be another important element of U.S. EV activity. Tesla, fueled by a $465 million DOE loan and a strategic partnership with Toyota, revived a shuttered former General Motors–Toyota joint venture-owned plant in Fremont, California, in 2010 to produce its Model S sedan line. And while the first Nissan LEAFs were not U.S.-made, the company is working to open its LEAF production complex in Smyrna, Tennessee, before the end of 2012. When that plant is operational, up to 150,000 LEAFs a year will roll down its assembly line.

In battery manufacturing, Michigan is the center of attention. A123 Systems, battery provider to the likes of Eaton, Fisker Automotive, Navistar, and Shanghai Automotive Industry Corporation, opened North America's largest lithium-ion automotive battery plant in Livonia, Michigan, in late 2010. And in Holland, Michigan, across the state, South Korea–based LG Chem—battery supplier for the Chevy Volt and Ford Focus Electric—expects to be producing thousands of batteries from its $350 million facility before the end of 2012.

As *The Economist* correspondents Iain Carson and Vijay Vaitheeswaran wrote in their book *ZOOM: The Global Race to Fuel the Car of the Future*, "Oil is the problem; cars are the solution." With the first mass-produced EVs now in showrooms across America, the first wave of automobile electrification is already upon us. It has become evident that the future for transportation in the 21st century is electric (including hybrid electric), for both the U.S. and the world. Whether through vehicle sales, charging-infrastructure deployment, or manufacturing activity, competition is heating up among cities, states, and nations to lead in this budding clean-tech sector.

BRIGHT MINDS, BRIGHT IDEAS: HUMAN AND INTELLECTUAL CAPITAL

The clean-energy economy cannot be defined solely by our capacity to produce clean electrons, the number of clean vehicles on our roads, or the efficiency of our buildings and electric grid. To locate today's leading clean-tech clusters and discover where future activity will emerge, we must look beyond technology deployment and take a more comprehensive approach embracing human capital. Where are researchers developing new technologies? Where are entrepreneurs turning these technologies into new businesses? And where are workers manufacturing the latest clean-tech products? Even though the clean-tech revolution is widespread, regions with high concentrations of clean-tech minds already exist, and it is these places that are driving industry growth.

In his book *Who's Your City?* Richard Florida analyzes factors that draw people to different places around the world. One conclusion, what Florida calls the "clustering force," suggests that it is the fundamental gathering of people that powers economic growth, as clusters attract new people in search of like-minded individuals. "When large numbers of entrepreneurs, financiers, engineers, designers, and other smart, creative people are constantly bumping into one another inside and outside of work, business ideas are formed, sharpened, executed, and—if successful—expanded," Florida explains.

This clustering force is no different for clean tech. Hubs of clean-tech activity can quickly reach critical mass and begin attracting entrepreneurs, investors, and consumers supportive of the industry. So in which U.S. states can you find the highest concentrations of these clean-techies?

According to 2011 research from the Brookings Institution, the largest employer of "clean economy" workers is California, with more than 300,000 people employed in that sector. (Brookings defines the clean economy as any activity that produces goods and services with an environmental benefit, like improved resource management or minimized pollution and waste.) Florida, Illinois, New York, Ohio, Pennsylvania, and Texas are also home to sizable clean-tech workforces, each with more than 100,000 clean-economy jobs. In terms of clean-economy jobs as a percentage of total jobs, state leaders include Alaska, Oregon, Montana, and Vermont—the clean economy makes up at least a 3 percent share of total jobs in those states. The clean-tech sector showed particularly promising growth in Brookings research. From 2003 to 2010, U.S. clean-tech jobs grew at a rate twice that of the rest of the economy: 8.3 percent versus 4.2 percent annually. But job counting is a challenging task, and differences in taxonomy and scope can quickly attract skepticism about even the most meticulous research. Until clean-tech or clean-energy jobs are officially defined and tracked by the federal government, accurate U.S. job statistics will remain elusive.

To identify hot spots for intellectual capital—places where individuals and companies are developing tomorrow's clean technologies—a review of the geographic dispersion of patents can be very revealing. From 2002 to 2011, a majority of clean-tech patent activity occurred in a small collection of states. Michigan, thanks to its dominant auto industry presence, led the way with more than 1,000 clean-energy patents granted, roughly a quarter of the U.S. total. California also performed strongly, as expected, taking home more than 700 patents across a variety of sectors. New York, propelled by fuel cell and wind-energy innovations, earned over 500 patents. And Connecticut, owing almost entirely to fuel cell activity, received nearly 300 patents during the nine-year span. Other states bringing in a large number of patents over the past decade include Illinois, Texas, Florida, and Massachusetts. As shown in the following chart, these top states continued to lead the way in 2010.

CLEAN ENERGY PATENTS GRANTED (2002–2010)

State	Rank	Patents Per 1 Million People	Total Patents
Michigan	1	103.1	1,024
Delaware	2	83.0	74
Connecticut	3	79.4	280
New Mexico	4	27.5	56
New York	5	27.3	535
Massachusetts	6	22.0	146
Wyoming	7	21.9	12
California	8	19.3	720
Oregon	9	18.2	70
Vermont	10	17.7	11

Source: Clean Edge, Inc., 2011. Heslin Rothenberg Farley & Mesiti data with Clean Edge analysis.

FOLLOW THE MONEY: FINANCIAL CAPITAL

Development of a regional clean-tech hub requires capital, whether in the form of R&D funding, early-stage venture capital, asset financing, or government incentives. For this reason, tracking investment trends is one of the more accurate ways to pinpoint areas of concentrated activity and also to identify locations primed for future growth.

Venture capital—money provided to startup firms—is particularly relevant for clean tech, given that the industry is based largely on commercializing new technologies.

A quick look at venture capital in the U.S. over the past decade provides a good depiction of clean tech's rise from niche sector to mainstream industry. At the turn of the century, the term "clean tech" had not yet even entered the investment lexicon, and the industry didn't amount to more than 1 percent of U.S. venture capital until 2001. But as the decade progressed, as technologies improved and market drivers became more apparent, clean tech began to garner attention from the most prestigious VC firms. By 2010, clean-tech venture investments exceeded $5 billion, 23 percent of all VC activity in the U.S. was clean-tech-related, and four of the five largest VC rounds in 2010 went to clean-tech companies. Better Place (EV battery-swap infrastructure) pulled in $350 million, BrightSource Energy (utility-scale CSP) $110 million, Abound Solar (thin-film PV cells) $110 million, and Trilliant (wireless smart-grid networks) $105 million, according to PricewaterhouseCoopers's *MoneyTree Report*. The only non-clean-tech company in the top five was Twitter, with a $200 million round.

From the perspective of U.S. states, California's dominance in the arena of clean-energy venture capital is undeniable. The table on the following page shows the top ten states for U.S. clean-energy venture capital activity, based on the home state of companies receiving funding. There is no close contention for the clean-tech VC state crown: 63 percent of all dollars go to California-based companies. From 2008 through 2010, California clean-energy companies closed 400 separate VC financing rounds. In this three-year span, 30 individual clean-tech rounds broke the $100 million mark, and California companies accounted for 20 of those. Led by companies in Silicon Valley, San Francisco, Los Angeles, and San Diego, the Golden State's attraction of venture capital is unmatched even when viewed from a size-adjusted per capita perspective. It doesn't hurt that California is also the epicenter of the VC industry itself. Sand Hill Road in Menlo Park—the Wall Street of the West—is home to the legendary early funders of Apple, Intel, and Google, and those same firms are now injecting millions into clean tech.

Although a distant runner-up, Massachusetts's attraction of clean-tech venture capital is notable. With a broad roster of start-ups, like A123 Systems and Boston Power in energy storage, Luminus Devices in solid-state lighting, and FloDesign in wind power, Massachusetts was the only state outside of California able to break the $1 billion and 100-deal barriers for clean-energy VC during the 2008–2010 period.

CLEAN ENERGY VENTURE CAPITAL INVESTMENT - TOP 10 STATES BY DOLLARS PER CAPITA (2008-2010)

State	Rank	Dollars Invested Per Capita	Total Dollars ($, Millions)	Total Deals
California	1	$231.09	$8,612.0	400
Massachusetts	2	$186.03	$1,233.7	103
New Hampshire	3	$165.47	$219.0	11
Colorado	4	$143.28	$730.1	33
Oregon	5	$75.53	$291.2	18
Vermont	6	$65.81	$41.0	4
Washington	7	$46.52	$313.8	42
Virginia	8	$30.04	$238.9	13
Maryland	9	$29.69	$170.4	8
New Mexico	10	$24.09	$49.0	5

Source: Clean Edge, Inc., 2011. Cleantech Group data with Clean Edge analysis.

STATE POLICY RANKINGS

State policies play a critical role in where technology is developed and deployed, where companies locate, and where money is invested. Please see the appendix for a summary of key incentives, regulations, and mandates that exist in each state, which reveals the stark differences that exist in our diverse national geography.

CLEAN-TECH ELITE: TOP TEN STATES

So far we've shown that examples of clean-tech leadership can be found in almost every corner of America, a direct result of the broad variety of sectors that the industry encompasses. And with today's instantaneous global connectivity, clean tech, like many other industries, will not be bound to a small number of geographic epicenters. It shouldn't be unusual to find a clean-tech company headquartered in California, funded by Massachusetts venture capital, manufacturing products in the heart of Ohio, and selling technology originally developed in a Colorado research lab.

But in looking at the results of our *State Clean Energy Leadership Index* research, it becomes evident that certain states consistently rise to the top of industry rankings, exhibiting strong competitive positioning in all three key areas of clean-tech activity: technology, policy, and capital. During the first global wave of clean-tech growth, states like California, Oregon, Massachusetts, New York, and Colorado have established fruitful industry clusters within their state lines.

What follows is a review of the most advanced clean-tech states—those ranking in the top ten of the *2011 State Clean Energy Leadership Index*. By taking a closer look at how these states have established top-tier positioning, we can learn important lessons about what success looks like. Each region will have its strengths and weaknesses, but common themes revealed among these leaders will serve as valuable insight for any region pursuing development of a clean-tech economy.

1. CALIFORNIA
California's dominance of the U.S. clean-tech industry is staggering.

In 2010, California-based clean-energy startups took in nearly $3 billion of venture capital investment—representing 63 percent of all U.S. clean-energy venture capital investment for the year. Coupling this strong industry presence with growth-inducing policies has allowed California to establish a leadership position in the deployment of many clean technologies. At the end of 2010, California's market for solar PV (1,022 megawatts of installed capacity) represented 48 percent of the U.S. total of 2,135 megawatts and was nearly four times the size of the next-largest U.S. market, New Jersey's 260 megawatts.

As an early supporter of clean forms of transportation, California also stands out from other states in automobile electrification progress. The Golden State's 440,000 hybrid electric vehicles in 2010 represented a quarter of the U.S. market. No other state exceeded the 100,000 mark. For all-electric vehicles, California's 18,435 registered EVs accounted for more than half of the national EV total. And racing to subdue any range-anxiety concerns, the state's nearly 1,700 public EV-charging stations by the end of 2011 far exceed any other statewide EV infrastructure deployment effort.

In terms of energy consumption, California's longtime commitment to energy efficiency has provided an inspirational case study. During 2010, the state's annual per capita electricity consumption figure (6,719 kilowatt-hours) was roughly half of the national average (12,119 kilowatt-hours per person). More important, as the national average has steadily risen over the past several decades—from 4,050 kilowatt-hours in 1960—California's per capita electricity consumption has remained relatively flat since the early 1970s, without any sacrifice in economic growth.

These clean-tech successes did not come overnight. They arrived only after many years of committed government support and thorough implementation of hard-nosed environmental policies under both Democratic and Republican administrations. When it comes to clean energy, California has made a habit of offering the largest incentives, adopting the strongest targets, and enforcing the strictest regulations. Key measures have included Governor Pete Wilson's signing of Assembly Bill 1890 in 1996, creating incentives for grid-tied solar PV systems (and deregulating investor-owned utilities); Governor Arnold Schwarzenegger's signing of the Global Warming Solutions Act (AB 32) in 2006, enacting a statewide greenhouse-gas-emissions reduction target; and Governor Jerry Brown's 2011 signing of RPS legislation mandating that the state get 33 percent of its electricity from renewables by 2020—the nation's most aggressive clean-energy target.

With its strong policy support, access to investment capital, large concentration of clean-tech companies and workers, and abundant solar, wind, and geothermal resources, California's top-dog position will not disappear any time soon. Clean tech has been a bright spot in the state's economy—over the past 35 years, energy-efficiency policies alone have saved consumers more than $56 billion and created more than 1.5 million jobs. And in recent years, California has consistently attracted more than half of all clean-tech venture capital investment in the U.S. But as the nation's clean-energy economy matures and competition among states intensifies, it will become more and more difficult for one state to lead in the dominant way that California does today.

Companies to Watch: California
Amyris
amyrisbiotech.com
NASDAQ: AMRS
Emeryville
Renewable fuels and chemicals developer

BrightSource Energy
brightsourceenergy.com
Oakland
Utility-scale solar (CSP) project developer

Silver Spring Networks
silverspringnet.com
Redwood City
Smart-grid technology developer and service provider

SunPower (majority-owned by Total)
us.sunpowercorp.com
NASDAQ: SPWRA
San Jose
Solar PV panel manufacturer

Tesla Motors
teslamotors.com
NASDAQ: TSLA
Palo Alto
EV manufacturer

2. OREGON

Tucked in the green timberland of the Pacific Northwest, Oregon is home to a culture of sustainability that is hard to ignore. In the metro area of Portland, where more than half of the state's population lives, networks of bike lanes, hybrid bus routes, EV-charging stations and light-rail and streetcar tracks are dramatically reshaping urban transportation. When Oregonians aren't commuting (or biking for fun), they're living, working, and socializing in many of the country's most environmentally friendly buildings—Oregon is number one in the nation in LEED projects per capita. Support for clean energy is a source of pride for many of the state's residents. Portland General Electric, Oregon's largest utility, is quick to boast about having the largest green-power-purchasing program in the U.S., with nearly 80,000 customers opting to pay a small premium each month to fund clean-energy projects.

During 2010, more than 7 percent of Oregon's in-state electricity generation came from wind energy (sixth most in the nation), a number that will increase in coming years as new utility-scale projects like the $2 billion, 845-megawatt Shepherds Flat Wind Farm begin feeding wind-derived electrons into the region's grid. Combine Oregon's wind power with other low-carbon sources—solar, geothermal, biomass, and hydroelectricity—and more than 63 percent of all kilowatt-hours generated in the state can be traced to climate-friendly power plants. But evidence of Oregon's clean-tech leadership extends beyond clean electricity to areas like smart-meter market penetration (25 percent of total meters by the end of 2010, number two in the nation), public EV-charging stations (number two per capita), and hybrid registrations (number three per capita).

As a result of some generous state incentives and a number of unique geographic and human capital advantages, Oregon has also been able to attract some of the industry's global powerhouses to the state. Drawn by manufacturing-friendly inexpensive electricity, proximity to California's solar market, and Portland's semiconductor-savvy workforce, Germany-based PV manufacturer SolarWorld chose in 2008 to locate its North American headquarters just outside Portland in Hillsboro, Oregon. Oregon's Business Energy Tax Credit program (BETC) also played a big role in the decision. In an April 2009 *Portland Tribune* article discussing the $11 million BETC tax incentive that SolarWorld received, former vice president Bob Beisner revealed the obvious. "It really put us over the edge. It was a key factor," he said. In 2011, the BETC program was restructured into several smaller programs, but Oregon incentives remain available for a wide range of activities including energy conservation, power generation, manufacturing, and transportation. SolarWorld's Hillsboro campus is now home to America's largest PV production facility, and the company employs more than 1,000 workers at the location. Along with SolarWorld, other solar-product makers like Sanyo, REC Solar, and MEMC Electronic Materials have helped make Oregon the nation's solar-manufacturing front-runner.

Apart from solar, Oregon has also become a popular destination for corporate wind energy operations, green-building-design firms, energy-efficiency consultancies, and energy storage manufacturers. Although Denmark-based Vestas Wind Systems' U.S. manufacturing activity is centered in Colorado, the world's largest turbine maker has long kept its North American headquarters in Portland. In 2012 the company had plans to move into a brand-new $66 million facility in Portland's trendy Pearl District. Just three blocks away, Spain-based renewable energy project developer Iberdrola Renewables houses its North American headquarters. It is industry clustering like this that has allowed Portland, and Oregon more broadly, to establish itself as a key U.S. clean-tech hub.

Companies to Watch: Oregon
Brammo Motorsports
brammo.com
Ashland
Electric motorcycle manufacturer

Gerding Edlen
gerdingedlen.com
Portland
Sustainable property developer

Puralytics
puralytics.com
Beaverton
Water-purification technology developer

SolarWorld
solarworld-usa.com
Frankfurt Stock Exchange: SWV
Hillsboro (North American PV cell and module manufacturing facility)
Germany-based PV product manufacturer

Vestas Wind Systems
vestas.com
NASDAQ: OMX; Copenhagen Stock Exchange: VWS
Portland (North American headquarters)
Denmark-based wind turbine manufacturer

3. MASSACHUSETTS

In 2010, Clean Edge worked with the Massachusetts Clean Energy Center to research and publish a report on the state's clean-tech activity called *A Future of Innovation and Growth: Advancing Massachusetts' Clean-Energy Leadership*. Two years later, this title still captures the essence of what has allowed Massachusetts to become a leader in clean energy, as it previously did in the high-tech and biotech sectors. World-class research institutions like MIT, an active venture capital community, a highly educated workforce, and supportive government leadership are among the strengths that make the state a hotbed for technology and company development.

While no other U.S. region can match California's clean-tech venture capital supremacy, Massachusetts puts forth its best effort, positioning the state comfortably in second place. In 2010, clean-tech companies in the Bay State attracted more than $400 million in venture investment, spanning 43 individual financing rounds, according to Cleantech Group data. The breadth of clean-tech activity in Massachusetts spans all sectors, but three areas in particular rise to the top: energy efficiency, solar PV, and energy storage.

With an extreme climate, high energy prices, and aging infrastructure, the state is situated to benefit greatly from energy-efficiency applications, and local government, utilities, and industry have all made strong efforts to focus on "negawatts" instead of megawatts. According to data compiled by the Consortium for Energy Efficiency, Massachusetts utilities budgeted $357 million in 2010 for energy-efficiency programs, second only to Vermont when viewed by dollars per capita. Massachusetts is also home to several key energy-efficiency service providers, including energy management firm EnerNOC and home energy-efficiency adviser Conservation Services Group.

For solar PV and energy storage, Massachusetts activity is centered on R&D and commercialization of new tech. Konarka and 1366 Technologies are two of the leading Massachusetts-based companies developing innovative solar technology, while companies like A123 Systems, Boston-Power, General Compression, Premium Power, and others give the state a solid cluster of storage innovation and commercialization.

Companies to Watch: Massachusetts

1366 Technologies
1366tech.com
North Lexington
Solar PV cell manufacturer

A123 Systems
a123systems.com
NASDAQ: AONE
Watertown
Lithium-ion battery/energy storage technology developer

Aspen Aerogels
aerogel.com
Northborough
Energy-efficient insulation maker

EnerNOC
enernoc.com
NASDAQ: ENOC
Boston
Building energy-management systems provider

FloDesign Wind Turbine
fdwt.com
Waltham
Wind turbine technology developer

4. NEW YORK

With the third-largest state GDP in the nation, roughly equivalent in size to the economy of Australia, the Empire State has an opportunity to play a sizable role in the U.S. clean-tech sector. New York might not match the comprehensive competitiveness shown by the top three states, but it is becoming an increasingly strong performer in the areas of clean-energy policy, energy-efficiency deployment, technology research, and product manufacturing.

Implementation of New York's ambitious clean-energy policies is led by the New York State Energy Research and Development Authority (NYSERDA), a nonprofit with an annual budget exceeding $600 million funded primarily by a small assessment on utility bills known as a systems benefit charge. NYSERDA's main activities include managing the state's many clean-energy incentive programs; leading participation in the Regional Greenhouse Gas Initiative (RGGI), a regional cap-and-trade program of nine Northeast and Mid-Atlantic states; and administering New York's RPS mandate, which requires that 30 percent of the state's electricity come from low-carbon sources by 2015.

The downstate and upstate regions of New York State, although starkly different, provide complementary strengths for a range of clean-energy advantages. While upstate New York is home to several prominent research centers and manufacturing facilities, like General Electric's GE Global Research headquarters, in Niskayuna, and its new advanced battery plant in Albany, downstate New York's status as the preeminent financial capital of the world provides ample access to investment capital.

At more than 27,000 residents per square mile (8.2 million total), New York City's density is also a key driver of clean-tech deployment in the state, particularly for energy-efficiency technologies. In her book, *Power Trip: The Story of America's Love Affair with Energy*, Amanda Little accurately portrayed the Big Apple's electric infrastructure: "The New York City grid encompasses more than 80,000 miles of cable—enough to circle the globe four times. Peel back the sidewalks of Manhattan and you'll find a larger concentration of copper than anywhere else on the planet. . . . All that metal can be found within 15 feet below street level, sandwiched in with water mains, sewage pipes, and telephone lines."

This density has allowed New York to become a leader in efficiency, with the state consuming fewer kilowatt-hours per capita than any state other than California. But as New York City's infrastructure continues to age and the city continues to grow at a blistering pace, the need for improved energy efficiency is higher than ever. New York utilities know this. In 2010, the budget for utility energy-efficiency programs in the state was $688 million, second highest in the nation and seventh in per capita terms.

New York will remain a hot market for clean tech as incentive policies, emissions regulations, and efficiency concerns continue to drive technology adoption. If the state can further leverage its finance industry influence—especially as major financial institutions become more involved in the sector—the Empire State has a real chance to join California and Massachusetts as one of the nation's key clean-tech investment hubs.

Companies to Watch: New York

e2e Materials
e2ematerials.com
Ithaca
Biocomposite particleboard material producer

EnergyHub
energyhub.com
Brooklyn
Energy management system provider

GE Global Research
ge.geglobalresearch.com
NYSE: GE
Niskayuna
Research lab working in electronic systems, clean energy,
biosciences, and nanotechnology

Primet Precision Materials
primetprecision.com
Ithaca
Lithium-ion battery material technology developer

Recyclebank
recyclebank.com
New York
Recycling rewards program manager

5. COLORADO

Although it's home to abundant clean-energy natural resources, Colorado's network of cutting-edge research facilities is arguably its most
valuable clean-tech advantage. Led by the Golden-based National

Renewable Energy Laboratory (NREL)—the principal research laboratory for the DOE's Office of Energy Efficiency and Renewable Energy—Colorado's research community also includes an assortment of university clean-tech centers, corporate R&D facilities, and nonprofit research headquarters. This concentration of research labs, accompanied by a strong traditional energy industry presence, gives Colorado a large workforce with training relevant to a variety of clean-tech sectors.

The combination of natural resource availability, a well-established R&D community, a talented workforce, and an actively supportive state government has allowed Colorado to grow into a top-tier clean-tech hub, and the state is now enjoying the rewards that come along with that achievement. Colorado has attracted several global clean-tech leaders to the state, including Vestas, the world's largest wind turbine manufacturer, and Germany-based SMA Solar Technology, the world's largest solar inverter manufacturer. Since making Colorado its North American manufacturing hub in 2008, Vestas has invested more than $1 billion in five facilities scattered across the state—two blade-manufacturing factories, a nacelle factory (a nacelle is the housing for a wind turbine's gearbox and other components), a tower factory, and an R&D center. Vestas employment in Colorado, already exceeding 1,000, is expected to grow to around 2,500 in coming years. SMA's 1-gigawatt solar inverter plant in Denver, the company's first production facility outside of Germany, opened in mid-2010 and is expected to employ 700 when operating at full capacity.

Colorado has enjoyed a noticeable influx of capital to the region as a result of its clean-tech activity. In 2010, solar thin-film PV developer Abound Solar was awarded a $400 million loan guarantee from the DOE to fund manufacturing-capacity expansion. And from 2008 through 2010, more than $730 million in venture capital investment was spread across 33 financing rounds to Colorado-based clean-energy startups, good enough for fourth place in the nation in terms of dollars per capita.

Companies to Watch: Colorado

Abound Solar

abound.com

Loveland

Thin-film solar PV module manufacturer

Albeo Technologies

albeotech.com

Boulder

Industrial LED lighting manufacturer

Gevo

gevo.com

NASDAQ: GEVO

Englewood

Biobutanol chemical and fuel technology developer

Ice Energy

ice-energy.com

Windsor

Efficient air-conditioning/distributed-energy storage system maker

Tendril

tendrilinc.com

Boulder

Smart-grid product and service provider

6. WASHINGTON

As the northern neighbor to second-ranked Oregon, Washington is also home to vast clean-energy resources and communities supportive of sustainable development. The state has not let this competitive advantage go to waste. During 2010, more than 71 percent of electricity generated in Washington came from low-carbon sources—wind, solar, geothermal, biomass, or hydro—second most in the nation. The Evergreen State has shown particular commitment to development of its wind resources, ranking fifth for peak wind capacity at the end of 2010, with more than 2,100 megawatts installed.

Another bright area for Washington is clean transportation. By October 2010, there were more than 58,400 hybrid electric vehicles registered in the state, fourth most of any state when viewed by hybrids per capita. Washington is also leading the way in development of the West Coast Green Highway, an initiative to advance use of EVs along the I-5 corridor. The first leg of this effort, led by the Washington State Department of Transportation, enables EV drivers to travel the 276-mile stretch of I-5 between the state's borders with Canada and Oregon free of any range anxiety.

Propelling Washington's clean-energy activities is a broad and effective set of regulations and incentives implemented by state governments, local communities, and regional utilities. In particular, Washington's energy-efficiency and clean-energy deployment efforts are catalyzed by the state's innovative policy of lowest-reasonable-cost integrated resource planning (IRP), which allows utilities to better recognize conservation and energy-efficiency measures as lower-cost resources. According to state representative Jeff Morris, more than 1,500 megawatts of coal have been moved out of Washington utilities' resource acquisition plans in favor of renewables, energy efficiency, and natural gas since IRP was passed in Washington in 2006.

Companies to Watch: Washington
3TIER
3tier.com
Seattle
Renewable energy risk analysis information provider

EnerG2
energ2.com
Seattle
Nanotechnology-structured energy storage technology developer

Hydrovolts
hydrovolts.com
Seattle
Micro-hydropower turbine maker

Itron
itron.com
NASDAQ: ITRI
Liberty Lake
Smart-meter manufacturer and smart-grid service provider

McKinstry
mckinstry.com
Seattle
Energy-efficient building systems engineering firm

7. NEW MEXICO

New Mexico's world-class solar resources, along with the vast open desert landscapes of the American Southwest, make the state an ideal setting for large-scale solar projects. In 2010, the state finally capitalized on these favorable characteristics, installing 40.9 megawatts of new PV capacity, a meteoric rise from the 1.4 megawatts installed in 2009. But this is merely the beginning for New Mexico's solar future. By mid-2011, 422 megawatts of utility-scale solar capacity was either under construction or in development, according to the Solar Energy Industries Association.

A 2010 road map for New Mexico's clean-tech economy by the

state's Economic Development Department pointed to innovation as a key area of focus for New Mexico, highlighting that R&D represents 8.4 percent of the state's economy, more than in any other state. Much of this activity takes place at Los Alamos and Sandia, the two nuclear-focused national labs located in the state, but the culture of innovation expands beyond government-funded nuke research.

Albuquerque-based Emcore, a developer of concentrating PV cell technology, was a bright spot for the state in 2010, earning ten solar PV patents from the U.S. Patent and Trademark Office. Led by Emcore, New Mexico ranked third for clean-energy patents granted per capita in 2010, according to law firm HRFM's Clean Energy Patent Growth Index.

New Mexico's clean-energy standing is heavily guided by solar industry activity, but with an RPS requiring that investor-owned utilities get 20 percent of electricity from renewables by 2020, the state has also begun to develop clean electrons from other sources. With 700 megawatts of wind energy capacity at the end of 2010, New Mexico was the tenth-ranked state for wind as a percentage of in-state peak generating capacity (8.72 percent).

Companies to Watch: New Mexico
Array Technologies
wattsun.com
Albuquerque
Solar-tracking-equipment maker

Emcore
emcore.com
NASDAQ: EMKR
Albuquerque
Concentrating solar PV cell developer

Energy Control
energyctrl.com
Rio Rancho
Automated demand-response service provider

Enerpulse
pulstar.com
Albuquerque
High-efficiency automotive spark plug replacement product
manufacturer

Iosil Energy
iosilenergy.com
Albuquerque
Silicon purification technology developer

8. MINNESOTA

As the highest-ranking clean-energy state in the Midwest, Minnesota's strategy is to lead by example. The state has become a top-tier performer in several sectors, including but not limited to wind energy, biofuels (both production and infrastructure development), and green building deployment. Minnesota is also an active manufacturing locale, with a robust workforce producing an array of clean-tech products including hybrid buses, efficient windows, solar panels, and wind turbine parts.

Wind power plays a major role in Minnesota's clean-tech industry, and during 2010 wind sources accounted for 9.7 percent of all in-state electricity generation. The state's 2,192 megawatts of wind capacity installed by the end of 2010 was enough to give it the fourth-largest wind market in the nation, behind only Texas, Iowa, and California. Minnesota continued its wind sector growth during the first quarter of 2011, installing a nation-leading 293 megawatts of new wind capacity.

Biofuels is another area of leadership for Minnesota. The state ranks fourth in ethanol production capacity and leads the U.S. with more than 350 biofuel fueling stations in operation.

In the realm of policy, Minnesota is driving clean-energy growth through its strong RPS, which mandates that utilities get 25 percent of electricity from renewables by 2025. The legislation created a separate, stronger RPS for its largest utility, Minneapolis-based Xcel Energy, requiring that renewable sources account for 30 percent of its electricity sales by 2020. Apart from the RPS and other regulatory mechanisms, Minnesota's state and local governments and in-state utilities offer a broad set of incentives that aid development of renewable energy and energy-efficiency projects.

Companies to Watch: Minnesota
Cymbet
cymbet.com
Elk River
Thin-film rechargeable battery maker

NatureWorks
natureworksllc.com
Minnetonka
Plant-based bioplastics manufacturer

New Flyer
newflyer.com
Crookston and St. Cloud (manufacturing facilities)
Diesel-electric and hydrogen fuel cell bus manufacturer

SAGE Electrochromics
sage-ec.com
Fairbault
Tintable, high-efficiency smart-window maker

Segetis
segetis.com
Golden Valley
Bio-based chemical and plastic maker

9. CONNECTICUT

Like other northeastern clean-tech leaders, Connecticut has established industry prominence through a combination of strong, comprehensive policy and a focus on energy efficiency. Connecticut utilities in 2010 budgeted the sixth-highest amount in the U.S. for energy-efficiency programs, and the state ranks fourth in electric productivity (dollars of state GDP per kilowatt-hour consumed). Connecticut's policy efforts are led by landmark 2011 legislation that created the Connecticut Clean Energy Finance and Investment Authority (CEFIA), the nation's first state-level green bank—an entity designed to leverage both public and private funds to drive investment and the deployment of clean energy. With $30 million from existing electricity bill surcharges and $18 million from the Connecticut Green Loan Guaranty Fund, the CEFIA will provide low-interest loans to clean-energy and energy-efficiency projects in Connecticut. The state also named leading clean-economy expert Daniel Esty, a Yale professor and coauthor of the best-selling *Green to Gold: How Smart Companies Use Environmental Strategy to Innovate, Create Value, and Build Competitive Advantage*, as commissioner of its Department of Energy and Environmental Protection.

To date, Connecticut has made its clean-tech-industry mark on one area in particular: fuel cells. Home to sector leaders like Fuel-Cell Energy, UTC Power, and Proton OnSite, the state has become a hot spot for manufacturing, deployment, and development of fuel cell technology. Of the 280 patents granted to Connecticut clean-energy companies from 2002 through 2010, 260 were fuel-cell related.

(Connecticut ranked third in the nation for clean-energy patents per capita from 2002 through 2010.) As a result of the state's concentration of fuel cell activity and sector-supporting policies, Connecticut has repeatedly been named one of the "top five fuel cell states" by the annual *State of the States: Fuel Cells in America* report, compiled by research firm Fuel Cells 2000. This focus on fuel cells, however, leaves the state vulnerable to a lack of diversification, something that the green bank is likely to work to address.

Companies to Watch: Connecticut
Apollo Solar
apollosolar.com
Bethel
Solar PV power electronics provider

FuelCell Energy
fuelcellenergy.com
NASDAQ: FCEL
Danbury
Stationary fuel cell maker

Optiwind
optiwind.com
Torrington
Small-scale wind turbine manufacturer

STR Holdings
strholdings.com
NYSE: STRI
Enfield
Solar PV component provider

UTC Power
utcpower.com
NYSE: UTX
South Windsor
Fuel cell manufacturer

10. VERMONT

Vermont's commitment to energy efficiency has been the state's most prominent example of clean-tech leadership. For more than a decade, Efficiency Vermont, the nation's first ratepayer-funded organization to focus exclusively on energy efficiency, has helped Vermont residents and businesses reduce energy costs by providing technical assistance and financial incentives for efficiency projects. In 2010 alone, Efficiency Vermont provided state residents with more than $115 million in savings from decreased electricity, fossil-fuel, and water use. Led by Efficiency Vermont, the state ranks number one in dollars per capita budgeted for utility energy-efficiency programs.

This focus on efficiency has helped Vermont become a leader in other clean-tech areas like green building and clean transportation. Vermont ranks second in the U.S. in LEED-certified projects per capita, trailing only Oregon. And at the end of 2010, more than 7,100 homes in Vermont were recognized as Energy Star–qualified, a certification awarded by the EPA for efficiency performance, giving the state the seventh-highest ranking Energy Star homes per capita. With more than 6,400 hybrids on the road in 2010, Vermont ranked second in hybrids per capita, behind only California.

Vermont's clean-tech activity might not draw as much attention as its top-tier brethren, but close attention to efficiency will have long-lasting payoffs, allowing the state to temper future demand for increasingly expensive electricity, polluting fossil fuels, and precious water resources.

Companies to Watch: Vermont

AllEarth Renewables
allearthrenewables.com
Williston
Solar tracker and small-scale wind turbine manufacturer

Dynapower
dynapower.com
South Burlington
Power-conversion equipment provider

Efficiency Vermont
efficiencyvermont.com
Burlington
Energy-efficiency service provider

groSolar
grosolar.com
White River Junction
Solar energy system integrator

Northern Power Systems
northernpower.com
Barre
Wind turbine manufacturer

UNDERPERFORMING STATES PLAY CATCH-UP

This chapter has focused largely on identifying regional front-runners in the U.S. clean-tech competitive landscape, but these are not the only places in America with activities worthy of mention. An account of today's U.S. clean-energy economy cannot be limited to just solar roofs in California, green buildings in Oregon, and research labs in Massachusetts. Now more than ever, states across the country are looking to create their own Silicon Valleys, with regions competing to attract the companies, jobs, and investment dollars that go along with clean-tech economic development. And even states occupying the bottom of Clean Edge's *State Clean Energy Leadership Index* are beginning to make industry waves.

Although ranked second to last in the 2011 *Leadership Index*, Mississippi has raised some eyebrows for its recent attraction of manufacturers. Among companies lured by the state's generous financing and tax-exemption offers in the past few years are solar-product makers Stion and Twin Creeks Technologies and biofuels developers KiOR, Enerkem, and Bluefire Ethanol. Missouri is another state on the cusp of becoming a hot spot for clean-tech manufacturing. The state ranked only 37th in our 2011 *Leadership Index* but has made headlines by luring companies like Smith Electric Vehicles and grid battery maker Exergonix to locate facilities in the state.

But for lagging states to truly compete against America's clean-tech powerhouses and better enable the U.S. to establish leadership on the global stage, their activities must move beyond just manufacturing to actual deployment of clean technologies. Luckily, some of the best opportunities for tech deployment can be found in states not among today's clean-tech leaders.

In the northern Great Plains, where fossil fuels still reign supreme, states like Wyoming, Montana, Nebraska, and the Dakotas are home to the nation's greatest wind resources—approximately 58 percent of all U.S. onshore potential. Development of these resources should play a major role in driving the American wind industry forward. And in the Southeast, where most states are lacking in policy support and remain stuck on nuclear and coal, biomass holds the key to a competitive clean-tech future. NREL estimates that, if fully utilized, biomass residues (from forests, agriculture, mills, and urban waste) could provide more than six times the region's current electricity demand.

The greatest opportunity for underperforming states, though, is improvement in energy efficiency. In the 2009 report *Assessing the Electric Productivity Gap and the U.S. Efficiency Opportunity*, researchers at the Rocky Mountain Institute (RMI) exposed an enormous potential to reduce the carbon footprint of electricity while growing the economy. Focusing on states' electric productivity—dollars of GDP generated per kilowatt-hour consumed—RMI found that by bringing all states in line with the average electric productivity of the top ten most efficient states, the country would save a total of 1.2 gigawatts annually, or roughly 30 percent of current annual electricity use. More important, RMI findings show that these efficiency improvements can be achieved all while maintaining 2.5 percent annual economic growth.

THE ROAD AHEAD

As we've detailed in this chapter, clean tech in the U.S. cannot be defined by one geographical region, nor can it yet be considered an industry with a nationwide presence. Without strong federal government leadership or policy direction, we've seen proactive states, cities, and local communities take charge in the pursuit of America's clean-energy future. Today, these early movers enjoy advantageous positions in the nation's competitive landscape. Some states have followed technology-specific approaches to clean-energy leadership—New Jersey in solar energy, Texas in wind power, and Connecticut in fuel cells. But the most successful regions exhibit strong performances across the board in technology development and deployment, industry-supporting government policy, and attraction of financial, human, and intellectual capital. While California's dominance over the field is undeniable, the Golden State is joined at the top by a selection of geographically diverse states including Oregon, Massachusetts, New York, and Colorado.

Benefits enjoyed by clean-tech leaders—job creation, increased private investment, improved infrastructure efficiency, and cleaner electricity supply—have piqued the interest of many previously dormant regions. This popularity has intensified domestic competition in the U.S. as new industry players look to establish their own regional clean-tech hubs. This heightened competition and broader industry participation can only help the U.S. become a more active global player in new-technology development, a richer market for deployment of clean-tech products, and a more lucrative target for international investment. In the next few critical years, bringing laggard regions and states up to speed, while ensuring that the leading clean-tech states continue to grow and innovate, will be crucial paths to improving America's global clean-tech competitiveness.

3

CENTERS OF INNOVATION

The Top 15 U.S. Cities for Clean Tech

Photos of Seattle's Georgetown neighborhood aren't likely to make it into any of the scenic Emerald City tourist brochures. Although not far from the evergreen hills of Puget Sound or the famous clear-day views of stunning Mount Rainier, Georgetown is a flat, lackluster industrial warehouse district whose most popular draw might be the tasty offerings of two neighboring local eateries, Pig Iron Bar-B-Q and Slim's Last Chance Chili Shack. But it's in this part of Seattle, on the city's southern edge, that you'll find a shining example of the type of leadership that makes cities such a key part of America's clean-tech future.

The McKinstry Innovation Center, a 24,000-square-foot office space atop a parking garage, houses a dozen Seattle startup companies and nonprofits, all engaged in different aspects of clean tech and sustainability. It's across the street from the corporate headquarters of center founder and funder McKinstry, a 52-year-old building-and-engineering contractor that has grown into one of the world's leading companies making new and existing buildings more energy efficient. McKinstry, now a $500 million firm with 1,800 employees in 16 U.S. locations, invested $5 million to open the Innovation Center in May 2010, with the goal of shepherding new-technology advances and growing Seattle's clean-tech economy. In addition to office and lab space and amenities, McKinstry provides business and innovation mentoring from its own management team. Tenants include Hydro-volts, maker of a small hydroelectric turbine for use in rivers and irrigation canals; EcoFab, a residential energy retrofit provider; and the nonprofit Washington STEM, which works to improve the state's science, technology, engineering, and math education, with backing from Boeing, Microsoft, and the Bill & Melinda Gates Foundation as well as McKinstry.

The center "is not a traditional incubator, but an *accelerator* to commercialization," says David Allen, McKinstry's garrulous executive vice-president. "These guys all pay rent, and there are great deliverables for us. It enhances our brand as a leader in this space and creates new innovations; we like those."

Like many of the top 15 U.S. clean-tech cities spotlighted in this chapter, Seattle has a rich history as an innovation center in areas ranging from aerospace to software to the way Americans buy, consume, and experience coffee. Now a number of local officials, financiers, and business leaders like McKinstry are seeking to make clean tech one of the Seattle metro region's key new industries for job and wealth creation. Businesses "are both doing the work and driving the conversation," says Ross Macfarlane, senior adviser for business partnerships at Climate Solutions, a Seattle-based nonprofit. "In some ways, the clean-tech leadership baton has been passed from the government to the private sector."

For more than a century, cities have served as the driving force of the developed world's economy, and that phenomenon is now playing out in emerging nations across the globe as the world turns solidly from rural to urban. The year 2008 marked the tipping point—the first time in human history that more than half of the world's population resided in cities—and the trend is only accelerating. As with so many other global trends, China offers the most dramatic example. As employment and social advancement opportunities from its expanding economy draw millions away from rural areas, China is now home to an astounding 120 cities with more than one million people, according to Yang Jiechi, the nation's minister of foreign affairs. Fifty percent of China's population—more than 660 million people—now lives in urban areas, and the figure is expected to reach 900 million in the next 20 years. "This is one of the most important avenues toward modernization," Yang says. This transformation has also coincided with China's rise to the top of global competitors in clean tech.

But in the cities of China and in other leading clean-tech hubs around the world, it's not just solar-panel or lithium-ion-battery factories that make cities such an important driver of clean-tech leadership. It's the concentration of intellectual and financial capital, business acumen, and university and research-lab R&D—nearly always abetted by progressive and supportive public-sector policies and practices—that create a metro area's successful clean-tech ecosystem. And success tends to build on itself. Once a city has established itself as a center of specific clean-tech activity—say, New York or Boston for energy-saving building retrofits or San Diego for next-generation biofuels—it tends to attract even more job seekers, entrepreneurs, and investors in that sector.

This phenomenon, known as clustering, is certainly not unique to clean tech, and we'll examine it in more detail shortly. But first, let's answer a question: In a book on U.S. competition on a global scale, why focus on cities?

Along with states, it is cities that are on the front lines of America's battle to develop and grow a leading 21st-century economy. The vast majority of economic activity, employment, and wealth creation in the U.S. occurs in and around big cities (90 percent of GDP in 2010). As much as some politicians and pundits romanticize small-town Main Streets as "the real America," the reality (according to the 2010 census) is that more than 75 percent of Americans live in and around urban areas. Viewed geographically, more than three-quarters of U.S. residents share just 3 percent of America's land area. With some notable exceptions, like Walmart's fabled Bentonville, Arkansas, corporate headquarters, the vast majority of large and small businesses are located there as well. "Cities are our fate and future," says California lieutenant governor and former San Francisco mayor Gavin Newsom.

For clean tech in the U.S., cities' leadership is at the forefront of building the types of projects and new industry sectors that will employ their citizens in quality jobs and boost often struggling local economies. Despite facing historic budget challenges in America's struggling economic climate, 75 percent of 400 mayors in all 50 states say they plan to increase their use of clean-energy technologies in the next five years.

That survey, released in June 2011 by the U.S. Conference of Mayors, found that the most promising clean technologies for city use are LED and other energy-efficient lighting, low-energy buildings, and solar electricity generation. The survey also pointed to economic development as a prime factor behind the clean-tech support. "The key drivers behind much of this activity are, not surprisingly, economic: to attract new businesses and jobs, reduce energy costs, and, more generally, develop a greener economy," said Tom Cochran, the Conference of Mayors' CEO and executive director, at the report's release. Attracting new businesses and employment was the number-two goal of cities' energy strategies, second only to maximizing energy efficiency. The vast majority of the nation's local leaders clearly see clean tech as an economic driver to be emphasized, not scaled back, during difficult economic times.

WHERE THE ACTION IS

Although we'd never downplay the intensity of local political rivalries, city-level politics are more likely to be free of the blue/red polarization that so often causes gridlock on Capitol Hill and in many state capitals. In the past decade, for example, urban leaders have been out ahead of national policy on carbon-emissions reduction through efforts such as the U.S. Conference of Mayors' Climate Protection Agreement, created in 2005 and signed by more than 1,000 mayors across the country. Signatories pledged to meet or exceed the Kyoto Protocol emissions-reduction goals of 7 percent from 1990 levels by the end of 2012 in their respective cities.

"I don't know if it's easier for cities to coalesce and move in the same direction, but more seems to get done at the local level," says clean-tech investor Michael Butler, chairman and CEO of Cascadia Capital, in Seattle. "At the federal level, there are so many checks and balances. Cities create demand, and that's key for the success of this sector. In Seattle we see building regulations driving innovation, making the built environment the number-one clean-tech industry here. That's a direct result of demand being created locally by policies."

In addition, clean tech is growing and maturing as an industry during a time of urban renaissance for many U.S. cities. We don't minimize the challenges of income inequality, crime, homelessness, and crumbling infrastructure that face virtually all large metro areas—problems all exacerbated by city budgets cut to the bone and beyond. But most cities have come a long way from urban America's low ebb in the 1970s, when the infamous "Ford to City: Drop Dead" newspaper headline appeared after President Gerald Ford refused near-bankrupt New York City's request for federal aid. Urban cores from Philadelphia to Los Angeles were desolate at best, with drugs and danger in abundance. Such issues clearly remain, and the nation's current economic crisis has even forced some communities to declare bankruptcy, most notably state capital Harrisburg, Pennsylvania, and the county that includes Birmingham, Alabama. But dozens of cities large and small have revitalized themselves. Smart, pedestrian, and mass-transit-oriented redevelopment, location incentives for business, and scores of other measures have helped restore cities to their historical role as places that attract, not repel, the ambitious and the community-oriented. Reversing a demographic trend that dated back to post–World War II days, the population of America's central cities has been on the increase since 1990.

In the introduction, we added Connectivity to our list of the Six C's—the global trends moving clean tech forward around the world. Although that referred mainly to today's online and cloud-based technology tools enabling collaboration and new business models, the same lessons certainly apply to the *in-person connectivity* that's made cities the hub of ideas and innovation since the days of ancient Athens. Many futurists and pundits have predicted that global Internet connectivity would obviate the need for people to congregate in cities, but the opposite has proved true. Even if urbanites these days often choose to gather in cafés and work spaces equipped with WiFi connections, only cities can enable what Ford Foundation president Luis Ubiñas calls "the unleashing of human energy that occurs when people are that close."

CLEAN TECH AND CLUSTERS

Although economists have studied the advantages of geographically concentrated industries since the late 19th century, Harvard Business School professor Michael Porter is widely credited with popularizing the modern concept in his 1990 book *The Competitive Advantage of Nations*. Creating a cluster from scratch is a daunting task, but the concept is fairly simple. As an industry develops in a given city or region, the suppliers, financiers, infrastructure providers, and academic trainers to that industry tend to cluster in the same area. The most famous examples are legendary: Detroit for auto and component manufacturing, Silicon Valley for high tech, Las Vegas for gaming and tourism, Los Angeles for entertainment.

Clean tech, however, is a bit different. When looking to create a cluster in clean energy, transportation, or water technologies, a city can play a much greater role beyond favorable policies that would support any industry, such as tax incentives and exemptions, cheap real estate, and workforce training. For one thing, cities can lead by example with sustainability-oriented policies that promote energy efficiency, mass transit, pedestrian and bicycle activity, and recycling. But much more significantly, city governments can be major catalysts for clean-tech industry development and job creation with their purchasing power. All large urban areas procure vast amounts of electricity, vehicles, transportation fuel, food and water, sanitation services, building materials, and scores of other products and services that fall under the wide umbrella of clean tech. (See our clean-tech taxonomy chart on page 26.) So it's not just a symbolic "walking the walk"—city governments can act as major customers, creating market demand for clean-tech players in their area.

Examples abound across the U.S. The San Francisco Bay Area is the nation's biggest solar PV industry hub, and San Francisco's city government does its part, with 7 megawatts of solar capacity on municipally owned facilities, including the city's largest reservoir (5 megawatts there alone), San Francisco International Airport, and the Moscone Center convention facilities. New York City operates the nation's largest electric transportation fleet—430 vehicles, including plug-in hybrid Chevy Volts, Ford Transit Connect cargo vans, and Navistar eStar utility trucks used by nine different city departments, including police and fire for non-emergency duties. New York is also the country's largest municipal buyer of biodiesel fuel. Some large cities own their own municipal electric utility; in our Top 15 U.S.

Clean-Tech Cities listing, later in this chapter, we'll discuss how this gives Los Angeles, Austin, Seattle, and Sacramento a potential strategic advantage in growing clean electricity and its related jobs.

CLEAN TECH'S THREE PILLARS: THE CITY VERSION

As we detailed in chapter 2, the clean-tech industry rests on the three pillars of technology, policy, and capital. Similar to states, cities must exhibit strength in all three areas in order to sustain and grow their clean-tech industries. A timely example of how technology, policy, and capital interact at the city level comes from an innovative program created to turbocharge the green-building-retrofit industry in New York.

The building sector is, pardon the pun, the absolute cornerstone of efforts to reduce energy use and emissions in the Big Apple. Buildings are responsible for a staggering 75 percent of the city's carbon emissions, compared with the nationwide rate of just below 50 percent. To meet the 2030 carbon reduction targets of the PlaNYC initiative from Mayor Michael Bloomberg's administration, 50 percent of greenhouse-gas reductions will have to come from the built environment. And although the city boasts some glittering examples of very green skyscrapers erected in recent years, such as the 54-story, LEED Platinum Bank of America Tower at One Bryant Park, the real need is energy retrofits of less glamorous older buildings. Some 85 percent of today's buildings will still be in residential or commercial use in 2030.

Launched in 2011, the New York City Energy Efficiency Corporation (NYCEEC, pronounced *ny-seek*) is a collaboration of city government, Deutsche Bank, and the nonprofit Natural Resources Defense Council's Center for Market Innovation. Jump-started with $37.5 million from the federal stimulus program, NYCEEC has created a revolving loan fund to help finance such retrofits in commercial buildings and low-income housing—projects that don't always jump to the front of the line of sexy investments. NYCEEC seeks to leverage its seed funding with up to ten times as much money from private investors and philanthropic donations, to start creating a thriving clean-tech sector from what has been more of a fragmented cottage industry.

"Our goal is to establish retrofitting as an ongoing marketplace," says NYCEEC's CEO, Susan Leeds, a veteran investment banking professional with stints at Deutsche Bank, GE Capital, and Prudential Securities. "We have policy, energy, finance, and investment people involved, but the place where it all happens is in the building. I think the city is taking a good approach to something that wouldn't happen solely from the private market. It needs government support to get it going, but it's not something that government can do on its own dime."

NYCEEC typifies the kind of collaborative effort among different communities that we see in the 15 leading U.S. clean-tech cities profiled in this chapter. Businesses, government agencies, investors, NGOs, universities, and community organizers come together in a myriad of ways to help make clean energy, transportation, water, and/or materials an important part of the metropolitan economy. This all-hands-on-deck approach has become ever more critical in the current climate of struggling local economies and strapped city budgets. Collaboration often brings conflict, of course, particularly between communities that haven't worked together in the past. But the cities making it work are seeing payoffs in attracting the companies and projects of the 21st century—and helping the U.S. stay competitive in the global clean-tech marketplace.

OUT IN FRONT: THE TOP 15 U.S. CLEAN-TECH CITIES

Clean Edge, along with other research partners including leading clean-tech job search and placement firm Hobbs & Towne, created a ranking of the top 15 U.S. metro areas for clean-tech job activity as part of our report *Clean Tech Job Trends 2010*. The rankings reflect data from Clean Edge and a range of research partners and publicly available sources on clean-tech investment activity, job postings, job presence, and patent activity. Although we compiled these rankings in 2010, we believe the overall list is still a good gauge of the leading centers of clean-tech activity and economic development in the U.S.

Clean-Tech Job Activity – Top 15 U.S. Metro Areas

Rank	Metro Area
1	San Francisco-Oakland-San Jose, CA
2	Los Angeles-Long Beach-Riverside, CA
3	Boston-Cambridge-Quincy, MA-NH
4	New York-Northern New Jersey-Long Island, NY-NJ
5	Denver-Aurora-Broomfield, CO
6	Washington-Arlington-Baltimore, DC-VA-MD
7	San Diego-Carlsbad-San Marcos, CA
8	Houston-Sugar Land-Baytown, TX
9	Chicago-Joliet-Naperville, IL-IN-WI
10	Austin-Round Rock-San Marcos, TX
11	Seattle-Tacoma-Bellevue, WA
12	Atlanta-Sandy Springs-Marietta, GA
13	Dallas-Fort Worth-Arlington, TX
14	Portland-Vancouver-Hillsboro, OR-WA
15	Sacramento–Arden-Arcade–Roseville, CA

Source: Clean Edge, Inc, 2010. Job Rankings are based on a proprietary weighting of job postings, investment activity, job presence, and patent activity.

City and state leadership in clean tech are obviously linked, and our rankings bear that out. Four of the top 15 metro areas for clean tech, including the undisputed leader, the San Francisco Bay Area, are found in the number-one state, California. Each of the next five leading states in our index—Oregon, Massachusetts, New York, Colorado, and Washington State—has its largest city in the top 15 rankings, as does the number 12 state, Illinois. (It should be noted that several of the top metropolitan statistical areas, or MSAs, such as New York, Chicago, and Boston, encompass suburban-area clean-tech activity in more than one state.) Some may be surprised to see three Texas cities in the top 15, but the Lone Star State ranks in the top 20 (at number 18) in our overall *Leadership Index* and is by far the nation's leading generator of wind power, as well as home to a host of energy companies expanding into the renewables field. The outlier cities in the top 15 are the Washington, D.C./Baltimore area and Atlanta. The District of Columbia is not included in our state rankings, and Georgia's capital and largest city, as we'll discuss in the profile below, has pushed ahead on clean-tech development that belies its state's lackluster ranking of 35th.

Size matters, too. The leading cities are those with the greatest number of clean-tech jobs and related activities, so larger metro areas with a clean-tech focus tend to rise to the top. But there are very notable pockets of clean-tech leadership in many of America's smaller and medium-size cities that should not be overlooked. After profiles of the top 15 cities, we'll look at some smaller cities in a Best of the Rest section that includes Toledo, Ohio; Reno, Nevada; Indianapolis, Indiana; Albany/Schenectady/Troy, New York; and Spokane, Washington.

1. SAN FRANCISCO

From a competition standpoint, other cities in the top 15 should be grateful that San Francisco, San Jose, and Oakland are combined into the same metropolitan area, because each of the three would likely reach the top rankings on its own. No other area in the U.S. comes close to matching the Bay Area's confluence of factors to create a thriving clean-tech industry. All three cities boast sustainability-minded policymakers, along with the citizens who elect them. The area's vibrant, diverse culture and world-class research universities and labs attract thousands of bright, often young minds from around the country and the world, creating one of the nation's best-educated workforces. Clean-energy resources, particularly solar, are strong.

But all of that actually pales in comparison with the Bay's greatest asset: the nexus of Silicon Valley innovation culture and the Sand Hill Road venture capital funding engine that turns ideas into wealth and job-creating companies. It's telling that, worldwide, more silicon now goes into the manufacture of solar PV cells than into semiconductor chips; Silicon Valley today is every bit the clean-tech leader that it has been in semiconductor, computer, software, Internet, and social networking technologies. "It's an ecosystem that knows how to develop companies and things—new products, processes, and business models—and put them on the global stage," says Matt Maloney, head of the clean-tech practice at Silicon Valley Bank. The area's Asia-focused, export-oriented business culture is another plus, with Bay Area companies selling into booming Asian clean-tech markets and attracting engineering talent from the same countries.

The analysis of most leading clean-tech metro areas focuses on sectors where they excel. With the Bay Area, it'd be easier to list major clean-tech sectors that are *not* well represented, like wind power. Just about every other key sector has a significant presence here: solar development and manufacturing, solar installation and financing, smart grid, energy-efficiency tools, EVs and their charging infrastructure, stationary fuel cells, biofuels and biomaterials, and many more. And it's not just clean-tech pure-play companies creating jobs and economic activity. Many of Silicon Valley's leading lights in high tech, notably Cisco, Google, Intel, and Applied Materials, have become important players in solar, smart grid, efficiency, and other clean-tech areas.

The Bay Area's business culture of innovation and risk taking is the envy of dozens of other clean-tech development efforts around the world, and the market usually offers a willing proving ground for new clean-tech deployments. "There's a heritage of tinkering—the Valley is set up in a lot of ways to experiment," says Maloney. "For something new, it's considered cool to try it out and test it here first."

With leadership comes the glare of the spotlight, however. The nation's highest-profile clean-tech failure to date was a Bay Area company, Fremont-based Solyndra, which went bankrupt in 2011 despite its $528 million federal loan guarantee. Much of the political finger pointing in Solyndra's aftermath ignored the inherently risk-oriented culture of technology startups—the same culture upon which the Bay Area thrives like no other.

2. LOS ANGELES

The automobile-centric, onetime smog capital of the country doesn't historically have the same green reputation as its Northern California rival. But not only has Los Angeles made great strides in improving its air quality; it's also in the process of building a vibrant clean-tech economy with a strong focus on clean transportation and electricity. Beyond the green ethos of Hollywood stars like Leonardo DiCaprio, Brad Pitt, and Ed Begley Jr., there's plenty of substance behind the glitz.

By one measure—a July 2011 report from the Brookings Institution and Battelle Memorial Institute called *Sizing the Clean Economy: A National and Regional Green Jobs Assessment*—the Los Angeles metro area added more than 26,000 clean-economy jobs from 2003 to 2010. Brookings's clean-economy definition is broader than what we define as clean tech, encompassing areas like environmental services and organic farming, but it does provide a useful metric on clean-tech trends.

Los Angeles is by far the largest American city with a municipally owned electric utility, the Los Angeles Department of Water and Power (LADWP), so its policies are set by the administration of clean-energy-promoting mayor Antonio Villaraigosa. Although the city's clean-tech reality has lagged behind its rhetoric in some areas, LADWP did reach Villaraigosa's goal of 20 percent (19.7 percent, to be precise) of its electricity from clean energy sources by 2010, up from just 5 percent five years earlier. The city aims to completely wean itself off coal-fired electricity by 2020. L.A. is also working with the Clinton

Climate Initiative to replace 140,000 streetlights with energy-saving LED bulbs, the most ambitious LED retrofit plan in the world.

The Los Angeles residential and commercial rooftop solar PV market is the nation's largest. The city, along with San Diego, is the closest metro area to the sun-baked inland deserts where some of the world's largest solar-generating plants, both PV and concentrating solar power, are being built. Southern California Edison (SCE), the utility serving the parts of the metro area outside LADWP's territory, is also a leader in clean-energy generation, as well as smart-grid development. SCE's program to deploy smart meters is the nation's largest, with a staggering goal of five million meters installed by the end of 2012. SCE also runs the nation's largest utility-administered rooftop solar PV program, aiming to install 500 megawatts of solar panels on roofs in its service territory by 2014.

Southern Californians have always embraced the leading edge of automotive technology, and L.A. arguably shares the EV industry lead among U.S. cities with Detroit and the Bay Area. It is home to EV manufacturers CODA Automotive, in Santa Monica, and Fisker Automotive, in nearby Anaheim, although the local jobs are in areas like R&D and marketing; both companies manufacture their vehicles overseas. The U.S. operations bases of global hybrid-vehicle leaders Toyota and Honda also call Los Angeles home, as does the North American headquarters of BYD Auto, the Chinese hybrid vehicle and battery leader whose investors include Warren Buffett. A range of public- and private-sector initiatives are deploying hundreds of EV-charging stations throughout the region, some of them solar-powered. Other notable area assets include a vibrant academic research community (Caltech, UCLA, USC, and many more) and Pasadena-based Idealab, Bill Gross's legendary private-sector incubator whose clean-tech launches include Energy Innovations, eSolar, and Aptera Motors.

Although Los Angeles public policy has been exemplary in encouraging clean transportation growth and LADWP's renewable-energy efforts, it's been less successful on the economic development front. The Clean Tech Corridor, a much-hyped business zone on the east side of downtown, had landed just one small clean-tech business as of winter 2012. But in the big picture, supportive city policies (including the October 2011 launch of the LA Cleantech Incubator, a public-private partnership that aims to house some 25 clean-tech startups), generally progressive utilities, and a growing clean-tech business sector make Los Angeles a very fertile ground for clean-tech companies, investors, and job seekers.

3. BOSTON

It's no surprise to see Boston among the top clean-tech cities. Massachusetts ranks third in our *State Clean Energy Leadership Index*, and some 70 percent of the state's population lives in the Boston metro area. Although there are notable pockets of clean-tech activity in other parts of the state, Boston lives up to its nickname as the indisputable hub of clean tech in Massachusetts—and as a consensus national leader as well.

The Boston area's unparalleled technology-education and research assets are the envy of all other regions, even the San Francisco Bay Area. That list of assets begins, of course, with the Massachusetts Institute of Technology, in Cambridge. MIT not only turns out some of the top clean-tech scientists and researchers in the world, it is also increasingly focused on entrepreneurship and commercialization. Advanced battery pioneer A123 Systems, solar cell maker 1366 Technologies, and bioplastics developer Metabolix are just a few of the many Boston-area clean-tech companies with roots in research breakthroughs at MIT labs. They're part of a big global club; the annual revenue of companies founded by MIT graduates is estimated to exceed $2 trillion.

In solar and energy-efficiency technology, MIT partnered with

Germany's renowned Fraunhofer Institute in 2008 to create the Fraunhofer Center for Sustainable Energy Systems (CSE). CSE also includes TechBridge, a group specifically devoted to accelerating the commercialization of its tech breakthroughs. Practicing what it preaches, in 2011 CSE retrofitted a century-old building on the South Boston waterfront to become its new headquarters, 5 Channel Center.

And it's not just MIT. A rich panoply of other universities, including Harvard, Boston University, Worcester Polytechnic Institute, and UMass Lowell, give Boston a wealth of tech resources and a highly skilled workforce. As in the Bay Area, Boston's strong high-tech heritage has laid the groundwork for clean tech as a cornerstone of the regional economy.

Energy-efficiency retrofits are a particularly thriving clean-tech area in Boston, where a harsh climate, high electricity rates, and aging building stock make efficiency gains pay off quickly. And the energy management sector in general, with industry leaders like building energy manager EnerNOC, is a key focus of the city's clean-tech efforts.

4. NEW YORK CITY

The congestion, energy, and intensity of the Big Apple are unmatched by any other U.S. city, and certainly don't fit the "green city" stereotype found in laid-back Austin or Portland. By some measures, however, that urban density makes New York the nation's most sustainable city. Thanks to the country's most used public-transit system, and living spaces often a fraction of the size that most Americans are used to, New Yorkers boast the nation's smallest per capita carbon footprint for city dwellers.

That's a point of pride for green-minded mayor Michael Bloomberg, who currently chairs the C40 Cities Climate Leadership Group, a global coalition of large cities (58 of them, actually) committed to carbon reduction and planning for climate change. But what of building a local clean-tech economy? Bloomberg and scores of other public- and private-sector leaders in New York have made it a top priority. The Brookings/Battelle report data count more than 152,000 clean-tech jobs in New York, and the city added nearly 48,000 clean-economy jobs between 2003 and 2010. The city hopes to significantly boost that figure with the new $2 billion NYC Tech Campus of Cornell University, on Roosevelt Island in the East River. The campus, to be partially powered by the city's largest solar and geothermal energy systems, is expected to eventually spawn dozens of technology start-ups, including many in clean tech.

New York has notable activity in clean transportation, rooftop solar PV and hot-water installations, and clean water technologies, but its key clean-tech sector by far is green buildings and energy efficiency. It has all the same factors that make this sector big in Boston—but much larger buildings and many, many more of them. A set of Greener, Greater Buildings laws, passed in 2009 as a key part of the city's PlaNYC sustainability strategy out to 2030, requires energy-efficiency upgrades in the city's largest buildings. It's a big target. There are a staggering 800,000 building lots in New York's five boroughs, but half of the city's total square footage is in less than 2 percent of the lots.

That's a lot of retrofit work and a lot of potential jobs, from small contractors to behemoths like Parsons Brinckerhoff, the project engineering firm founded in New York in 1885 (one early project was the city's first subway line, the IRT, opened in 1904). The NYCEEC collaboration aims to fill in the financing piece that so often goes missing after mandates are put in place, with the dual goals of energy savings and economic stimulus. "Everything in energy retrofits requires labor," says NYCEEC's CEO, Susan Leeds. "By putting this money to work, we'll have economic activity happening—new jobs and the greening of existing jobs by upgrading workers' skill sets." In 2011, New York's landmark Empire State Building became the world's largest and oldest building to win LEED Gold certification for its retrofit. Johnson Controls, Serious Energy, and many other firms upgraded more than 6,500 windows (among other improvements) to cut the skyscraper's energy consumption by nearly 40 percent.

5. DENVER

In the previous chapter, we detailed Colorado's remarkable transformation from a fossil-fuel and mining state to a clean-energy leader, and the majority of the state's clean-tech jobs and economic activity are centered in the Denver metro area. Clean tech is very broad-based here, with both companies and deployments in solar, wind, green building, smart grid, vehicle efficiency, and other sectors.

Denver is the second-largest market in the U.S. for jobs in green building, EVs and EV infrastructure, and clean water technologies, according to data compiled for Clean Edge's *Clean-Tech Job Trends 2010* report by Seattle-based research partner PayScale, owner of the world's largest salary database. (PayScale's rankings are based on the percentage of total workers in the metro area employed in specific clean-tech industry sectors.) The Brookings/Battelle report found that Denver's solar industry jobs (both PV and thermal technologies) grew 42 percent from 2003 to 2010, while positions in battery technologies grew by one-third.

Like all the top clean-tech cities, Denver enjoys a very strong university-and-research community. The crown jewel is the DOE's National Renewable Energy Laboratory (NREL), at the foot of the Rocky Mountains' Front Range in the western suburb of Golden. Although it's at the mercy of federal budget cuts, NREL employs more than 1,500 people and is a key source of clean-energy technology development and workforce training. NREL's technology commercialization programs, like the Innovation and Entrepreneurship Center, augment its strong research component. Local clean-tech startups like Boulder Wind Power, founded by former NREL chief engineer Sandy Butterfield, show the lab's ability to help pollinate the local clean-tech economy.

The University of Colorado–Boulder, the University of Denver, and Colorado State University (CSU), in Fort Collins, all have notable clean-tech bona fides as well. CSU engineers and planners are working with the DOE on an ambitious project called FortZED, which aims to make downtown Fort Collins a net-zero energy community that generates as much clean electricity as it uses.

In October 2011, Denver landed GE's coveted thin-film solar panel factory, beating out rivals from some ten other states for the largest solar-panel-manufacturing facility in the U.S. The facility is slated to produce 400 megawatts of panels and employ 355 workers, with commercial production beginning in 2013. That's a big fish to hook, but Denver is accustomed to it. More than 20 wind and solar companies elected to relocate or expand to Colorado between 2009 and 2011, most of them in the Denver region. Perennial world wind turbine leader Vestas of Denmark has all its major U.S. manufacturing in the Denver area, with three plants making turbine blades and nacelles.

Denver's clean-tech economy has reaped many benefits from the strong leadership of former Colorado governor Bill Ritter, which we detailed in the previous chapter. Ritter's successor is two-term Denver mayor John Hickenlooper, who launched a sustainability program called Greenprint Denver in 2006 and is now bringing pro-clean-energy policies to the statehouse.

6. WASHINGTON, D.C.
If only some of the members of Congress who oppose the clean-tech economy could look literally in their backyards, they'd see the beginnings of revitalization in a city that faces huge financial struggles. The Washington metro area added more than 20,000 clean-economy jobs from 2003 to 2010, for a total of more than 70,000, with the solar PV industry as its fastest-growing sector.

As in any other industry with a keen interest in federal policy, the nation's capital is home to dozens of clean-tech lobbying and advocacy groups. The American Council on Renewable Energy, Advanced Energy Economy, the Coalition for Green Capital, GridWise Alliance, and many other key industry organizations are based here, as are the trade associations for individual sectors in solar, wind, biofuels, geothermal, hydrogen, and more.

The federal government and, notably, the military are large and growing purchasers of clean-tech products and services, so companies serving that market want to be where the action is. The U.S. Army, for example, buys solar-fueled mobile power stations from SkyBuilt Power, in Arlington, Virginia, for deployment in off-grid remote areas including Afghanistan. (The Pentagon has a mandate to use 25 percent renewable energy by 2025.) SkyBuilt's investors include the venture capital arm of the Central Intelligence Agency (known as In-Q-Tel) and Gamesa, a leading Spanish wind turbine manufacturer.

The area is also one of the nation's leading regions for green power purchasing. The D.C. city government, the Montgomery County Clean Energy Buyers Group in Maryland, and the Washington Suburban Sanitary Commission water/wastewater utility all rank in the top 12 local-government buyers of green power nationwide. And four of the area's leading universities—American, Catholic, Georgetown, and the University of Maryland—are among the top 20 green-power-purchasing academic institutions; no other U.S. city has more than two. Since it effectively functions as its own state, the District has a state-like RPS mandate, passed by the city council in 2005, to receive at least 20 percent of its electricity from clean sources by 2020.

7. SAN DIEGO

Southern California's surf-and-sun destination demonstrates how clean-tech leadership can grow out of a city's existing industries. San Diego is leveraging its strength in biotech, defense technologies, software, and data communications to build growing sectors in biofu-els/biomaterials, smart grid, energy storage, and the deployment and integration of EVs.

"We've considered ourselves an innovation economy for a long time, and we do well with cluster development," says Jacques Chirazi, who manages the city's clean-tech program for Mayor Jerry Sanders. "Our goal now is to create the jobs and the companies of the future."

With more than 70 research institutions in the area, notably the Scripps Institute and the University of California–San Diego, the city has been a particularly fertile ground for producers of algae-based and other advanced biofuels. San Diego's company roster includes Sapphire Energy, a 2011 *Wall Street Journal* Top 10 Clean-Tech Company whose backers include Bill Gates's Cascade Investment, and Synthetic Genomics, founded by human genome pioneer J. Craig Venter. The company's six-year partnership with ExxonMobil, inked in 2009, included a $600 million cash infusion.

Despite a more conservative political culture than those of San Francisco or Los Angeles, San Diego has emerged as a key clean-tech test bed and boasts California's highest percentage of rooftop solar installations. "When it comes to green, our politics is mostly focused on economic development and job creation," says Chirazi.

Local utility San Diego Gas & Electric, although infamous to some for a September 2011 power outage that affected six million people, is among the nation's leaders in clean-energy generation, smart-grid activities, and the integration of EVs. San Diego has one of the largest deployments of EV-charging stations in the DOE's EV Project, with 1,510 locations in the metro area by the end of 2011. Even the world-famous San Diego Zoo is on board with clean tech. The zoo has hosted an annual conference since 2009 on biomimicry, the practice of designing cleaner, more efficient products and systems by mimicking designs and processes found in nature.

CleanTECH San Diego, a networking/promotional group headed by former city economic-development official Jim Waring, lists more than 800 clean-tech companies in the metro area. Although we think that's casting a pretty wide net, the city is nonetheless a strong number three among California cities, with very high aspirations to make clean tech a big part of its innovation economy.

8. HOUSTON

The nation's oil-and-gas capital is perhaps the best example of the distinction between what's traditionally thought of as "green" and the new clean-tech economy. Houston doesn't earn high marks for sustainability planning, mass transit, or bicycle paths. But in terms of total jobs and economic activity related to clean tech, the city outpaces more "environmentally conscious" locations such as Seattle, Portland, and Texas's green capital of Austin.

A great deal of this activity is in what could be called the clean side of fossil fuels—technologies that cut energy use and emissions by making engines of all kinds, pipelines, and even oil refineries more efficient. You won't usually see workers in these sectors on clean-energy-touting brochures next to solar installers or wind-turbine assembly-line employees—and they may not even view themselves that way. But they're every bit as important in reducing the nation's fossil-fuel consumption. Houston teems with startup companies like Emissions Technology, developer of a catalyst system that makes diesel engines run cleaner with less fuel, and Orbital Traction, designer of energy-efficient transmissions for products including all-terrain vehicles, farm equipment, and marine outboard motors. There is notable activity in biofuels as well.

As an energy capital, Houston brings an industry focus and knowledge of infrastructure, financing, and market dynamics that's invaluable for clean-energy ventures that must compete with traditional fossil-fuel players. "Ten years from now, I think the big clean-tech cities will be the old energy-center cities, like Houston and Denver," says Marc Cummings, the Seattle-based director of policy and external affairs at the DOE's Pacific Northwest National Laboratory for energy and efficiency research. "That's where people really understand how this industry works. There may be some recalcitrance about clean tech today, but they know how technology, capital, and policy interact."

Houston's best example of that crossover may be Horizon Wind Energy, a large wind farm operator launched as Zilkha Renewable Energy in 1998 by offshore-oil-lease trader Selim Zilkha. The company was renamed Horizon when Zilkha and his partners sold it to Goldman Sachs in 2005; two years later, Goldman sold it to Portugal's national utility, Energias de Portugal, for more than $2 billion. Horizon operates 27 wind farms across the U.S., with capacity of more than 3,400 megawatts—including 400 megawatts at the Lone Star Wind Farm, in central Texas—and is now involved in solar development as well. A former Horizon executive, Michael Skelly, even ran for Congress in former president George H. W. Bush's onetime district in 2008. Skelly now runs Clean Line Energy, a Houston-based developer of high-speed transmission lines to harness electricity from renewable energy projects around the country.

Wind is king among renewable energy sources in Texas, and the city of Houston is the nation's largest local government purchaser of green power for its own operations, according to the EPA's Green Power Partnership program. Wind from utility Reliant Energy supplies 34 percent of the government's electricity needs, and those 438 million annual kilowatt-hours are the fifth most of any purchaser in the U.S., trailing only Intel, Kohl's Department Stores, Whole Foods, and the Commonwealth of Pennsylvania. Houston has an academic crown jewel in Rice University, and the Rice Alliance for Technology and Entrepreneurship has helped launch more than 300 tech companies, including many in clean tech, since its founding in 1999.

9. CHICAGO

Clean-tech acolytes in Chicago are prouder than ever of the city's legendary handle, the Windy City. Thanks to its proximity to the rich wind resources of the Midwest and a determined economic development effort, the Chicago metro area is home to the global or North American headquarters of more than a dozen wind power manufacturers and project developers, more than any other U.S. city. These include some of the largest wind players in the world, including Spain's Acciona Energy, India's Suzlon, Germany's Nordex, and, perhaps most notably of all, China's Goldwind—that country's largest wind turbine manufacturer. The Chicago area's wind industry jobs grew an average of nearly 40 percent annually from 2003 to 2010.

Chicago Mayor Rahm Emanuel has pledged to continue the environmental and clean-tech leadership of his predecessor, Richard M. Daley, who made the city the nation's green-roof capital (including the one on City Hall) and worked to lure solar, biomass, and other clean-energy companies to the city. Chicago-based nationwide solar installer SoCore Energy has been a notable success, and is a key partner in the solar deployment plans of Walgreens (also headquartered in the area). Walgreens led all U.S. retailers with 130 rooftop solar PV installations planned by the end of 2011, and the drugstore chain also aims to be the nation's largest host of EV-charging stations, with some 800 targeted by the same time. "We have all the pieces that make Chicago the perfect place to be the center of gravity as it relates to new technology in the field of alternative energy," Emanuel told attendees at the Midwest Energy Forum in 2011. In March 2012, Emanuel announced the Chicago Infrastructure Trust, which, like NYCEEC in New York City, will leverage private capital to fund energy-efficiency retrofits in municipal buildings; initial investors include units of Citibank and J. P. Morgan.

The Chicago area is also rich in education resources and research labs, but faces a continuing challenge in converting tech advances into jobs that stay in the local region. Much of the R&D for the lithium-ion-battery technology powering the Chevy Volt, for instance, came out of Argonne National Laboratory, the nation's oldest national research institution, in the Chicago suburbs. But most of the 300 jobs manufacturing the batteries went to Michigan. Chicago can look to Boston and the Bay Area as models of how to better translate research advances into local economic drivers.

10. AUSTIN

Showing leadership that belies its small size (the MSA's population ranks just 35th in the U.S.), Austin has been a clean-energy-development, deployment, and policy leader since the early days of the clean-tech revolution a decade ago. Austin's prominence stems from a technology-focused economy, a progressive city government, a strong academic community, and its famous "Keep Austin Weird" and "Third Coast" ethos, which keeps the Texas state capital at the leading edge.

In October 2011, Austin became the nation's largest city purchasing 100 percent clean energy for government operations. That goal was set in 2007 by the former mayor and the world's best-named politician, Will Wynn; the city actually reached its goal one year early, under current mayor Lee Leffingwell. Austin now procures all of its public-use electricity through the GreenChoice option of municipal utility Austin Energy, often considered the nation's leading utility in its commitment to the deployment and sale of clean energy. PayScale's national ranking of clean-tech job markets by sector lists Austin as number five in smart grid, sixth in solar, and fourth in clean water technologies.

Austin Energy is one of the funders of the Austin Technology Incubator (ATI), one of the nation's earliest and most successful nurturers of local startup companies. Demonstrating the multidisciplinary partnerships of a clean-tech leader, ATI's backers also include the

University of Texas, the city of Austin, the state government, and federal grants from the DOE and the U.S. Department of Commerce. ATI has worked with more than 200 companies since 1989 in IT, life science, and clean tech. Recent "incubated" clean-energy companies in Austin that are now in commercial operation include utility-scale energy storage provider Xtreme Power and LED lighting developer Firefly. Austin has also done a good job luring larger clean-tech companies from other states to add locations there, such as California-based SunPower's new operations center, opened in 2011 with 450 employees.

11. SEATTLE
The Pacific Northwest, dubbed Ecotopia for its striking natural beauty and decades-long heritage of environmentalism, is logical and fertile ground for growing a strong clean-tech economy. The cities of Seattle, Portland, and Vancouver, British Columbia, have all made that a goal, and have succeeded in many ways. The effect of the economic downturn, particularly on the building sector, has made job creation efforts fall short of high expectations. But it's fair to say that the Northwest sets the bar higher than other U.S. regions. Looking at the overall national picture, Seattle (along with Portland) is widely recognized as a clean-tech leader among U.S. cities.

Seattle's public policy has led the way with leading-edge green building policies that have helped create the city's largest clean-tech cluster: companies whose products and services reduce energy use in the built environment. Clean Edge termed this sector "green building design services" in *Carbon-Free Prosperity 2025*, a regional report we prepared with Climate Solutions for policy and business leaders in the Northwest in 2008. Seattle, for example, has required LEED Silver or better certification for all public structures over 5,000 square feet since 2000, and in October 2011 began requiring property managers at some 9,000 buildings to report their annual energy use to the city. Such policy leadership helps create a market for local firms like McKinstry. "A city or region's support for specific clean-tech sectors is not just attitudinal," says Tom Ranken, CEO of the Washington Clean Technology Alliance. "The regulatory framework makes a big difference."

Other key clean-tech sectors in the Puget Sound area are smart grid, with companies often populated by software engineers formerly at Microsoft and other local tech firms, and biomass/bioenergy. Local forest products giant Weyerhaeuser has a major R&D initiative for technologies that convert wood waste to energy and fuels, including a joint venture with Chevron called Catchlight Energy. Propel Fuels operates more than 30 biodiesel and E85 ethanol stations in the Seattle area and California, and Targeted Growth is an emerging leader in refining jet fuel from camelina, a fast-growing plant. Even the city's trash produces renewable energy: Since 2010, municipal utility Seattle City Light has powered about 5,000 city homes with 6 megawatts of electric generation from a Waste Management landfill gas generator at the Columbia Ridge landfill, in Oregon.

Another notable Seattle clean-tech player is renewable energy risk-analysis firm 3TIER, which helps developers assess the feasibility of solar, wind, and hydroelectric projects around the world. Nearly half of 3TIER's employees hold master's degrees or Ph.D.'s.

12. ATLANTA

As we have pointed out, the Deep South is the least advanced region in the U.S. for clean-energy deployment, policy support, and financing. But pockets of change are beginning to emerge, with states like South Carolina and Mississippi landing manufacturers of EV batteries, solar panels, and biofuels. As the South's business capital, Atlanta is making notable strides in embracing clean tech as part of its diversified economy.

Atlanta's clean-tech sector is an interesting mix of pure-play startups and old-line manufacturers moving into clean-tech products. Overall, there are more than 43,000 positions in Atlanta's clean-tech job market. Exide Technologies, a 124-year-old vehicle battery manufacturer, has made a new focus on hybrid batteries part of its financial turnaround strategy after emerging from Chapter 11 bankruptcy protection several years ago. Exide employs 40 hybrid battery engineers at a lab opened in 2010 and plans to hire up to 200 factory workers to make hybrid batteries at a plant in the nearby city of Columbus. City icon Coca-Cola is a global leader in developing clean water technologies and has invested some $70 million in clean-tech venture funds from leading VC firms Element Partners and RockPort Capital Partners. And few old-line companies anywhere have undergone a bigger transformation than Atlanta modular carpet maker Interface, whose late founder and chairman, Ray Anderson, took the company from a large-scale, petroleum-based polluter to a leading provider of green building materials from clean and recycled sources and a pioneer of sustainability in operations.

The area's top clean-tech pure play is solar cell manufacturer Suniva, in suburban Norcross. A spinoff of the DOE's University Center of Excellence for Photovoltaics at Georgia Tech, Suniva opened the South's first solar PV cell plant in 2008. Subsequent expansions have upped the plant's capacity to 170 megawatts. Atlanta also boasts one of only three landfill covers in the U.S. to produce solar power. The 1-megawatt cover on the Hickory Ridge Landfill contains ten acres of PV panels and is one of the largest solar installations in Georgia. Norcross is also home to Comverge, a leading provider of energy management software and services to utilities and their commercial and residential customers.

13. DALLAS–FORT WORTH

In an area not particularly known for an entrepreneurial business culture, clean-tech jobs in the Dallas–Fort Worth metroplex tend to be found in the green initiatives of larger companies—and in the public sector. The city of Dallas is, surprisingly, among the nation's leaders in clean-energy policies and initiatives.

Dallas was one of the first U.S. cities to issue a green building standard for private-sector construction, both residential and commercial, back in 2003. The city is the nation's second-largest purchaser of green power for city operations, behind Houston (more than 300 million kilowatt-hours in 2010), and its sprawling DFW airport procures enough green power to rank eighth among municipal buyers.

The automobile-centric area is also home to two of the nation's most notable EV deployment projects. ECOtality is in the process of deploying more than 200 EV-charging stations in the metroplex, while NRG Energy will add 70 of AeroVironment's eVgo Freedom Stations by the end of 2012.

Large Dallas companies with significant clean-tech activity include HKS Architects, a global firm considered a green-building leader; regional utility TXU Energy, one of the first in the nation to offer incentives for residents to sign up for solar rooftop installations from SolarCity; and transmission provider Oncor, which is erecting new power lines to bring wind power from the West Texas plains to the state's population centers. China's largest privately owned wind company, Mingyang, chose Dallas for its first office outside China—the result of a highly publicized 2009 trade mission to China led by former mayor and current U.S. Senate candidate Tom Leppert.

14. PORTLAND

With Oregon as the number-two state in our *State Clean Energy Leadership Index*, it's no surprise to see its largest city and economic center on the list of top clean-tech metro areas. Portland's relatively small size and recent sluggish economy, however, have tempered much of its clean-tech job growth.

Nonetheless, Portland stands out as a leader in a wide range of clean-tech sectors, including green building/green design, wind power operations, and solar PV manufacturing. Industry is supported by progressive city policies, a skilled tech workforce, an academic/ research community that's quite robust for a smaller city, and a rich collection of relevant nonprofits and NGOs. Oregon ranks first in the nation in LEED-certified buildings per capita, and the vast majority of that green-building activity is concentrated in the Portland metro area.

In the suburb of Hillsboro, Germany–based SolarWorld operates the largest solar-PV-module factory in the U.S., with capacity of 350 megawatts, and other solar companies such as MEMC and Sanyo maintain operations in the region. Downtown Portland is home to about 400 employees at the North American headquarters of Vestas, Denmark's industry-leading wind turbine manufacturer. More than a half-dozen other wind manufacturers and developers have offices in the area, making Portland the number-one U.S. city for wind power industry jobs, according to PayScale.

In 2012, Vestas was slated to move into new offices in a renovated building in the city's hip Pearl District, a project that brings together three of the city's leading clean-tech players. Vestas will be based in the former depot of the legendary Meier & Frank department store, where Clark Gable once worked as a necktie salesman before moving on to a more high-profile career. The building will be partially powered by a 112-kilowatt array of SolarWorld panels on the roof, and the project manager is Portland's Gerding Edlen, one of the world's leading green-building developers. As in Seattle, companies that design, engineer, and build or renovate green buildings form a key cluster of clean-tech leadership and employment in Portland. Although job growth has taken a hit during the real estate downturn, Portland remains a key center of green-building-design services. Other notable green-design companies in the Rose City include Brightworks, Interface Engineering, SERA Architects, and CH2M Hill, which is based in Colorado but has 700 employees in the Portland region.

Portland is also a leader in creative financing of clean-tech projects, a key area of innovation in the area of strapped city budgets. One example, Clean Energy Works Oregon (CEWO), allows property owners in Portland (and throughout Oregon) to finance up to $30,000 in energy-efficiency improvements with no money down, repaying the loan through a monthly charge on their utility bills. Started, like NYCEEC in New York, with federal dollars, with the city government as one of several partners, CEWO aims to retrofit 6,000 homes and more than 3.5 million square feet of commercial space by the end of 2013.

15. SACRAMENTO

With less acclaim than the three other California metro areas on our top-cities list, the state capital has quietly emerged as a national leader in both clean-tech economic development and clean-energy deployment. Sacramento is the home of public-policy makers who administer generally progressive clean-energy legislation such as AB 32, the nation's only state-mandated cap-and-trade system for carbon emissions. But the private sector is also vibrant and diverse, with more than 100 clean-tech-related companies based in the area. Solar, biomass/biofuels, and energy efficiency are the leading sectors for companies belonging to CleanStart, an initiative launched in 2005 to develop a local clean-tech cluster.

Like another state capital, Austin, Sacramento has done a good job of bridging the city government, business, and academic communities to move clean tech forward. The Greenwise Initiative of Mayor (and onetime NBA basketball All-Star) Kevin Johnson aims to double the region's clean-tech job total to 28,000 jobs by 2020 while reducing per capita energy use 15 percent and overall water use 20 percent. The nearby University of California–Davis is a rich resource, housing the Plug-In Hybrid & Electric Vehicle Research Center and many programs in solar and efficiency technologies. Engineering professor Dr. Andrew Frank is considered the father of plug-in hybrid technology. UC-Davis has spawned several area clean-tech startups, like SynapSense, a leading provider of energy-saving systems for large data centers.

Also like Austin, Sacramento has a progressive, municipally owned electric utility, the Sacramento Municipal Utility District (SMUD). Although, as a "muni," it's exempt from California's nation-leading RPS mandates, SMUD has sought to meet and often exceed those clean-energy targets for its electricity mix. It's aiming for 37 percent renewable energy by 2020, better than the state mandate of 33 percent. SMUD's clean-energy legacy, particularly in solar, dates back more than a quarter-century. The utility opened one of the world's first utility-scale solar PV plants in 1984, doing so adjacent to the decommissioned Rancho Seco nuclear power plant—a fitting symbol of transition to renewable energy.

BEST OF THE REST: FIVE NOTABLE POCKETS OF CLEAN-TECH LEADERSHIP IN SMALLER CITIES

Although large cities dominate our leaders list, and with good reason, we don't want to overlook some smaller cities that have made clean-tech development and jobs a key component of their regional economies. These five metro areas often face financial and budgetary challenges just like their larger brethren but have made the clean-technologies sector a key piece of economic revival in activities ranging from R&D to manufacturing to deployment.

Toledo, Ohio, has emerged, surprisingly, as one of the nation's best examples of transformation from old-line industry to clean tech. The onetime Glass Capital of the World thrived for decades supplying glass to the auto plants of nearby Michigan, but Detroit's economic crash became Toledo's, too. In recent years, however, Toledo's business, government, and academic leaders have leveraged the city's glass-manufacturing expertise into another silicon-based industry: solar PV panels.

Some 6,000 people work in the solar industry in the Toledo area, helping make Ohio the number-two U.S. state in solar production (behind Oregon) in the first quarter of 2011. First Solar, the largest American solar manufacturer, started here before moving its headquarters to Arizona but still runs a thin-film solar factory in suburban Perrysburg. Xunlight, founded by University of Toledo physics professor Xunming Deng, employs 100 people making thin-film modules. And in July 2011, Spanish solar firm Isofoton selected the nearby town of Napoleon for its first U.S. plant, with 120 employees initially and potentially more than 300. Although the solar industry hasn't replaced as many total jobs as Toledo has lost in recent years, it's clearly a regional bright spot and a model for other Rust Belt cities seeking to create a 21st-century industry cluster.

Indianapolis, Indiana, is another Midwest manufacturing hub seeking economic revitalization through clean tech. Long synonymous with automotive excellence (and, of course, speed), Indy is becoming a notable center of electric vehicle and EV battery technology. Public-private partnerships like Hoosier Heavy Hybrid and Project Plug-IN are seeking to build the industry, and Indiana is the second-largest recipient of federal stimulus funds for EV and hybrid technologies, trailing only Michigan. Lithium-ion-battery specialist EnerDel supplies batteries for a range of vehicles, from the $88,000 Fisker Karma all-electric sports car to the U.S. Army's new hybrid Humvee. Altairnano is another lithium-ion-battery maker, with local production at a 70,000-square-foot facility in nearby Anderson. Indianapolis-based auto component manufacturers like Allison Transmission are adding a new focus on hybrid and EV-supporting technologies.

Indianapolis's clean-tech aspirations took a hit in February 2012, when Bright Automotive, an EV pure play focused on commercial utility vans, shut its doors in Anderson. The company may have been an ancillary victim of Solyndra's bankruptcy, as it failed to get a $314 million DOE loan guarantee needed to build its factory.

Altairnano's corporate headquarters is in **Reno, Nevada**, another unexpected clean-tech locale, with a diverse range of companies in solar, wind, geothermal, waste-to-energy, biofuels, and energy storage. Reno has arguably the nation's largest business cluster in the sometimes overlooked clean-energy sector of geothermal power. The area's largest company is Ormat Technologies, one of the world's leading pure-play geothermal companies competing with the likes of Chevron. Ormat Technologies is a $400 million subsidiary of Israel-based Ormat Industries, founded in 1965 and still run nearly half a century later by the husband-and-wife team of Lucien and Dita Bronicki. Ormat operates more than 500 megawatts of geothermal plants around the world, including six in northern Nevada. Smaller geothermal players in the Reno–Lake Tahoe area include Terra-Gen Power, Ram Power, Magma Energy, and Nevada Geothermal Power.

Reno's emerging entrepreneurial business culture has also spawned Windspire Energy, a global pioneer in small (1.2-kilowatt) 30-foot wind turbines for use in residential areas and on urban rooftops; wind farm developer Nevada Wind; and biodiesel refiner and seller Bently Biofuels.

Casual observers might be surprised to learn that the **Albany, New York**, area is a top technology R&D hub in the U.S., if not the world. Its crown jewel is the 525-acre campus of GE Global Research, in Niskayuna, home of more than 100 different labs and the unit's world headquarters, overseeing GE's other research centers in Bangalore, Munich, and Shanghai. The Niskayuna labs earned 560 U.S. patents in 2008 alone. Although GE Global Research serves all aspects of the $150 billion company, clean-tech activities under GE's Ecomagination umbrella (with its $1.5 billion annual R&D budget) are a major focus. GE Global Research director Mark Little formerly ran GE Energy's power generation unit in Schenectady and holds a Ph.D. in mechanical engineering from the area's leading research university, Rensselaer Polytechnic Institute, in Troy.

The New York State Energy Research and Development Authority (NYSERDA), one of the nation's most active state agencies promoting clean energy, houses and incubates about a dozen companies at the Saratoga Technology + Energy Park. Tenants include solar thermal hot-water developer the Radiant Store and mobile-power provider Electrovaya. Fuel cell technology is another key cluster in the region, with players like MTI Micro Fuel Cells and Plug Power. Clean-economy jobs account for 6.3 percent of all employment in the area, one of the highest concentrations in the nation.

Spokane, Washington, boasts a low cost of living, a high quality of life in a beautiful if remote location, and an emerging clean-tech economy with a focus on the smart-grid sector. The Spokane area is the home of Itron, the largest publicly traded pure-play clean-tech employer in the U.S. (and fourth largest in the world). Based in nearby Liberty Lake, it is the world's leading manufacturer of smart meters for electricity and water, with 9,000 employees worldwide. Itron anchors a small cluster of clean-tech providers including fuel-cells developer ReliOn, demand-side management specialist Ecova, and Commuter Cars, maker of the Tango urban electric vehicle.

In this chapter, we've highlighted 20 large and medium-size U.S. metro areas, from Seattle to Boston and Albany to San Diego, where clean tech is viewed as a significant economic driver. They are far from alone. Although it hasn't always been a smooth or easy ride, dozens of American cities have aspirations to create jobs, build industry clusters, and lure companies away from other cities (and nations) to become notable clean-tech destinations.

Clean tech's broad reach across the diverse sectors of energy, transportation, construction, materials, and water means that many different cities and regions can succeed—and help drive America's competitiveness in this key 21st-century industry. Although cities' approaches and focuses vary widely, most of the leading clean-tech metro areas share some common characteristics. They have leadership and cooperation from business, government, finance, and academia, with a spirit of innovation in all of those disciplines. Even in an era of inconsistent federal support and daunting financial challenges, America's cities have aggressively moved to make clean tech a key pillar as they build their regional economies in this century.

4

THE BIGGEST CLEAN-TECH DEVELOPMENTS RESHAPING THE WORLD

In *The CleanTech Revolution*, we identified the foremost clean-tech sectors and examined the latest market trends and growth opportunities emerging around the world. What immediately became apparent in our investigation was the remarkable diversity of the industry, with applications ranging from utility-scale renewables to plant-based plastic packaging materials. But the one unifying theme of all clean technologies was an intention to improve products and processes without sacrificing performance. Using less energy, producing cleaner electricity, traveling more efficiently, wasting fewer resources—these are all missions of clean-tech entrepreneurs, companies, and technologies.

"I find out what the world needs, then I proceed to invent," said Thomas Edison. This quote provides great context to the underlying motive that drives clean tech. The industry exists to profitably solve many of the world's most challenging problems, and for this reason, successful clean-tech innovations have a great ability to transform.

They can change the ways in which we power our buildings, fuel our vehicles, grow our economies, and live our lives.

In this chapter we will present and analyze the four most influential clean-tech developments that are likely to impact our world in the next five to ten years. We will analyze the drivers behind each major trend, explore the core and enabling technologies and value chains, and review—both in the U.S. and globally—where clean-tech leadership is taking root. At the end of our discussion of each development, we'll provide a list of the key companies to watch and highlight likely near-term, medium-term, and long-term trends.

Based on our research and review, the four biggest clean-tech developments reshaping the world are:

Smart Grids and the Utility of the Future. The development of an intelligent 21st-century power grid and the rise of distributed-energy technologies—like solar PV and stationary fuel cells—will forever reshape the business of energy production and delivery.

The Fast Lane to Vehicle Electrification. The need to curb the world's dependence on oil is driving us to find a new way to fuel the world's vehicle fleet. Electric vehicles and efficiency-boosting hybrid drivetrains have become the de facto technology for future transportation.

Green Building: Deep Retrofits and Net-Zero Ambitions. By combining aggressive energy-efficiency measures with on-site energy generation, efforts to develop net-zero energy buildings—buildings that generate the same or more energy than they consume—are now much more than a pipe dream.

One Person's Trash, Another Person's Treasure: The Vast Potential of Waste-to-Resource Technologies. Innovative technologies that convert municipal, agricultural, and industrial waste streams into electricity, fuel, and value-added products are increasingly achieving a classic win-win around the world, producing clean energy and sustainable offerings while reducing emissions and solid waste otherwise headed to landfills.

SMART GRIDS AND THE UTILITY OF THE FUTURE

Knowledge is power. But, as Arlington, Virginia–based Opower is proving, knowledge also saves power. The company gathers massive amounts of energy-usage data from utilities, runs the information through its proprietary analytics software, and delivers detailed monthly home-energy reports to utility customers with analysis of their energy-consumption performance. Armed with this intelligence, participating consumers average energy savings of around 1.5 to 3.5 percent each month. That might not seem like a staggering amount, but when aggregated across a large network of households, the savings can be huge. Since the company's launch in 2007, Opower's users had saved 500 gigawatt-hours. "We've saved enough energy to power the Empire State Building for more than 10 years," touted Opower's website in 2011. "Think of it this way," says Om Malik, founder of technology-business online publishing and research firm *GigaOM* in his profile of the company. "If Opower was working with all the utilities in the U.S., and had access to all the homes in the U.S., it could be saving a total of $5 billion a year." That's an inspiring potential for growth.

Opower's success thus far is noteworthy, given that home-energy management has been a rather shaky clean-tech sector—both Google and Microsoft threw in the towel in mid-2011 and discontinued their respective short-lived products in the space. Opower, backed by more than $64 million from top-tier venture investors Kleiner Perkins Caufield & Byers, Accel Partners, and New Enterprise Associates, has established partnerships with more than 50 U.S. utilities, including PG&E, Commonwealth Edison, and MidAmerican Energy. In 2011, the company expanded overseas to the U.K. through a deal with First Utility, launched a smart-thermostat device in partnership with Honeywell, and teamed up with Facebook and the Natural Resources Defense Council (NRDC) to create a social media app that allows participants to access their energy-consumption data and easily benchmark their behavior against others.

Opower is just one of many clean-tech companies leveraging today's information and smart-grid technologies to transform a utility industry that has been very slow to change since its early days at the dawn of the 20th century. As smart-grid deployment efforts become more robust, greater monitoring and control of the world's energy systems will create vast opportunities for novel applications, services, and business models. And with targeted utility regulation reform, aimed at sparking innovation rather than protecting entrenched monopolies, the utility of the future can achieve significant benefits for consumers and investors alike.

A SMARTER GRID

Driven by an accumulating convergence of forces, the global electric grid is finally undergoing a long-overdue restoration and giving rise to a 21st-century "smart grid," an electricity network that promises increased efficiency and reliability, two-way delivery of electrons, automated grid monitoring and control, and increased transparency of real-time energy use for consumers. In *The Clean Tech Revolution*, we chose smart grid as one of the eight major clean-tech sectors driving industry growth. Five years later, factors necessitating grid upgrades—aging grid infrastructure, outdated system monitoring and control, growing energy demand, and an increasing supply of intermittent and distributed renewable energy—have only intensified.

The fragility of our power grid was on display on a sweltering Thursday afternoon in September 2011, when a transmission line near Yuma, Arizona, tripped offline, cutting power to six million people across Southern California, Arizona, and even parts of Mexico. The suspected cause was human error from a single utility employee in

Arizona during routine substation maintenance. Typically, an outage of this kind can be isolated to the local grid, but in this case the power interruption quickly severed energy flow on a line critical to electricity supply in the populous San Diego metro area. Problems multiplied when San Diego's unstable grid caused the automatic shutdown of the nearby San Onofre nuclear power plant, another major supplier of power to the region.

Although the blackout lasted just 12 hours, its effects were wide-ranging. Businesses closed their doors. Schools sent students home. Streets became gridlocked as traffic lights went dark. All outgoing flights were grounded from the San Diego International Airport. And ten miles of California oceanfront was closed when the power failure shut down a number of pumping stations, causing nearly two million gallons of sewage to spill into a beach-adjacent lagoon. In total, the incident cost the San Diego economy around $100 million in damages from lost business, spoiled food, and overtime pay for government workers. And the lights weren't even out for a full day! The economic consequences of power outages and interruptions like this are severe, costing Americans billions each year.

Overhauling an energy system that in the U.S. alone delivers more than $350 billion in annual electricity sales is no small task. Yet even in the face of lingering global economic disorder, smart-grid development has become a growing area of focus for governments of the world's largest economies. Interested in meeting skyrocketing energy demand, China's government led all nations with more than $7.3 billion in stimulus-related smart-grid spending in 2010, according to Austin, Texas–based research-and-consulting firm Zpryme. The U.S. was a close second with $7.1 billion in federal investments, followed by Japan, South Korea, and Spain, each exceeding $800 million in smart-grid government spending.

Unlike smart-grid efforts in developed nations that center on integrating advanced data communication systems, China has focused on strengthening grid stability and expanding delivery capacity. China's electricity demand is expected to double in the next decade, and the nation plans to meet much of the new demand with vast wind-energy resources located far from population hubs. For this reason, implementing a strong smart grid is vital to continuing the country's accelerated rate of economic growth. According to Zpryme, China's smart-grid market will reach $61 billion by 2015, with a third of this derived from advanced transmission and distribution equipment. China may seem at a disadvantage, since it essentially has to build a national grid from scratch, but that means it can also use the latest and best technologies available. Judging by government-led investment thus far, China will be a market full of opportunity for smart-grid vendors for some time to come.

In the U.S., the idea of a smart grid has begun to appear on the general public's radar. The tipping point arguably came during Super Bowl XLIII in February 2009, when General Electric debuted its *Wizard of Oz*–themed smart-grid ad campaign. (GE is a manufacturer of smart meters and other smart-grid products.) In the 30-second spot, the Scarecrow character danced along the top of transmission lines crooning "If I only had a brain" as a voiceover promised 100 million football fans across America that smart-grid technology "will make the way we distribute electricity more efficient simply by making it more intelligent."

Unfortunately, performing brain surgery on our energy grid requires major spending from utilities—on top of the billions already being spent by the federal government. And because of the way the utility industry operates, this investment will swiftly be passed on to ratepayers in the form of price hikes. For consumers accustomed to a 99.9 percent reliable grid, never questioning that lights will shine on the flip of a switch, incurring new costs for relatively intangible consumer-side benefits is difficult to support, making the smart grid a hard sell for utilities and product vendors like GE. It will take much more than a singing scarecrow to convince the American public.

A few years after GE's Super Bowl pitch, smart-grid deployment in the U.S. remains somewhat tempered by a skeptical and cost-averse public, poorly performing demonstration projects, and a prolonged economic storm that has decimated budgets for governments, corporations, and individuals alike. Still, the move toward a smarter grid inches ahead, most noticeably with the installation of advanced metering infrastructure (AMI, which includes smart meters) that is bringing 21st-century data communication to the 20th-century grid. By 2010, advanced metering market penetration in the U.S. had exceeded 8 percent, a considerable increase from four years earlier when penetration was less than 1 percent. But smart-meter deployment is scattered, with states like Arizona, Oregon, Idaho, Pennsylvania, and Wisconsin each reporting between 20 and 30 percent advanced meter penetration in 2010, while eight states reported a less than 1 percent share for smart meters.

Across the Atlantic, the EU has taken a more aggressive stance with a 2006 directive requiring electric smart-meter market penetration of 80 percent by 2020. Ahead of even this schedule, Sweden essentially achieved full deployment of remotely readable electric meters by 2009, and Italy reached more than 90 percent smart-meter penetration by the end of 2011. Strong metering targets from France, Spain, and the U.K. will help further establish European smart grids that better monitor energy delivery and enable a variety of advanced energy services for utility customers large and small.

Smart grid is not all about the meter, however. Grid technologies that simplify the integration of distributed generation, on-site energy systems, and energy storage can have a major impact—especially in the developing world, where one and a half billion people live without electricity. Utilizing distributed power production in local microgrids makes it possible to bypass expensive buildout of electricity systems reliant on large centralized power plants and heavy-duty transmission lines. This leapfrogging of traditional infrastructure isn't a far-fetched scenario, as many parts of the developing world have already done the same thing with telecommunications—moving immediately to cell phones without ever deploying a system of conventional telephone lines.

THE EVOLVING BUSINESS OF ENERGY DELIVERY

The utility industry, whether because of its highly regulated nature, its low risk tolerance, or both, is famously averse to innovation. Compared with the pharmaceutical industry, which regularly invests more than 10 percent of revenue in R&D, or top tech companies like Microsoft and Google, each of which spend upwards of 14 percent of sales on R&D, utility R&D commitment is virtually nonexistent, averaging well below 1 percent of annual revenue. Despite utilities' historical fear of change, however, technology advances have nonetheless revolutionized their business. Developments in aerospace have brought about significant gas-turbine efficiency improvements, drilling-industry innovations have enabled cheaper extraction of shale gas resources, and IT and communication breakthroughs have improved how we control the flow of electrons, natural gas, and even water.

A growing roster of companies has emerged to assist utilities in their reluctant adoption of the latest technologies. Offering the ability to monitor energy delivery and consumption in real time and automate grid operation, companies like Itron, Silver Spring Networks, and Schneider Electric have built thriving global businesses by targeting utilities. As a startup in the nascent smart-grid sector, Silver Spring's ability to land early partnerships with major utility players like Florida Power & Light and Pacific Gas and Electric (PG&E) has been essential to the company's survival and success in penetrating the risk-averse utility market. Itron, headquartered in Liberty Lake, Washington, just outside Spokane, is one of the world's largest meter manufacturers, offering metering equipment to utilities across the globe. With a long history in the business of traditional meters, the company serves more than 8,000 utility customers in more than 130 countries. As the smart-grid opportunity has gathered steam, Itron has focused increasingly on its smart-metering activity and the selling of related smart meters and network communication systems. Similar stories can be told for other leading meter makers, like Switzerland-based Landis+Gyr and Echelon, in San Jose, California. But metering extends beyond electricity, and Itron is exploring increasingly attractive opportunities in smart metering for gas and water markets.

"Water, in particular, is an intriguing long-term play," says Jesse Berst, founding editor and chief analyst of the industry newsletter *Smart Grid News*. "Water shortages are predicted in many parts of the world. Smart water meters offer measurements and analytics that can dramatically improve usage and reduce losses."

With advanced communication-and-control systems in place, utilities can shave peak electricity demands and increase grid stability through dynamic interaction with their consumers. So-called demand-side energy-management applications such as demand response can cut peak electricity loads, briefly throttling back the most energy-intensive functions like air conditioning and refrigeration during times of high demand.

Utilities generally like demand response because it allows them to limit use of expensive "peaker" plants—usually natural-gas-fired plants built solely to supply electricity on peak-demand days—which can quickly eat away at bottom-line profits. But that doesn't mean they want to do it themselves. This is where companies like Boston-based EnerNOC and Norcross, Georgia–based Comverge come in. These demand-response service providers are in the business of helping large commercial energy users save electricity. They work directly with utility customers to dim lights slightly, shut off computers not in use, and the like, earning revenue from how much electricity they save—so-called negawatts. By the end of 2010, Ener-NOC had more than 5,300 megawatts of demand-response capacity under management—the equivalent of about ten conventional natural-gas-fired plants. During the 2011 summer cooling season alone, Comverge reduced more than 16 gigawatt-hours of electricity demand—equivalent to taking nearly 2,000 households off the grid for an entire year. As the number of grid-tied appliances and grid-powered electric vehicles grows, we believe the opportunity for demand-response services will expand at a rapid pace, creating a new breed of "virtual" power plant.

POWER TO THE PEOPLE?

Disruption of the traditional utility business model by clean technology advancements won't be limited to what happens behind the meter. As prices continue to drop for on-site clean-energy-generation technologies like solar panels, small-scale wind turbines, stationary fuel cells, and on-site storage, the entire process of purchasing energy stands to be turned on its head, with the potential to cut traditional utilities out of the picture entirely.

And this isn't a far-off flying-car scenario. In this case, the flying cars are already here, and they are growing in number by the day. Take the business of distributed solar PV project financing. Companies like SolarCity, Sungevity, and SunRun are finding nationwide success through solar power purchase agreements (PPAs), in which they install, own, and maintain solar installations on customers' homes and businesses. The customer pays a small monthly lease—with little or no upfront fees—to tap the power provided by on-site PV systems. Essentially, PPAs operate in the same way you pay for television service, with a Comcast-owned modem or DirecTV dish feeding channels to your TV. In the case of solar PPAs however, instead of paying for access to the Food Network, you're paying for the power to run your blender. In coming years, as solar power reaches grid parity in markets around the world, it will be increasingly common to see solar PPAs offer energy at fixed monthly payments that undercut rates for grid-fed electricity.

Utilities' aversion to innovation is partly due to regulatory schemes that deter adoption of new technologies and efficiency measures. This is especially true in the U.S., where federal policies overlap with state-level rules. Environmental laws, however well-intentioned, can also delay and deter new clean-energy-generation plants and their necessary transmission lines. Utility regulation in the U.S. stems from its earliest days, when the high cost of electricity generation made it useful to establish monopolies that could reliably deliver power free from the risks of competition. A century later, with intentions of empowering customers and driving innovation, more than a dozen states have tinkered with some form of deregulation, and further free-market structures have been pursued in Europe.

Injecting competition via deregulation is not always a positive solution, however; California ratepayers ruefully remember how Enron was able to game the state's newly deregulated system in the early 2000s and send electric rates through the roof. Neither side of the deregulation debate is likely to find itself in full favor any time soon, but this stalemate is not a bad outcome. With deregulation best discussed on a case-by-case basis, educated deliberations are needed to establish the best way to move forward.

"Changes in regulation are needed to create a new business model for energy utilities," says a 2011 report from the American Council for an Energy-Efficient Economy (ACEEE) titled *The Old Model Isn't Working: Creating the Energy Utility for the 21st Century.* What the industry needs, it says, is "a model that changes the fundamental financial motivations for utilities from commodity sales of energy . . . to providing energy services at the lowest cost to both customer and utilities."

Utilities need to be able to value efficiency-derived negawatts the same as new generating capacity, recovering costs for efficiency programs in the same way they would traditional fossil-fuel-capacity additions. To eliminate the current incentive to sell ever more centralized baseload electricity, revenue generation needs to be separated from electricity sales—a concept known as decoupling. And utilities will need to create new models for participating in the increasing trend toward distributed energy sources like solar PV, which compete at the retail level (the cost of energy on the customer side of the meter), rather than at the wholesale, power-plant level. Net metering laws, which require utilities to credit their customers (whether property owners or rooftop solar operators like SolarCity) for electricity generated on-site, will also help push utilities into 21st-century realities.

In order to survive in this rapidly changing landscape, utilities need to shift from selling the greatest possible quantities of fossil-fuel-generated electricity to providing the most reliable clean power. Within this reformed framework, renewables and energy efficiency will increasingly stand on their own. Saving a kilowatt-hour of electricity through utility efficiency programs, for example, would cost the utility about 2.5 cents, according to the ACEEE, compared with the 5 cents or more that it costs to generate that same kilowatt-hour from a new natural gas plant or other source of generation. Tapping on-site renewables, instead of expensive, occasionally used gas-fired peaker plants, would provide additional cost savings.

What does all of this disintermediation and change mean for the smart grid and the companies that service it? The 21st-century utility industry is moving away from a model reliant on a single organization responsible for power generation, grid operation, and monopolistic control of electricity delivery. The smarter the grid gets, the more third-party devices, software platforms, and energy management services are monitoring and controlling energy flow. And with the advent of transparent energy-usage data and affordable distributed-generation technologies, utility ratepayers—both residential and commercial—are starting to enter a brave new world of innovative options for on-site generation and energy management. As regulation reform takes hold and utility innovation picks up speed, tomorrow's energy industry, even for the slow-moving utility sector, is fast approaching. The utility of the future, in fact, may not look like a utility at all.

FUTURE OUTLOOK
Short Term (0–5 years)

- Extensive worldwide smart-meter deployment
- Increased use of energy management systems and demand-side response activity, primarily in large industrial and commercial buildings
- Widespread utility revenue decoupling, enabling utilities to focus on efficiency rather than new capacity
- New breed of energy service companies (PV leasing, demand response, home energy management) transforms the role of utilities

Medium Term (5–10 years)

- Major deployment of distributed generation and increased grid-scale energy storage capacity
- Smart appliances enable demand-response activity to extend into the home
- Extensive introduction of time-of-use pricing schedules from utilities

Long Term (10+ years)

- On-site energy generation is ubiquitous for home, business, and industrial facilities
- Self-sustaining microgrids supplement existing centralized electricity system, enabling greater security, reliability, flexibility
- Emerging vehicle-to-grid (V2G) services enable EV fleet to serve as large-scale virtual storage source

Companies to Watch

ABB Group
abb.com
Zurich, Switzerland
Power distribution and automation technology developer

Comverge
comverge.com
Norcross, Georgia
Demand-response service provider

Echelon
echelon.com
San Jose, California
Smart-metering and utility network provider

EnerNOC
enernoc.com
Boston, Massachusetts
Demand-response service provider

General Electric
ge.com

Fairfield, Connecticut
Smart-meter manufacturer

Itron
itron.com
Liberty Lake, Washington
Smart-meter manufacturer

Landis+Gyr (subsidiary of Toshiba)
landisgyr.com
Zug, Switzerland
Smart-meter manufacturer

Opower
opower.com
Arlington, Virginia
Home energy management software maker

Silver Spring Networks
silverspringnet.com
Redwood City, California
Utility communication network and smart-grid service provider

SolarCity
solarcity.com
San Mateo, California
Solar installation, financing, and leasing firm

THE FAST LANE TO VEHICLE ELECTRIFICATION

It's a rainy May day in Manhattan, and Fifth Avenue foot traffic is sparse as New Yorkers disappear into taxis to escape the springtime downpour. But in this reality, where more than 90 percent of taxis in the Big Apple are electric-powered, the streets remain silent and smog-free as cars zip to and from their destinations. In New York, Boston, and Chicago, electric vehicles (EVs) represent about one-third of all cars on the road. And in America's factories, one out of every four vehicles manufactured is all-electric.

Is this a glimpse into the future? A scenario in which volatile gas prices and climate-changing pollution have finally reached a tipping point, spurring a fundamental transformation of our transportation system? Not in the slightest. In actuality, the year is 1899, and Jacob German has just been arrested on the streets of New York for driving his electric taxi at an astounding 12 miles per hour, earning the first speeding ticket on record in the United States.

As we all know, this early age of electric cars did not last long. For a myriad of reasons—including demand for longer-range vehicles, discovery of more accessible crude oil, gasoline-engine innovations such as the muffler and the electric starter, and Henry Ford's assembly line—petroleum-powered vehicles were quick to overtake EVs as the transportation technology of choice. Over the next century, EVs would remain little more than a novelty. And while interest in electric-drive technology reappeared as a result of air quality concerns in the 1960s, global oil crises in the 1970s, and strengthened environmental regulations in the 1990s, EVs failed to find commercial success for the same fundamental reasons they faded into obscurity in the early 20th century: high price tags and range limitations.

Fast-forward to the present day. Toyota's hybrid electric Prius was the number-one-selling car in Japan in 2009 and 2010, mass-produced EV models from Chevrolet and Nissan have each won car-of-the-year awards, and massive efforts are under way across the globe to deploy reliable networks of EV-charging stations.

After a few false starts, EVs have finally emerged as a promising solution to the resource constraints and environmental concerns brought on by the global rise of the automobile—and the need to fuel it. In 1950, only 53 million passenger vehicles were on the world's roads. This number had skyrocketed to 500 million by 2000, and by 2010 the global passenger vehicle fleet had ballooned to 750 million. Driven by accelerated growth in China and India and sustained sales in the U.S., passenger vehicles are expected to total 1.5 billion by 2050. "It would be unrealistic to assume that a passenger fleet of this size will only be populated by gasoline-powered vehicles," says a 2011 report from the Harvard Kennedy School. "One would have to assume either that the global transportation fleet will be twice as efficient in 2050 as it is today, or that the world's oil supply will be sufficient to meet the demand of a fleet that is twice as large." With current oil demand already pushing oil prices to economy-crippling highs, the smart money is on a future of improved fleet efficiency.

Moving to improve vehicle efficiency, the Obama administration in November 2011 proposed new Corporate Average Fuel Economy (CAFE) standards that would roughly double the nation's fuel efficiency to 54.5 miles per gallon by 2025. Across the Atlantic, the EU is also addressing the topic of fuel economy, utilizing a CO_2-emission reduction timeline to enforce vehicle efficiency improvements. Both policies call for sizable improvements in fuel economy, a boon for vehicles like EVs, which present the potential to achieve significant fuel efficiency gains and remove the need for oil altogether.

From an environmental perspective, today's transportation sector is already a major contributor to climate change—accounting for a quarter of global carbon dioxide emissions—and is a culprit in the degradation of air quality, agriculture, ecosystems, and human health all over the world. If car ownership grows as expected in the coming years, a fundamental shift in the world's transportation system will be needed to avoid horrific oil-induced environmental catastrophes.

For the U.S., economic realities alone necessitate a move away from strictly gasoline-powered vehicles. Estimated direct costs of America's oil addiction reached as much as half a trillion dollars in 2008, and in 2010 crude oil imports accounted for more than half of the entire trade deficit. With America's transportation sector responsible for nearly three-quarters of the nation's oil consumption, any effort to reduce oil use must start behind the wheel. Diversification of the transportation sector's energy supply is the quickest way the U.S. can ease economic malaise caused by oil dependence.

While the case to move beyond petroleum-based transportation is clear, electricity is not the only game in town, and advocates of natural gas, biofuels, and hydrogen fuel cells argue that these technologies also offer viable ways to provide a sustainable transportation fuel supply. Some even argue that simply making internal combustion engines (ICEs) more efficient will adequately curb demand for oil. Each of these may have a role to play in a future that sees 1.5 billion passenger vehicles on the road, but none will fully derail the electrification of transportation that is under way. Natural gas, although cleaner-burning than oil and abundant in the U.S., still produces harmful tailpipe emissions and is currently best suited for vehicle fleets that have access to fast-fill fueling stations. Biofuels were a gleam in investors' eyes during the early 2000s and still offer great potential, but unfavorable carbon life-cycle realities, food-versus-fuel debates, and slow-moving progress in advanced biofuel technologies have tempered the sector's prospects. And the fuel cell, an integral piece of the utopian hydrogen economy, still faces cost challenges that make high-priced EVs look like bargains in comparison. It's certainly not an either/or scenario, and we still see prospects for advanced biofuels derived from sustainable feedstocks like algae and agricultural waste. But we believe that electricity is the number-one weapon of choice in the global effort to cure transportation's dependency on oil.

As a transportation fuel, electricity has many positive features: Its prices are stable and relatively low; it is not dependent on imports, as electricity is typically generated domestically; and in all-electric vehicles it enables a tailpipe-emissions-free vehicle fleet that will have a decreasing impact on the environment as the electric grid becomes increasingly powered by clean electrons. Although EVs require specialized charging stations or home-based hookups, the actual fuel distribution system—the electric grid—is already in place. That gives electrons a major advantage over hydrogen and (to a lesser extent) natural gas, which require significant new infrastructure buildouts.

THE 21ST-CENTURY ELECTRIC VEHICLE

You don't transform a trillion-dollar industry overnight. After several failed attempts to introduce all-electric vehicles to the world's auto market, it was gasoline-electric hybrids that played arguably the most important role in paving the way for an achievable EV future. Combining an ICE with a battery-powered electric powertrain, hybrids typically achieve 20 to 30 percent better fuel economy than comparable non-hybrids. Toyota's Prius, the world's longtime best-selling hybrid model, was introduced into the Japanese market in 1997, hit the American market in 2000, and in September 2010 surpassed the two million cumulative sales mark in the U.S. Toyota's success has not only granted the company commercial success; it has also proved to other carmakers that fuel efficiency can drive vehicle sales. By 2010, more than 30 different hybrid models were available globally, a substantial increase from just three models ten years earlier. If Toyota's projections are accurate, hybrids will make up 20 percent of the auto market by 2020.

While hybrid vehicles utilize electric motors to assist conventional gasoline engines, the batteries that power their electric motors are small enough to be charged through on-vehicle processes like regen-erative braking, making it unnecessary to draw upon the grid for energy. Plug-in electric vehicles, on the other hand, rely much more on electric motors as a primary source of propulsion, requiring larger batteries that must collect power directly from the grid. Plug-ins can be all-electric, operating exclusively on energy stored in the grid-charged battery, or plug-in hybrids, which also use grid-charged batteries to power electric motors but still depend partly on combus-tion engines.

This is the logic that led General Motors to include a small gas-powered engine on its Chevrolet Volt, a plug-in hybrid that can travel 40 miles on all-electric power before the conventional engine kicks in to provide an additional 300 miles of range. Because 80 percent of U.S. drivers travel 40 miles or less each day, plug-in hybrids like the Volt allow for primarily all-electric travel with the safety net of tra-ditional gas-powered operation. "Batteries require a lot of space, they add a lot of mass to the car, and they're expensive," said Jon Lauck-ner, GM's former VP of global program management, who now heads the company's venture capital arm, on the eve of the Volt's unveiling in September 2008. "Whether the Volt evolves into a fully battery-electric vehicle will depend on the cost and the capabilities of batter-ies as we go forward."

Many other carmakers, initially reluctant, have also either already introduced a plug-in hybrid or are planning to offer one in the near future. Toyota, looking to expand on the success of its Prius brand, planned to begin offering a plug-in version of the vehicle in Japan, the U.S., and Europe in 2012. With an advertised range of 15 miles of pure-electric drive per 1.5-to-3-hour charge (depending on outlet voltage), the plug-in Prius can cover roughly half of an average Amer-ican's daily mileage in full-electric mode.

Leapfrogging the ambitions of PHEV makers, a number of auto companies are pursuing development of pure all-electric vehicles—

with some already available to the mass market from major manufac-turers (e.g., Nissan's LEAF, Ford's Focus Electric, and Mitsubishi's i) and several more models to be released soon. All-electrics face the difficult task of drawing power entirely from an onboard battery sys-tem, but they operate completely independent of gasoline, an attri-bute that plug-in hybrids cannot claim. For carmakers that succeed in developing adequate battery systems, the electric motor presents some valuable advantages over the ICE: It's more energy efficient, emits no tailpipe emissions, runs practically silently, requires less maintenance, and—contrary to popular belief—enables superior power performance.

When the gas engine of Croatian auto engineer and racing enthu-siast Mate Rimac's 1986 BMW 3 Series blew up during a race, he decided against scrapping the classic vehicle. Instead, Rimac worked with a team to convert the BMW into a 900-horsepower electric-drive supercar capable of accelerating from 0 to 60 miles per hour in 3.3 seconds—enough speed to get a jump on the Enzo Ferrari, which gets to 60 in 3.4 seconds with 660 horsepower. "I believe that the electric motor is a much better machine compared to the ICE, in almost all aspects," Rimac told *Wired* magazine in 2011.

Nissan's LEAF is no Ferrari beater, but with the car's range of around 73 miles per charge, the Japanese automaker is placing a big bet on the widespread acceptance of all-electric vehicles. The LEAF hit U.S. and Japanese markets in late 2010, serving as a direct competi-tor to Chevy's Volt. Nissan's Smyrna, Tennessee, production facility—scheduled to come online in late 2012—will have the capacity to build 150,000 LEAFs each year.

"The first cars in the industry were electric cars," Nissan CEO Car-los Ghosn told online magazine *Yale Environment 360* in May 2011. "So when people say you're pioneering electric cars, we're going to say that electric cars always existed. What we're pioneering is affordable electric cars—that's where the revolution is taking place."

Traditionally, auto manufacturing has been a game dominated by big players, with little opportunity for the little guy. Mass EV production, however, is uncharted territory for all carmakers, and this has provided smaller firms with a good deal of confidence. Among the startups looking to become big-time EV makers is Tesla Motors, in Palo Alto, California, which is well known for its high-end Roadster and hoping to find success with the new Model S luxury sedan.

For EV electricity storage, there is a need to capture energy in a battery that is small, lightweight, safe, and fast-charging and produces consistent, high-quality power in a wide range of environmental conditions. But this presents many technical challenges. In the words of world-famous car collector Jay Leno, "Electricity is like an animal. You put it in a jar and it either escapes or it dies." The maturation of lithium batteries—which now dominate the EV market—was largely enabled by years of real-world application in consumer electronics, powering devices like laptops and cell phones. Watertown, Massachusetts–based A123 Systems, for example, got its start making lithium-ion products for Black & Decker power tools but now provides EV battery packs to a number of carmakers, including Smith Electric Vehicles and Shanghai Automotive Industry Corporation.

Significant progress in battery technology has been made in the past several years, but if the electric vehicle is to be an affordable, high-performance, long-distance mode of transportation, major battery technology breakthroughs will be needed, particularly in cost reduction. The United States Advanced Battery Consortium has taken on aggressive cost-reduction targets; however, with South Korea, Japan, and China supplying more than 90 percent of the world's advanced batteries, it may be up to Asian technology companies like Sanyo, Samsung, and LG Chem to make these cost targets a reality.

Many formidable barriers stand in the way of transitioning to an electric-powered passenger vehicle fleet. First and foremost is the higher purchase price of most hybrids and especially of plug-ins and all-electric vehicles versus comparable ICE models. The success of all-electric vehicles and plug-in hybrids also depends on establishing a reliable network of charging stations. It takes well over 100,000 gas stations to keep the U.S. vehicle fleet running, and this degree of fuel accessibility must be replicated for EV charging if consumers are to overcome range-anxiety concerns. With cars spending more than two thirds of their time parked at home, residences should be the first priority for any EV-charging infrastructure buildout, followed by charging availability at the workplace, and finally public charging stations at commercial centers and along main routes to provide supplemental juice when needed.

A wide variety of players are tackling the EV-charging challenge, from major automakers and EV startups to charging-station-technology developers and national and local governments. Innovative business models, like battery swapping from Better Place, are also moving forward and have the potential to disrupt the entire EV-charging paradigm. The Palo Alto–based startup, led by software industry veteran Shai Agassi, offers a subscription service in which drivers swap out depleted EV batteries for a fully charged replacement in minutes, rather than the hours it would take to recharge a drained battery. Among markets testing Better Place's battery-swapping model are Denmark, Israel, Japan, and the San Francisco Bay Area.

There are a host of questions regarding EVs that remain to be answered. The big ones, relating to vehicle costs, charging availability, battery performance and safety, limited range, and consumer acceptance, have been the subject of much study and scrutiny. However, less obvious topics must not be ignored: How will utilities accommodate the electricity load from a grid-tied EV fleet? Will EV growth create new natural resource supply constraints for battery materials like lithium? And as EVs gain wide acceptance and truly begin reducing gasoline consumption, what happens to government highway funding that has historically been procured through gas taxes? Issues like these will also have great impact on the extent to which EVs are able to gain worldwide market share.

EVs ON THE WORLD STAGE

No single city, country, or continent is going to dominate the EV industry. Instead, the arrival of EVs will present wide-ranging opportunities to regions all over the globe. Some places will emerge as test beds for EV deployment, others will become centers for manufacturing, and still others will grow into research clusters leading technology development.

As a leader in automobile and battery manufacturing and home to the largest, fastest-growing car markets in the world, Asia is arguably the most important region for the future of EVs. China, currently the world's largest vehicle market, is aiming to have five million electric cars, trucks, and buses on its roads by 2020, with EVs nearing 10 percent of all vehicle sales by that time. China's $15 billion government investment in vehicle electrification, announced in early 2011, will no doubt help send the country in its desired direction. India will also be an increasingly important market for EV sales, with its car market expected to eclipse China's as the world's largest within a few decades. Not to be overlooked, two- and three-wheel EVs also have great potential for success throughout Asia, where highly polluting two-stroke-engine scooters, motorcycles, and three-wheelers (also commonly known as tuk-tuks) rule the roads.

Commitment to EV-market development in Europe varies by country, but when compared with the U.S., Europe's higher gas prices and shorter average trip distances could be a favorable recipe for greater EV adoption. Europeans' taste for smaller cars—in contrast to the American bigger-is-better mentality—could also allow for swifter EV acceptance. Conservative estimates put European Union EV totals slightly above three million by 2020, but this will depend largely on the level of government support and the pace of technology advancement and cost reductions. Europe is not lacking EV makers, with Renault, BMW, and Volkswagen each having already introduced EV models or are about to do so. Yet European companies lag significantly in funding of EV battery manufacturing, making up only 6 percent of the global investment total in 2010.

The U.S. is making a noticeable push toward vehicle electrification, but it will take lasting commitment from the federal government, states, automakers, and the American public for the U.S. to achieve a strong position of leadership in the emerging global EV sector. Efforts like the $1.5 billion in Recovery Act grants for U.S.-based EV battery manufacturers are crucial, but much more will be needed if America is to avoid simply replacing its dependence on Middle Eastern oil with a dependence on Asian-made batteries. EV-charging infrastructure initiatives and vehicle-purchasing incentives will help speed EV adoption, but enduring support will be needed if EVs are to gain market share in a U.S. vehicle fleet that takes roughly 20 years to turn over. President Obama has announced a target of putting one million EVs on American roads by 2015—an ambitious kickoff to the EV era, but only the beginning of transforming America's 250-million-strong vehicle fleet.

FUTURE OUTLOOK
Short Term (0–5 years)

- Diverse-fuel-source vehicles (electric, natural gas, biofuel) hit the mass market
- PHEV/EV models available from all major manufacturers
- Public charging infrastructure established in select markets

- EV hubs emerge (driven by early adopters and supportive government policies)

Medium Term (5–10 years)

- Hybrid and advanced efficiency technologies (stop-start idling, regenerative braking, etc.) become ubiquitous in most new autos
- Advancements in battery technology strengthen appeal of EVs (longer range, lower cost, safer)
- Fast-charging (level 3) infrastructure emerges

Long Term (10+ years)

- New lightweight materials enable significant fuel efficiency improvements in all types of vehicles
- With the availability of next-generation biofuels, PHEVs can operate fossil-fuel free
- Decreased battery costs bring EV costs in line with conventional ICE vehicles

Companies to Watch

A123 Systems
a123systems.com
Waltham, Massachusetts
Lithium-ion-battery maker

Better Place
betterplace.com
Palo Alto, California
EV-battery-swapping service operator

BYD Auto
byd.com
Pingshan, Shenzhen, China
EV maker

Chevrolet
chevrolet.com
Detroit, Michigan
Auto manufacturer

ECOtality
ecotality.com
San Francisco, California
EV-charging-station provider

LG Chem
lgchem.com
Seoul, South Korea
EV battery manufacturer

Nissan
nissan-global.com
Yokohama, Japan
Auto manufacturer

Shanghai Automotive Industry Corporation
saicgroup.com
Shanghai, China
Auto manufacturer

Tesla Motors
teslamotors.com

Palo Alto, California
EV maker and electric-drive-technology developer

Toyota
toyota.com
Aichi, Japan
Auto manufacturer

GREEN BUILDING: DEEP RETROFITS AND NET-ZERO AMBITIONS

Situated on the northeast shores of San Francisco Bay in Richmond, California, the mixed-use Ford Point property is an inspiring example of history-conscious green building development. Originally constructed in 1930 as the largest Ford Motor assembly plant on the West Coast, the site now houses several businesses, restaurants, and an expansive event space, the Craneway Pavilion. On Craneway's roof sits a 1-megawatt solar installation that provides half of the building's electricity needs—a stark contrast to a time when 80,000-gallon oil tanks powered the factory. Among the extensive accolades the building renovation has received is the California Preservation Foundation Design Award for Sustainability, granted for its use of existing structure, utilization of natural lighting, and on-site renewable-power generation.

Ford Point is also home to the Rosie the Riveter National Historical Park, a reminder of the important role Richmond played as a military boomtown in the 1940s. During World War II, the Ford plant was converted to a wartime production facility, churning out more than 60,000 tanks, trucks, and other vehicles to support pivotal overseas military campaigns. Today, U.S.-based solar PV manufacturer SunPower aids in America's 21st-century battle for energy security and economic competitiveness, housing an R&D facility not far from where armored tanks once left the assembly lines.

With such a rich history, Ford Point's redevelopment may be unique, but the project is representative of a broader global transition to sustainable, energy-efficient building practices, incorporating and improving the existing built environment whenever possible.

As the world's largest source of energy demand and the number-one contributor of greenhouse gas emissions, the built environment is a prime culprit in today's global energy crisis. In most countries, buildings are responsible for roughly half of all energy use, and in terms of electricity consumption, powering residential, commercial, and industrial buildings can make up three-quarters of total demand. If we are to alleviate economic and environmental pains already present at today's level of global development—and make room for a future that sees China add ten billion square feet of new building space each year—improving the energy and water efficiency of our buildings is an inescapable necessity.

The end goal is to create ultra-efficient structures, zero-energy buildings (ZEBs), which produce as much power as—or even more than—they use. A growing stock of energy-neutral and net-energy-positive buildings will be essential to achieving sustainable growth, given the pace of new construction around the world. True ZEB developments remain rare today, but with energy neutrality as the ultimate objective, near-net-zero projects can offer enormous potential to ease energy and resource demands of the world's residences, office buildings, and factories. At Frito-Lay's Casa Grande manufacturing facility in Arizona, for example, investment in a large-scale biomass boiler, a 5-megawatt solar PV installation, and an advanced water-recovery system has enabled the company to achieve a 90 percent reduction in electricity usage, 80 percent reduction in natural gas consumption, and 50 percent reductions in both water usage and GHG emissions.

Many countries have indicated ambitions for building sector efficiency with targets for milestone achievements. In Europe, for example, France is aiming for all new buildings to be energy positive by 2020, Germany is targeting all buildings to operate free of fossil fuels by the same year, and the U.K. intends all new homes to be carbon-emission-free by 2016.

In the U.S., federal government support comes from an assortment of DOE programs focused on research, funding, and deployment, but actual regulation of building-energy performance is done with individual state codes. Given this fragmentation of building standards, rating systems like the U.S. Green Building Council's LEED standards are crucial to tracking progress. In 2011, the International Living Building Institute, with offices in Portland, Seattle, and Vancouver, launched a certification program for net-zero energy buildings, the first of its kind. Just as LEED-certified projects saw incredible growth in the past decade, increasing from only a handful of LEED projects in 2000 to more than 8,000 by 2010, we expect net-zero-energy projects to flourish in coming years as benefits of reducing building-energy demand become more apparent.

Although the Frito-Lay facility's on-site energy generation is impressive, its actions to reduce the factory's energy demand were critical to achieving its goals. The first step in improving building-energy performance should always be demand-side efficiency improvements. Connecting an expensive PV array to a building with uninsulated walls and leaky windows makes about as much sense as trying to fill a bathtub without first plugging the drain. As a general rule, all cost-effective efficiency measures should be explored before installing on-site generation technologies. Not only are efficiency improvements much cheaper, but once a building is operating at optimal efficiency it will take much less on-site power generation to achieve net-zero—or near-net-zero—energy performance.

COOL AIR AND BRIGHT LIGHTS

Buildings need power for a wide range of needs, from lighting, air conditioners, refrigerators, and water heaters to computers, televisions, and other energy-hungry electronics. But it might come as a surprise to learn that 60 percent of energy use in the building sector can be traced to just three activities: space conditioning (heating and cooling), lighting, and water heating.

With such a large portion of building-energy demand stemming from such a small number of activities, concentrating efforts on improving these processes offers the largest gains in the shortest period of time. Like a military general focusing on an enemy's weaknesses in order to inflict the most damage, building-efficiency efforts must focus on enhancing performance of the most energy-intensive processes. But improved efficiency can't come at the expense of quality or comfort, as building tenants will complain about cold showers, stuffy air, and dreary lighting much quicker and more intensely than they will cheer energy savings, no matter how significant.

The most basic battle for building efficiency is how to keep the outside out and the inside in. Buildings that can effectively seal themselves off from sweltering summer highs and bitter winter lows require much less energy to maintain comfortable indoor temperatures all year round. Reducing energy losses through a building's outer surfaces (known as the building envelope) can come from simple weatherization tasks like plugging holes and increasing insulation, or through more intensive renovation endeavors such as upgrading windows, walls, and roofing. Initiatives like the U.S. DOE's Weatherization Assistance Program (WAP) are crucial to capitalizing on efficiency opportunities. WAP was formed in 1976 to reduce energy costs for low-income households, and by 2008 the program had provided weatherization services to more than six million households, creating average annual energy savings of $413 per household. The program's activities have become increasingly aggressive since it received an additional $5 billion in funding through the 2009 Recovery Act—although ramping up retrofit activity to allocate this influx of funds has proved a difficult task. With an estimated $1.65 in energy-related benefits for every dollar invested in the program, WAP's cost-effectiveness is a key factor in its longevity, especially during times of economic malaise like those faced today.

Beyond government-driven programs, technology developers are also advancing building-envelope performance with innovations that improve the ability to combat harsh outdoor climates. As part of the major retrofitting of New York City's iconic Empire State Building, for instance, Sunnyvale, California–based Serious Energy provided a superinsulated refurbishing to the building's 6,514 windows, using a dedicated on-site processing center to reuse 95 percent of the building's existing glass. Window improvements were only one of the renovations expected to reduce the Empire State Building's energy use by 38 percent, save $4.4 million annually in energy costs, and pay for themselves in three years.

But even adequately sealed buildings need a significant amount of power to keep indoor temperatures as desired—space heating and cooling account for 28 percent of energy consumption in commercial buildings and 40 percent in residential buildings. In California, air-conditioning alone makes up at least 30 percent of the peak summer electricity load. And because high peak demands can force utilities to produce additional capacity from expensive and rarely used peaker power plants, cutting air-conditioning-related electricity load can ease the severity of demand peaks, thus improving grid stability and reducing electric system costs.

Ice Energy, in Windsor, Colorado, has taken an innovative approach to solving the challenges of A/C electricity demand. Rather than worrying primarily about how much energy is needed to run A/C units, Ice Energy focuses instead on *when* units consume energy. The company's Ice Bear Energy Storage System draws power from the grid at night, when electricity is least expensive, using this nighttime energy to create ice. Then, during the next day's peak hours of electricity demand, the stored ice is used to chill refrigerant in the existing A/C system and deliver cool air to the building. By eliminating the need to power A/C unit compressors (which would normally be used to cool the refrigerant), Ice Energy enables a shift of A/C power demand to off-peak hours, an achievement that will have enormous benefits if implemented at a large enough scale. It's still uncertain if the company will succeed or not, but after seven years on the market, more than 7,000 Ice Bear systems had been sold, shifting more than six million hours of commercial A/C power demand to off-peak hours, according to the company.

In many cases, slashing energy use is as simple as changing a light-bulb. Worldwide, roughly 20 percent of electricity consumption goes to lighting, and in U.S. commercial buildings, close to 35 percent of total power is used to keep the lights on. Lighting has grown more efficient with the rising popularity of compact fluorescent lightbulbs (CFLs), which reduce electricity use by three-fourths and last up to ten times as long as traditional incandescent lights. However, concerns about CFLs' mercury content, poor light quality, and promised vs. actual longevity have opened the door for the next improvement in lighting technology, light-emitting diodes (LEDs), which use up to 85 percent less energy and can last 25 times longer than incandescent bulbs.

LED costs are falling quickly, particularly in the market for standard 60-watt replacement bulbs. Just a few years ago, you'd have been hard-pressed to find a 60-watt equivalent LED priced under $60, but today several brands offer LED replacement bulbs for around $20. Warner Philips, CEO of Netherlands-based Lemnis Lighting and great-grandson of Royal Philips Electronics founder Anton Philips, sees the LED replacement bulb on the verge of a tipping point. "Big chunks of the market are going to start shifting at $15," he said, "and we think that the entire mass market is going to shift at below $10. That's really the critical psychological price point for consumers." As LED technology costs decline, lighting quality is improved, and countries begin enforcing stricter lighting efficiency standards, the increased use of LEDs will result in significantly reduced energy consumption for the building sector.

GETTING TO ZERO

A net-zero-energy building cannot be achieved through efficiency alone. After a building's energy footprint has been reduced by a reasonable amount through efficiency measures, it becomes appropriate to explore supply-side strategies that can offset most, if not all (or even more), of the remaining energy demand.

Productive interaction with the sun is the greatest opportunity for buildings to create their own heat, light, and electricity. So-called passive solar design—the use of windows, skylights, and other features that optimize a building toward the path of the sun throughout the year—can go a long way in heating and cooling indoor spaces. Designs that provide shade from the high sun during hot summers and collect direct heat from the low sun during cold winters dramatically reduce the amount of energy needed to keep temperatures as desired. Large south-facing windows can also provide ample light during the daytime, greatly limiting the need for electric-powered lighting.

On-site power generation, once associated with an alternative, "off the grid" lifestyle, is now available to the masses thanks to substantial declines in the cost of solar PV technology. For most buildings, a well-designed PV installation—set on a rooftop or ground-mounted on adjacent property—will cover a significant portion of electricity demand at a reasonable cost. As costs break through the installed price barrier of $2 per peak watt, and building-integrated PV (solar cells embedded in roofing material) becomes widely available, solar will become increasingly ubiquitous. And with a growing number of solar leasing options available from companies like SolarCity, SunRun, and SunEdison, it's easier than ever to disperse upfront costs and finance solar PV just as you would with a car.

Solar water heaters also have great potential to shrink building-energy footprints, with water heating accounting for roughly 15 percent of energy consumption in a typical U.S. household. Using the sun's energy to heat water can reduce those costs up to 90 percent. China, long before its recent rise to global leadership in solar PV manufacturing and other clean-tech sectors, was the world's largest manufacturer and user of solar water-heating systems. By 2010, China had installed enough rooftop solar thermal collectors to supply hot water for 120 million households. The country's commitment to this sector hasn't gone unnoticed by international players, as evidenced by the nearly $100 million that Himin Solar Energy Group, China's largest solar water-heater maker, received in a 2008 investment led by Goldman Sachs. Solar water heating is growing more popular in the U.S., but not at a pace that reflects any sense of urgency. The boldest U.S. deployment initiative is California's goal to install 200,000 solar water-heating systems by 2017. Being a technology that is already cost-effective, solar water heating deserves much more attention as a tool to reduce building-energy demand.

But buildings are using more than just the sun to make energy. Technologies like small-scale wind turbines and stationary fuel cells are gaining more attention as means to generate power. In 2010, for example, well-funded Sunnyvale, California, startup Bloom Energy installed 12 fuel cell units at Adobe's San Jose, California, headquarters. These Energy Servers (dubbed "Bloom Boxes") convert air and biogas into enough power to supply roughly one-third of the facility's electricity while producing zero net carbon emissions.

Local and on-site heat production is also becoming common through the increased use of ground-source heat pumps, combined heat and power generation, and district heating systems. In particular, ground-source heat pumps (also called geothermal heat pumps) offer a great opportunity to reduce household-space heating demand, which accounts for nearly 30 percent of total energy consumption in the U.S. residential building sector. Utilizing the earth's temperature a few feet underground (which remains constant and relatively mild year-round), ground-source pumps can provide both heating and cooling to buildings—moving heat from the ground inside during the winter, and discharging heat from inside into the ground during the summer. Led by activity in North America and Europe, the global capacity of ground-source heat pump systems grew by more than 800 percent from 1995 to 2005, a pace of growth that continues today as energy-efficient space heating and cooling become increasingly important.

In combination with aggressive energy-efficiency measures, supply-side renewable-energy-generation technologies like those discussed here are enabling both newly constructed and existing structures to become energy neutral. And while net-zero energy will certainly not be attainable for every building, the increasing number of ZEB and near-zero examples around the world are transforming basic expectations about how buildings should interact with energy.

GLOBAL BENEFIT, LOCAL MOTIVES

At the global level, reducing the energy demand of the built environment will have a greatly positive impact. It will ease resource constraints, enable sustainable growth, and lessen the harmful effects of anthropogenic climate change. But these benefits are not the primary cause of support for energy-neutral building development. Instead, it is national and regional self-interests that are truly driving action.

For rapidly developing nations like China and India, accommodating projected population growth at current building-efficiency levels is unimaginable. However, if new construction can operate with a minimized energy footprint, expansion is more likely to be achieved without sacrificing citizens' quality of life. For the developed world, the high energy costs of existing building stocks are bleeding economies that are already hurting. In these cases, efficiency improvements can redirect money from monthly utility bills to more stimulative areas of the economy.

The world's population shot past seven billion in late 2011. Many might associate this with a need to build more, but what we really need to do is build *smarter*. "Seven billion people standing shoulder to shoulder could fit in the city limits of Los Angeles," noted *National Geographic* in its yearlong 2011 series on population growth. "We're not running out of space, we're running out of resources." For any community, city, or nation hoping to maintain environmental or economic health in coming years, the importance of green building, energy retrofits, and eventual energy and resource neutrality cannot be overstated.

FUTURE OUTLOOK

Short Term (0–5 years)

- Weatherization and retrofit initiatives significantly improve energy efficiency of existing building stock
- LED prices fall to $10 for a 60-watt-equivalent bulb, begin achieving mass-market deployment
- Building automation enables reduction in lighting and A/C- and-heating-related energy consumption

Medium Term (5–10 years)

- Net-zero energy performance within reach for most new buildings, enabled by improved design, efficient appliances and lighting, and advanced on-site power-generation technologies
- LEDs become more popular than CFLs
- Growth of rooftop PV deployment continues to skyrocket as cost for solar power reaches grid parity in most major markets

Long Term (10+ years)

- Newly commercialized on-site generation technologies (e.g., stationary fuel cells) turn buildings into mini power plants
- Mass deployment of active and responsive building components (e.g., electrochromic tint-adjusting glazed windows, building-integrated PV)
- Net zero extends beyond individual buildings to entire campuses and communities

Companies to Watch
Bloom Energy
bloomenergy.com
Sunnyvale, California
Stationary fuel-cell maker

Bridgelux
bridgelux.com
Livermore, California
LED manufacturer

ClearEdge Power
clearedgepower.com
Hillsboro, Oregon
Stationary fuel-cell developer

CH2M Hill
ch2m.com
Englewood, Colorado
Engineering and construction firm

Cree
cree.com
Durham, North Carolina
LED technology developer

Himin Solar Energy Group
himinsun.com
Dezhou, Shandong, China
Solar water-heater maker

Ice Energy
ice-energy.com
Windsor, Colorado
Energy-efficient air-conditioning technology developer

Johnson Controls
johnsoncontrols.com
Milwaukee, Wisconsin
Building-energy automation provider

Royal Philips Electronics
usa.philips.com

Amsterdam, Netherlands
Lighting manufacturer and LED technology developer

Serious Energy
seriousenergy.com
Sunnyvale, California
Energy-efficient window maker and building-energy service provider

ONE PERSON'S TRASH, ANOTHER PERSON'S TREASURE: THE VAST POTENTIAL OF WASTE-TO-RESOURCE TECHNOLOGIES

At the Magic Hat Brewing Company, in Burlington, Vermont, the craft-brewed #9 Not Quite Pale Ale and Circus Boy Hefeweizen aren't the only things creating a buzz. Since 2010, the microbrewery has been using a 500,000-gallon biodigester to convert brewing by-products— yeast, grains, and wastewater—into clean-burning biogas that serves as a drop-in replacement for natural gas, providing energy to run the facility. Built by Waltham, Massachusetts–based startup PurposeEnergy (company tagline: "Saving the Earth. One Beer at a Time"), the system produces 330 kilowatts of electricity, along with steam that's used in the brewery's boilers. PurposeEnergy founder/CEO and MIT-trained engineer Eric Fitch says Magic Hat will be able to save more than $15,000 a month on its energy bill, a result of nearly eliminating the brewery's need to purchase natural gas.

"The cost for them to remediate this by-product can be about as expensive as the cost of energy itself," Fitch told *Mass High Tech* magazine in a 2010 profile about the project. "With an anaerobic digester they can get a two-fer, producing methane for energy and breaking down the grain." PurposeEnergy's technology earned it a spot on *Entrepreneur* magazine's 2011 list of 100 Brilliant Companies, and the company has raised roughly $3 million in venture capital to fund its pursuit of brewery waste-to-energy opportunities. "The reason why we chose a brewery of Magic Hat's size is, if it works, you've just shown to every major brewery you're doing something that works," Fitch said. "Building the first one is always hard, but the next ones will be easier and easier."

Finding value in waste streams is by no means unique to the brewing industry, and capitalist-minded entrepreneurs and business are increasingly seeing dollar signs where they once saw only trash (and the costs of disposing of it). Whether dealing with manufacturing by-products, agricultural waste, industrial heat loss, or just everyday household garbage, waste-to-resource technologies are generating new business models for their ability to turn the world's leftovers into valuable electricity, heat, fuel, and materials. And waste-to-resource efforts aren't only about dollars and cents. If employed at a large enough scale, these practices can go a long way in reducing harmful pollution, easing resource constraints, and moderating the global economy's undesirable dependence on fossil fuels.

REDEFINING WASTE: TURNING TRASH INTO CASH

The world's population creates a staggering amount of waste. In the U.S. alone, more than 11 billion tons of solid waste is produced each year, about half from agricultural processes and a third from mining activities. American homes and businesses produce 250 million tons of municipal waste each year, or roughly four and a half pounds of garbage per person every day. While recycling efforts in the U.S. have increased over the years, more than half of all municipal waste still ends up in landfills. A similar story can be told in other countries, where most trash is either shipped to landfills or incinerated, releasing harmful toxins and pollutants into the atmosphere.

Beyond solid waste, an enormous amount of energy is lost as unused heat that can and should be recovered. Thermal power plants supply most of the world's electricity by using coal, natural gas, or nuclear energy to boil water to run steam turbines, essentially converting heat into electrical energy. But they typically do so at thermal efficiencies of only 30 to 50 percent. The remaining heat—50 to 70 percent of what's created in the process—is discarded into the environment. Industrial activities are also extremely wasteful in this regard—steelmaking, oil refining, and other chemical and manufacturing processes experience vast heat loss in the form of steam, exhaust, gas flares, and leftover hot water. And in the built environment, an immeasurable amount of heat escapes from poorly sealed commercial and residential buildings around the globe. Yet the important topic of heat loss generally flies under the radar, as it doesn't leave behind an unsightly trail of evidence like solid waste or visible exhaust fumes.

Discussion about and management of waste has traditionally focused on limiting its negative impacts, with most efforts centered on safe collection and disposal. But this paradigm is rapidly evolving, and forward-thinking companies and communities are increasingly finding ways to repurpose their waste streams into resources that can reduce operational costs and generate new revenue. In simpler words, they are turning trash into cash.

DUMPSTER DIVING FOR TOMORROW'S ENERGY

Every day two full freight trains and a fleet of 600 garbage trucks arrive at the Waste Fired Power Plant in Amsterdam, delivering municipal solid waste (MSW) from homes and businesses in the Dutch capital and its surrounding communities. The facility, run by municipal waste-management company Afval Energie Bedrijf (AEB), uses controlled combustion technology from German waste-to-energy developer MARTIN to convert 1.4 billion tons of solid waste into 1 million megawatt-hours of electricity every year—enough to power three-quarters of Amsterdam's households. Waste-to-energy is nothing new for Amsterdam, which, since 1917, has captured waste incineration steam for use in electricity generation. The latest facility, built in 2007 and the largest plant of its kind in the world, represents Amsterdam's fourth generation of energy-producing waste incineration. Excess heat from waste incineration also augments Amsterdam's district heating system, which serves more than 50,000 homes. The plant's ability to recycle recovered metals and turn 99 percent of received waste into usable electricity and heat is critical to the region's waste management, especially as dense infrastructure and sub-sealevel topography leave little option for landfill disposal.

MSW waste-to-energy facilities are not completely benign, as incineration of garbage does emit CO_2 and leaves behind ash residue, but technology improvements and tightening of pollution regulations have eliminated much of the concern about toxic emissions from today's waste-to-energy projects. By 2006, emissions of dioxins from waste-to-energy incineration plants in the U.S. had been reduced by more than 99 percent from 1990 levels, while mercury emissions were cut by more than 90 percent, according to the EPA. In terms of carbon emissions, MSW waste-to-energy is far preferable to fossil-fuel power generation. Roughly two-thirds of MSW consists of organic material (such as food scraps and yard trimmings), so burning this biomass emits CO_2 that is already part of the earth's natural carbon cycle—it would decompose and release carbon anyway. Although burning of petroleum-based products like plastics and rubber in the garbage mix releases additional CO_2, it's still a more favorable emissions equation than burning fossil fuels (especially coal) to produce the equivalent electricity. "Net GHG emissions from [waste-to-energy] facilities are usually low and comparable to those from biomass energy systems," says the United Nations Intergovernmental Panel on Climate Change (IPCC).

But even with recent improvements in pollution control, energy recovery through combustion (or any other method) is still a secondary option in the waste management hierarchy, behind initial resource-use reduction and reuse through recycling or composting. In the U.S., roughly one-third of municipal waste is recycled, and successful composting programs in cities like San Francisco and Portland, Oregon, are showcasing the value of organic waste reuse. Environmental groups like the Sierra Club are critical of waste-to-energy, seeing it as an impediment to recycling programs and not a true renewable source of electricity. The debate is contentious. But in a world that faces fast-increasing rates of waste accumulation and a dire need for low-carbon electricity production, we believe that waste-to-energy technology deserves careful consideration.

Thermal processing of new garbage is only part of the waste-to-energy picture. Much of today's MSW energy activity occurs in the capturing of gases from landfills, where old waste slowly decomposes via anaerobic digestion (the breaking down of organic material by bacteria in an oxygen-deprived environment), releasing methane and other biogases that can be used to generate power and heat in lieu of natural gas. Methane digesters are also viable for use in wastewater treatment plants.

With a growing number of waste-to-energy technologies available, sustainable-minded nations are exploring options to advance responsible waste management and renewable energy production in one fell swoop. By 2010, more than 900 MSW waste-to-energy plants were in operation worldwide, 50 percent more than seven years earlier. They convert 200 million tons of waste into 130,000 gigawatt-hours of electricity each year, according to estimates from market research firm Pike Research, in Boulder, Colorado. "Waste-to-energy plants serve an important dual purpose," says Pike Research president Clint Wheelock. "They help alleviate the growing municipal-solid-waste problem while simultaneously providing much-needed renewable energy and heat sources to local populations."

North America's largest recycler and handler of trash, Waste Management, is diving headfirst into the waste-to-energy opportunity. In 2010, Waste Management's more than 150 landfill-gas and combustion waste-to-energy facilities produced enough energy to power 1 million homes—an amount the company is intent on doubling by 2020. Forward-thinking CEO David Steiner has also led the firm to become a key investor in emerging waste-to-resource technologies, funneling millions into early-stage companies developing new ways to convert garbage into valuable energy, materials, and chemicals. Among the more prominent startups partnering with Waste Management are Agilyx, which is developing technology to turn plastic into synthetic crude oil; Enerkem, working to convert organic waste into cellulosic ethanol; and Genomatica, producing green chemicals from existing waste streams.

Beyond energy from municipal waste, another integral component of the global waste-to-energy opportunity is power and heat generation from agriculture and forestry by-products, wood waste, and animal manure. These organic biomass waste streams are used as co-firing fuel in modified coal power plants, combusted in combined heat-and-power facilities, and converted into usable biogas. Because of its vast availability, non-MSW biomass waste makes an attractive substitute for fossil fuels. In 2010, the U.S. generated a world-leading 48,000 gigawatt-hours of electricity from biomass power—most of which was derived from wood and agricultural residues.

Although nearly all waste-to-energy activity is related to electricity or heat production, innovative companies like New York City–based Tri-State Biodiesel (TSB) are also using existing waste streams to make waste-derived transportation fuel—a commodity that will only become more desirable in a future of volatile oil prices. Operating in New Jersey, New York, and Connecticut—as its name would imply—Tri-State Biodiesel collects used cooking oil from local restaurants and sends it to an upstate New York refinery, where it undergoes a chemical process that yields biodiesel fuel. TSB's biodiesel blend, which can be used as a transportation or heating fuel, is then marketed to businesses in the region. In early 2011, a South Bronx gas station installed four nozzles to sell the company's fuel to local vehicle fleets. While TSB's influence may seem immaterial when put up against America's 20-million-barrel-a-day oil appetite, the company's continued operation is a positive sign for the prospects of regionally focused waste-to-fuel businesses. "We had to raise $2.3 million to get the company off the ground in 2005, but now we are profitable," Tri-State Biodiesel CEO Brent Baker told the *Huffington Post* in 2011. In today's economic climate, that's well worth some bragging rights.

Down the road, waste-to-fuel sources may also play a part in cleaning up the aviation industry, which is responsible for roughly 3 percent of global CO_2 emissions each year. In November 2011, Alaska Airlines flew 75 passenger flights using a fuel blend with 20 percent biofuel derived from used cooking oil, part of the Seattle-based airline's ongoing effort to lessen its environmental footprint. The synthetic biodiesel used in Alaska's test flights came from Dynamic Fuels, a joint venture between Springdale, Arkansas–based meat-processing giant Tyson Foods and Tulsa, Oklahoma–based fuels producer Syntroleum. Dynamic's technology utilizes animal fats, greases, and vegetable oil waste streams to whip up its renewable diesel products, but the batch for Alaska Airlines was exclusively a cooking oil mix. "Think McDonald's fryer grease," Bob Ames, Tyson's vice president of renewable energy, told the *Seattle Times*.

Some waste-derived fuel technologies are already competing head-to-head with traditional petroleum fuels, but many of the most promising biofuel applications—namely, renewable jet diesel and cellulosic ethanol—remain uncompetitive with conventional fuels due to high production costs. But a legion of corporations, scientists, and entrepreneurs are dedicated to advancing next-generation biofuels, and organizations ranging from Boeing to the U.S. Navy are investing billions to make them viable. We foresee these efforts overcoming many technological challenges in the near future, opening up further possibilities to turn vast amounts of today's waste into valuable fuel.

CARBON AS A FEEDSTOCK

With concerns about climate change solidifying around the world, governments and businesses are increasingly looking for ways to reduce harmful greenhouse gas emissions. While carbon capture and sequestration technologies (the goal of so-called clean-coal projects) are proving prohibitively expensive and impractical, efforts to use carbon as feedstock in production of building materials, chemicals, plastics, and algae for biofuels are beginning to find some success— helping shift perception of carbon dioxide from a harmful pollutant to a pervasively available by-product with potential value as a raw material.

Coming out of stealth mode in late 2011, Piscataway, New Jersey–based startup Solidia Technologies has received $29 million in financial backing from high-profile investors like Kleiner Perkins Caufield & Byers for its low-energy building material, which sequesters carbon dioxide during production. Solidia's technology, developed by Rutgers University professor Richard Riman, combines CO_2 with minerals in a low-temperature process that churns out high-performance building material with a much lower energy and carbon footprint than traditional materials.

If deployed at a large enough scale, the company's technology holds much promise to reduce GHG emissions, particularly as a cement replacement; cement production accounts for approximately 5 percent of global CO_2 emissions annually. "It's a ton of CO_2 per ton of cement. It's a messy, very energy-intensive, very polluting industry," said Kleiner Perkins partner Bill Joy at an MIT event soon after Solidia exited stealth mode. "Solidia is based on aspiration for an ability to build materials with the kind of strength that high-strength concrete has, without all the embodied energy." Other leading companies pursuing captured-carbon cement production include Khosla Ventures–backed Calera, in Los Gatos, California, and U.K.-based Novacem.

As a feedstock, CO_2 can be used in the production of much more than just cement-substitute building materials. Waltham, Massachusetts–based Novomer, a green chemistry startup backed by several venture firms and U.S. government grants, is using captured carbon as a primary raw material in the production of industrial coatings, specialty polymers, and packaging that consist of more than 40 percent CO_2 by weight. Novomer's technology, which earned it a spot on the MIT-published *Technology Review*'s 50 Most Innovative Companies list in 2011, was originally developed at Cornell University by company cofounders Geoff Coates and Scott Allen. "Before CO_2 was even seen as a greenhouse gas, Geoff Coates had the idea of using it as a low-cost raw material to make commercially viable products," Novomer VP Peter Shepard told *ICIS Chemical Business*, a leading chemical industry publication. The company is only in the early stages of commercial production, but in 2010 it entered into an agreement with Netherlands-based materials provider DSM to jointly develop coating resins using the CO_2-sequestering technology.

CO_2 is also critical to the production of algae, an increasingly popular feedstock for developers of next-generation biofuel technologies. Among the several companies tapping waste CO_2 to grow algae are Colorado-based Solix Biofuels (tapping CO_2 from the nearby New Belgium Brewery) and Bill Gates–backed, San Diego–based Sapphire Energy (using CO_2 from German gas supplier and engineering firm Linde for its demonstration facility in Columbus, New Mexico).

CAPTURING WASTE HEAT AND WATER

Waste heat may not elicit the negative environmental impacts of polluting solid waste or climate-changing carbon dioxide, but heat loss from power generation and industrial processes offers an immense opportunity to salvage value from a vastly abundant waste stream.

Combined heat and power (CHP), or cogeneration, is the process of recovering heat that would normally be wasted during the generation of electricity at power plants and industrial facilities and using it to supply local heating or cooling needs. Today, more than two-thirds of the fuel used to generate power in the U.S. is lost as heat. If the U.S. were to achieve 20 percent of generation capacity from CHP by 2030 (up from roughly 10 percent today), the DOE estimates that it would save more than 5 quadrillion BTUs of fuel each year, equivalent to half the total energy consumed by U.S. households. Cogeneration technologies aren't new to the energy sector and, in fact, have been around since the industry's earliest days. In the late 19th century, Thomas Edison's first commercial power plant, Pearl Street Station, was actually a cogeneration facility, producing electricity while also delivering heat to nearby buildings. Waste heat resources remain drastically underutilized, but significant CHP deployment is under way in the U.S., Europe, Asia, and around the world. Outside of the U.S., CHP has found much success in China, Russia, and several European nations. Denmark and Finland, in particular, get more than half of space heating and water heating from district heating systems supplied mainly by CHP plants. With a proven track record and known investment costs, there are few more sure things we can do to improve overall energy efficiency.

Interest in thermoelectric processes that convert waste heat directly into electricity is also on the rise. In 2011, Alphabet Energy received $12 million in venture funds from TPG Biotech, Claremont Creek

Ventures, and others to further develop its thermoelectric technology that uses silicon nanowires to turn heat into electricity as electrons move from the hot to the cold side of a semiconductor. While other thermoelectric technologies depend on a mix of expensive materials, Hayward, California–based Alphabet's use of low-cost silicon as the primary thermoelectric material could give the company a key advantage. "We're piggybacking off of the semiconductor industry to build a scalable business," founder and CEO Matt Scullin told *Bloomberg Businessweek* in September 2011.

The 29-year-old Scullin is a UC Berkeley grad who, in true entrepreneurial style, paid for his Ph.D. in materials science by DJing events and consulting for venture capitalists. Arun Majumdar, director of the DOE's Advanced Research Projects Agency–Energy (ARPA-E), introduced Scullin to waste heat technology while serving as his Ph.D. adviser at Berkeley. Alphabet Energy's first target application is capturing exhaust gas from industrial and power plant facilities, with further possibilities in automotive, aerospace, and military markets. The company's potential for success will be determined largely by results of its initial pilot demonstrations, along with its ability to produce inexpensive thermoelectric materials.

Similar to waste heat, wastewater—water that has been dirtied by human activities in factories, buildings, homes, and agricultural fields—also offers much value in the multiple ways it can be reused. Properly treated wastewater can be reused as everything from irrigation water to ordinary drinking water, and at treatment facilities methane can even be captured from sewage much as it is from landfills.

The simplest and most inexpensive reuse opportunities involve gray water—wastewater generated from domestic activities that has not yet been contaminated by sewage. Louisville, Kentucky–based WaterSaver Technologies' AQUS system is one of many elegant solutions recouping value from recycled water. AQUS captures water from the bathroom sink, filters and treats it, and uses it to provide water for toilet flushing; it's as simple as that. By eliminating the need to waste fresh water in the toilet, the company estimates that its AQUS system can reduce water usage in a two-person household by 10 to 20 gallons a day, or approximately 5,000 gallons a year. As water shortages are becoming an ongoing concern for a growing number of regions around the world, simple tinkering like this is essential to sustainable resource management. By capturing tangible value from a previously discarded supply, wastewater reuse also makes possible significant earnings for technology developers and monetary savings for consumers.

REDUCE, REUSE, RECYCLE . . . RECOVER

The popular "3R" mantra for waste management—reduce, reuse, and recycle—serves as a catchy reminder of how we can improve efficiency and sustainability everywhere from the family kitchen to the industrial assembly line. And these strategies shouldn't be sold short, especially for management of municipal waste. San Francisco's long-time commitment to recycling and composting initiatives enabled a remarkable 77 percent landfill diversion rate by 2010. But waste is an inherent part of almost everything we do, and at the global level, even after efforts to reduce consumption and salvage existing resources, a significant amount of waste still remains.

Enter the fourth R: recover. By viewing waste as a potential resource rather than an unwanted—and often harmful—by-product, governments, businesses, and entrepreneurs are changing the way the world thinks about what it throws away. Waste-to-resource technologies range from century-old practices to lab-stage technologies. Through recovery of previously discarded materials, heat, emissions, or even wastewater, each creates valuable products that are cutting costs, creating revenue, and diminishing human environmental impacts all while mimicking natural cycles that ensure that one person's waste stream becomes another person's valued feedstock.

FUTURE OUTLOOK
Short Term (0–5 years)

- Growth of municipal-scale food-waste composting for commercial and residential customers
- Waste heat increasingly captured through on-site and district-wide combined heat and power systems
- Wastewater recycling becomes an essential element of resource management strategies

Medium Term (5–10 years)

- Achievement of commercial production of advanced biofuels (e.g., algal biodiesel, cellulosic ethanol, waste-derived jet fuel)
- Widespread use of building materials manufactured with sequestered carbon dioxide (e.g., new forms of cement/concrete)
- Increased replacement of petroleum-based products with waste-derived materials

Long Term (10+ years)

- Emergence of closed-loop manufacturing facilities that reuse all of their waste and energy streams
- Significant ramp-up of processes that generate power and fuel from municipal waste with improved efficiency and zero emissions
- Commercialization of cost-competitive thermoelectric devices that generate electricity directly from captured waste heat

Companies to Watch

Alphabet Energy
alphabetenergy.com
Hayward, California
Thermoelectric device maker

Calera
calera.com
Los Gatos, California
Carbon-sequestering building material developer

Covanta
covantaenergy.com
Morristown, New Jersey
Waste-to-energy project developer

MARTIN
martingmbh.de
Munich, Germany
Waste-to-energy project developer

PurposeEnergy
purposeenergy.com
Waltham, Massachusetts
Brewery waste-to-energy technology developer

Sapphire Energy
sapphireenergy.com
San Diego, California
Algae biofuel developer

Solidia Technologies
solidiatech.com
Piscataway, New Jersey
Carbon-sequestering building material developer

Solix Biofuels
solixbiofuels.com
Fort Collins, Colorado
Algae-based-biodiesel producer

Tri-State Biodiesel
tristatebiodiesel.com
New York, New York
Used-cooking-oil-derived-biodiesel producer

WaterSaver Technologies
watersavertech.com
Louisville, Kentucky
Household wastewater-recycling system maker

5

THE CLEAN-TECH IMPERATIVE

On September 22, 2011, the U.S. House of Representatives' Committee on Oversight and Government Reform held a hearing titled "How Obama's Green Energy Agenda Is Killing Jobs." The session came three weeks after federal loan guarantee recipient Solyndra, a solar cell manufacturer in Fremont, California, declared bankruptcy and shut its doors. During the proceedings, Republican committee chairman Darrell Issa of California joined several colleagues in severely criticizing federal financial support of the U.S. clean-tech industry. Issa said the Obama administration had "systematically waged a war on carbon-based energy in pursuit of new green energy."

On the same day that Congress was battling it out on Capitol Hill, Chinese solar PV manufacturer Hanwha SolarOne secured a five-year, $100 million loan from Standard Chartered Bank, the Korea Development Bank, and other large lenders. German steelmaker Dillinger Hütte announced that it would enter the wind power market by building a €135 million ($178 million) factory to make foundations

for offshore wind platforms. KMC Constructions, a major infrastructure builder in India, said it planned to issue an IPO to raise funds
for its entry into the solar energy market. The U.K.'s Department of
Energy and Climate Change announced details of a four-year, £200
million ($309 million) fund to help support low-carbon technologies.
And the government of Scotland announced the launch of a £327 million ($505 million) fund to support the construction and renovation
of energy-efficient housing in the country over the next three years.

More than a decade into the 21st century, the U.S. is still struggling to find its footing in the transition to a clean-energy economy.
With partisan sniping and legislative gridlock seemingly at all-time
highs, at least at the federal level, there's been little national priori-
tization of clean tech. Goals like an increasingly domestic and low-
carbon energy supply, clean air and water, technology innovation,
global economic competitiveness, and, above all, job creation all enjoy
deep support across the American political spectrum. Yet inside the
Beltway, the U.S. often seems stuck in a battle between old and new
energy sources, with partisans choosing sides along the same red-vs.-
blue, Fox News–vs.–MSNBC divide that infests so many other critical
national issues.

Mustering the necessary political will, across-the-aisle collaboration, and national leadership to make clean tech a top national priority will not be an easy task. But it is critical to our future as an
innovative, prosperous, and thriving global economic leader.

THREE IMPERATIVES: ECONOMY, SECURITY, AND CLIMATE

ECONOMY: REGAINING OUR MOJO

With every day that goes by, be it September 22, 2011, or any other, the
world's steady and inexorable transition to a clean-energy economy
unfolds. Someone in the world is going to provide the wind turbines,
electric-vehicle batteries, solar PV cells, solar thermal generating

plants, energy-efficiency management software, and countless other products and services that the new clean-energy infrastructure will demand. As we detailed in chapter 1, on the global landscape and competitive threat, governments from Beijing to Berlin to Seoul have made clean energy a key national priority, pursuing and funding agendas to build the clean-tech infrastructure and industries of the 21st-century economy. As *The Economist* magazine put it, in a broader U.S. economic context in November 2011, "As the superpower's clout seems to ebb towards Asia, the world's most consistently inventive and optimistic country has lost its mojo."

Government and private-sector support have helped China, Germany, and the U.S. lead the world in clean-tech investing in recent years. But in the U.S., this leadership is in a precarious position as federal programs (tax credits, loan programs, and other initiatives) begin to dry up. "This area has total policy support from the Chinese and other nations," says Cathy Zoi, formerly the DOE's assistant secretary for energy efficiency and renewable energy and now a partner at Silver Lake Kraftwerk, a clean-tech private equity fund in Menlo Park, California. "Without the U.S. also seeing that clean energy is an important part of our economy, we will fall behind." Microsoft chairman Bill Gates, along with other corporate and technology titans, has called for a more than threefold increase in federal R&D funding for clean energy, from $5 billion to $16 billion, even in budget belt-tightening times. "It's essential to protect America's national interests and ensure that the United States plays a leading role in the fast-growing global clean-energy industry," Gates wrote in *Science* magazine in November 2011.

Zoi and Gates echo a large consensus of economists and international trade experts who believe clean tech is a key global growth industry of this century—and not just in the industrialized world. A 2010 World Wildlife Fund report titled *Getting Back in the Game* estimated that the U.S. could create between 280,000 and 850,000 new jobs by capturing just 14 percent of the market for clean technologies in developing nations. The International Energy Agency estimates that such countries will need $27 trillion in clean-tech investments over the next four decades.

All of the top ten clean-tech competitor nations that we discussed in chapter 1 are large and growing markets for deployment of clean technologies. Some markets are admittedly more fair and open than others, and there will doubtless be trade disputes in clean tech, particularly with China. But even nations with trade barriers can offer great opportunities in clean tech. Although China has flooded the U.S. (and global) markets with low-cost solar PV cells, the overall U.S. solar industry was actually a net exporter to China in 2010, with a positive trade balance between $247 million and $540 million, according to a 2011 GTM Research report for the Solar Energy Industries Association. That's because U.S. manufacturers supply most of the polysilicon feedstock and capital equipment that China needs to make the cells. But that could be a risky long-term position, and the U.S. position could fluctuate wildly if the country doesn't remain a player in core solar PV technology production.

The U.S. must aspire to create world-leading clean-tech products and services that will be demanded by markets across the globe—especially our own. But in today's globalized economy, U.S. companies and government entities can't do this on their own—nor should they try. Collaboration with clean-tech partners and financiers in China, Japan, Germany, the U.K., and many other countries will be critical. Joint ventures, collaborative offshore R&D, and cross-border cooperation on open-source initiatives are key pieces of U.S. strategy to meet the economic imperative of clean tech in this century.

SECURITY: OLD STORY, NEW URGENCY
The national security imperative for moving away from fossil fuels is nothing new. Ever since President Jimmy Carter declared in 1980

that the nation was prepared to use military force to defend its access to Middle Eastern oil through the Persian Gulf—the so-called Carter Doctrine—U.S. troops have literally been on the front lines of America's energy usage. The U.S. military itself is also the largest single user of energy in the world. So it makes sense for the Pentagon to be taking a very active role in clean-tech development and deployment—and it is. Naysayers who still associate solar energy and electric vehicles with tree-hugging ex-hippies may find this incongruous, but to military leaders it's increasingly a matter of life and death.

"There is an urgent need for our nation to lead the world in renewable energy and conservation," says U.S. Marines Major General Anthony Jackson, a 37-year Corps member who commands seven Marine bases in Southern California and Arizona. "We need to get a grip on the permanent vise that that three-letter word—oil—has had around our necks. I know the cost of that. I know it up close and personal."

Limited domestic oil resources and the intricacies of global energy distribution make true U.S. "energy independence" more a political sound bite than a near-term attainable reality. Nonetheless, the ability to greatly reduce U.S. demand for petroleum from the Middle East, Venezuela, Nigeria, and other volatile regions has innumerable benefits for national security and economic stability. That's why a growing chorus of voices from the usually politically conservative security community has been urging a major push for clean energy, particularly in transportation fuels, for the past several years. Former secretary of state George P. Shultz, retired senator and ex–Navy secretary John Warner, Reagan administration national security adviser Robert McFarlane (Republicans all)—as well as former CIA director James Woolsey and ex-NATO director General Wesley Clark (Ret.)—are among those actively campaigning for a cleaner and more efficient use of energy by the U.S.

In November 2011, the State Department created a new Bureau

of Energy Resources. Its wide-ranging mission includes working to increase U.S. clean-tech exports, promote renewable energy in developing countries, and avoid supply and price shocks. "You can't talk about our economy or foreign policy without talking about energy," said Secretary of State Hillary Clinton in announcing the bureau. "With a growing global population and a finite supply of fossil fuels, the need to diversify our supply is urgent."

Without much fanfare, the Pentagon—particularly the Navy and the Marine Corps—is well into an aggressive effort to develop and deploy clean tech on a widespread basis. Biofuel-propelled aircraft, solar- and wind-powered base facilities, and a wide range of combat applications have made the U.S. military a major force in clean tech. We consider the Pentagon a critical player in the nation's effort to be a global clean-tech leader, and we call for stepped-up military efforts in our Seven-Point Action Plan, in the next chapter. "To the Marine Corps, it isn't about money or global warming," says Colonel Bob "Brutus" Charette, head of the Marines' Expeditionary Energy Office, formed in 2009. "It's about saving lives."

CLIMATE: AS IMPERATIVE AS EVER
The unfortunate fact that climate change has dropped out of the American political dialogue doesn't make it any less urgent as a national and global issue. While the political wind (some might say hot air) blows back and forth, scientific evidence is steadily mounting that the damaging effects of global climate change, if not already present, are imminent.

Global greenhouse gas emissions increased by the largest one-year amount ever in 2010, according to the DOE. In November 2011, the United Nations Intergovernmental Panel on Climate Change concluded for the first time that at least some of the world's extreme weather events, which are increasing in frequency, can be attributed to the warmer, moister atmosphere. While Fox News pundits may scoff that major blizzards like 2010's "Snowmageddon" in Washington, D.C., are evidence *against* global warming, climate experts say the opposite is true—both summer and winter storms are more severe as the climate warms.

Even a prominent climate change skeptic, University of California–Berkeley physicist Richard Muller, concluded in October 2011 after two years of research that global warming evidence is solid. Muller's research was partially funded by the Charles Koch Foundation, noted for supporting climate skepticism and anti-regulatory efforts, including the Tea Party. Koch and his brother David run Koch Industries, whose diverse businesses include oil and gas refineries and pipelines. Muller's two-year Berkeley Earth Surface Temperature Study researched the validity of previous climate studies. "Now we have confidence that the temperature rise that had previously been reported had been done without bias," Muller told the Associated Press.

As we noted back in the introduction, climate continues to drive significant clean-tech business activity in Kyoto Protocol signatory regions like Europe and Australia. In November 2011, Australia passed the nation's first carbon tax, which required the top 500 Aussie polluters to pay for emissions beginning in July 2012. Although opponents promised to make the tax a referendum issue in the next national election—meaning that a defeat of Prime Minister Julia Gillard could jeopardize the measure's future—it nonetheless made Australia one of the first large economies outside Europe to impose climate-related penalties.

Although President Obama has called for an 80 percent reduction in U.S. CO_2 emissions by 2050, he has not made it an urgent national priority. We believe it's long past time for the U.S. to lead on this issue. Although the primary motivator for our drive to prominence in clean tech will be economic leadership and job creation, climate change will always be present—and increasingly so—as a reminder of the global consequences of carbon emissions. The two go hand in hand.

"We don't believe in this false choice between economy and environment," says Mark Vachon, vice president of General Electric's Ecomagination clean-tech initiative, which accounts for more than $20 billion in annual revenue for the company. "We're going to design answers that provide success in both realms. Climate change is real, and there are trillion-dollar markets for the products and services that address it. This is what a great and good company should do."

WE'VE DONE THIS BEFORE: LESSONS FROM U.S. HISTORY

American leadership in technology innovation and deployment is not an abstract concept. U.S. history is replete with examples of nationwide, many-hands-on-deck initiatives to build out infrastructure deemed critical to the nation's economy, security, and continued global prominence. Transportation, energy, manufacturing, communications, and space exploration are among the areas that have benefited from these initiatives. All have had one thing in common: strong government leadership, from the White House on down, that mobilized both the public and private sectors toward an ambitious goal in the national interest. It's exactly this type of leadership that we think is necessary to make the U.S. the world's number-one clean-tech nation.

LESSON 1: THE TRANSCONTINENTAL RAILROAD

On July 1, 1862, President Abraham Lincoln signed the Pacific Railroad Act, laying out a vision for private companies (ultimately the Central Pacific and Union Pacific railroads) to connect their lines from California to the Missouri River and authorizing the U.S. Treasury to issue $16,000 worth of bonds (roughly $350,000 in today's dollars) to fund the construction of each 40-mile section of railroad. Seven years and more than 2,000 miles of new track later, Americans could travel coast to coast by rail for the first time.

When Lincoln and Congress officially authorized this effort, the nation was 15 months into arguably the greatest crisis it would ever endure, the Civil War. Unspeakably bloody battles raged that year at Shiloh, in Tennessee, Antietam, in Maryland, and dozens of other sites. Yet even under these most trying of circumstances, Lincoln saw the strategic importance of the railroad for his penultimate goal, the preservation of the Union. The historic endeavor did not unfold without corruption scandals, atrocities against Native Americans living near the rail route, and other unfortunate aspects. But it was an early example of public-private partnership, employing thousands of workers, which successfully completed infrastructure that was critical to the nation's economic success and emerging global leadership.

LESSON 2: THE WORLD WAR II MANUFACTURING OVERHAUL

In our more than a decade in the clean-tech industry with our company Clean Edge, we've often heard advocates call for a Manhattan Project–type effort to ramp up the industry. This referral to the nation's secret 1940s initiative to develop nuclear power and weapons technologies has some merit, but we believe that a much better World War II model was the unprecedented overhaul of the nation's manufacturing infrastructure to support the war effort.

One month after the Japanese attack on Pearl Harbor, President Franklin D. Roosevelt established the War Production Board in January 1942, under the direction of former Sears Roebuck executive Donald Nelson. An even more powerful Office of War Mobilization would follow in the next year as the administration sought to convert a huge percentage of the nation's industrial infrastructure to wartime production. Many companies initially resisted, fearing loss of market share in consumer goods. But a combination of government sticks and carrots, the latter being lucrative production contracts funded in part by war bonds, hastened the transition.

From the Bath Iron Works shipyard in Maine to the Richmond, California, Ford Motor assembly plant mentioned in the previous chapter, factories throughout the country retooled to make warships, tanks, munitions, fighter planes, and scores of other key products. The Ford plant alone, renamed the Richmond Tank Depot, assembled 49,000 military jeeps and processed or finished some 91,000 tanks, armored personnel carriers, and other combat vehicles in the next three years.

With that type of scenario replicated across the nation, U.S. GDP soared from $88.6 billion in 1939 to $135 billion in 1944, and unemployment (as a percentage of the labor force) fell from 14.6 percent in 1940 to 1.2 percent in 1944. A key part of this effort was the unprecedented training of a new workforce to replace workers joining the armed forces, including the millions of women on assembly lines who inspired Rosie the Riveter's iconic "We Can Do It!" image and spirit.

We see promising examples of retooling for clean tech in today's America, such as the former Toledo, Ohio, glass factories now producing solar PV panels, and General Motors and Toyota's once-shuttered joint NUMMI plant, in Fremont, California, gearing up to assemble all-electric Tesla sedans. But imagine what a nationwide initiative could do—with even a small fraction of the effort of World War II. The establishment of a national smart infrastructure bank, which we recommend in our Seven-Point Action Plan in chapter 6, could be an effective tool to finance a 21st-century version of a manufacturing overhaul for clean tech.

LESSON 3: ARPANET

Throughout human history, military imperatives have spawned disruptive technology breakthroughs, and the U.S. has certainly played a major part in this phenomenon. The U.S. Navy's wireless radio advancements during World War I (under young assistant secretary of the Navy Franklin D. Roosevelt) helped lead to the genesis of the

Radio Corporation of America (RCA) and a multibillion-dollar industry. Boeing's KC-135 Stratotanker aircraft for refueling Navy planes
was redesigned in the 1950s to become the company's first successful commercial airliner, the 707. There are dozens of other examples,
but few if any Pentagon technologies would have more impact on the
nation and the world than ARPANET.

The Department of Defense created its Advanced Research Projects
Agency (ARPA) in 1958 in direct response to the Soviet Union's Sput-
nik launch a few months earlier. Later renamed DARPA (the D standing for Defense), the agency's mission was (and remains) to research
and develop leading-edge, forward-looking technologies ahead of
the nation's adversaries, be they Cold War Soviets or today's terrorist
threats. Technologies like unmanned drones and global positioning
systems have come out of DARPA, but nothing really compares to the
rudimentary packet-switched computer network of the late 1960s that
would become the Internet.

DOD and university scientists created ARPANET not (as is widely
believed) to survive a nuclear exchange but simply to establish a
reliable way for the few large university research computers at the
time to share scientific data. The first link among such computers,
at four universities in California and Utah, was established in late
1969. ARPANET reached the East Coast in 1970, expanded overseas (first to Norway) in 1973, and was declared fully operational,
with some 50 nodes, in 1975. The network's communications protocols would be formalized as the Internet protocol suite (TCP/IP)
in 1982, ultimately leading to the worldwide Internet, which began
carrying commercial traffic in the mid-1990s. But it was a university
student, Marc Andreessen at the University of Illinois, who created
the Mosaic graphical browser (renamed Netscape Navigator) in 1993
and helped to revolutionize Internet use and launch a multibillion-
dollar industry.

The ARPANET-Internet evolution is a useful model: technology developed by the U.S. military, and perfected and upgraded in academia, that spawned thousands of entrepreneurs and corporate innovators who built businesses and changed the world. It's one of the reasons why we're encouraged by the Pentagon's commitment to clean tech described earlier in this chapter.

LESSON 4: THE APOLLO PROGRAM

We are certainly not the first to select America's successful moon-landing effort as a model for initiatives to excel in the development and commercialization of clean technologies. The Apollo program is often cited by advocates and is the namesake for the Apollo Alliance, a national coalition of environmental and labor groups that lobbies for federal and state policies to grow jobs in clean tech. Apollo is a great model for many reasons: President John F. Kennedy's vision that inspired a generation of new scientists, engineers, and entrepreneurs; the national pride in its ultimate success when astronauts Neil Armstrong and Buzz Aldrin walked on the moon in July 1969; and perhaps most influential of all, the technologies developed in the program whose descendants are still used today in military, scientific, and commercial applications.

Athletic shoes, freeze-dried foods, fire-resistant textiles, home insulation, water purification systems, and above all the modern microprocessor chip can all trace their roots to National Aeronautics and Space Administration R&D in the Apollo program. NASA's need to dramatically reduce the size, weight, and power consumption of computer circuitry on board a space capsule spurred key semiconductor technology advances that helped downsize computers from the room-size behemoths of the 1950s. "There was a major shift in electronics and computing, and at least half the credit goes to Apollo," said Stanford University aeronautics professor and former NASA engineer G. Scott Hubbard. "Without it, you wouldn't have a laptop. You'd still have things like the UNIVAC."

And it was at NASA's Ames Research Center in Sunnyvale, California, in the mid-1960s that 11-year-old Steve Jobs saw his first computer terminal and, as he told biographer Walter Isaacson, "fell totally in love with it." That's pretty good proof that a visionary national effort to lead the world in a technology-based undertaking can have far-reaching, unforeseen positive consequences even decades into the future.

TODAY'S POLITICAL REALITIES— AND HOW TO OVERCOME THEM

Given today's polarized American politics, a unified, visionary national effort on just about anything seems like a very elusive concept. After some encouraging bipartisan signs in the previous decade, like the Warner-Lieberman Senate bill to reduce carbon emissions, support for energy initiatives, at least at the federal level, has largely fallen along political party lines. Clean energy sources like solar and wind power enjoy the most support among Democrats, while Republicans tend to favor coal, oil ("drill, baby, drill"), and nuclear power.

The Republican charge that President Obama "waged war on carbon-based energy" didn't begin with the Solyndra bankruptcy fallout in autumn 2011; it started appearing on some right-wing websites more than 18 months earlier. During the Obama administration, Republicans have opposed much more than controversial carbon cap-and-trade measures; extremist members think even some energy-efficiency technologies are a bad idea. Take lightbulb efficiency. In 2007, Congress passed the Energy Independence and Security Act, signed by President George W. Bush, which included a mandated 25 to 30 percent increase in lightbulb efficiency starting in 2012. The measure, widely supported by U.S. lighting manufacturers, will gradually phase out conventional incandescent bulbs in favor of next-generation incandescent, compact fluorescent, and LED technologies.

But what a difference four years can make. In early 2011, a Republican-sponsored House bill sought (and failed) to repeal the measure. "Telling Americans which basic household necessities they can and cannot buy is something government should never do," said Texas Republican Jeb Hensarling. Another congressman, Michigan Republican Fred Upton, actually voted to repeal the very bill he had sponsored four years earlier.

So if our politicians can't even agree on improving lightbulbs, what hope do we have for policies that will address the clean-tech imperative and position the nation to be the global leader in clean and efficient energy, transportation, building, and water technologies?

The answer, as with many important issues, lies below the Beltway radar. Americans across the opinion spectrum tend to agree that politicians have lost touch with the people, and this is dramatically true on clean energy and environmental issues. Opinion polls consistently show high levels of public support for clean energy.

While members of Congress railed against government support of clean energy in the wake of Solyndra's implosion, the public did not go along. In October 2011, an overwhelming 77 percent of Americans (including 65 percent of Republicans) agreed that "the U.S. needs to be a clean-energy technology leader and should invest in the research and domestic manufacturing of wind, solar, and energy efficiency technologies," according to a poll by researcher ORC International for the nonpartisan Civil Society Institute. In the same poll, 69 percent of total respondents (including 59 percent of Republicans) agreed that putting progress toward clean-energy sources on hold during the current economic slowdown was "a bad idea." "American opinion focuses not on whether Washington should help usher in a renewable, clean-energy future," says institute founder and president Pam Solo, "but how it should proceed in doing so."

"Americans' deeply embedded values include clean air, fairness in the marketplace, innovation, and entrepreneurship," says Matthew

Lewis, communications director at the ClimateWorks Foundation, which funds carbon-reduction initiatives and technologies in the U.S. and overseas. "These are all values that define the clean-energy industry. We have this winning product that's very popular—what we have to do is assemble the right sales teams and close the sale."

SUPPORT IN THE HEARTLAND

Although Capitol Hill is mired in partisan gridlock, there are notable and growing examples of clean-tech economic success—and politicians championing it—throughout more politically conservative regions of the nation. Current and recent Republican governors like Kansas's Sam Brownback, Iowa's Terry Branstad, and Mississippi's Haley Barbour, regardless of their party's rhetoric in Washington, D.C., have strongly supported clean-energy companies and jobs in their states. "Experience has taught us that investment in the renewable-energy economy is creating jobs across all employment sectors," wrote Brownback, the former senator and onetime Republican presidential candidate, in a September 2011 op-ed in the *Wichita Eagle*. Eight of the 23 governors in the Governors' Wind Energy Coalition to lobby for wind-power-supporting policies are Republicans, including Maine's Tea Party–backed Paul LePage.

Iowa is arguably the best model of heartland clean-tech success, with the wind industry supplying more than 20 percent of the state's electricity; more than 3,000 jobs in wind manufacturing, construction, maintenance, and related areas at some 200 companies across the state; and more than $12 million in annual lease payments to farmers and ranchers housing wind turbines on their land. The October 2011 Iowa State–Texas college football game in Ames, Iowa, was named the "Wind Bowl," as it matched the state with the nation's highest percentage of wind-generated power (Iowa) against the state with the largest overall amount of wind energy (Texas); Texas won,

37–14. Republican congressman Steve King likes to call his sprawling rural district in western Iowa "the number-one renewable-energy congressional district in all of America."

BUSINESS VOICES ARE KEY

Mobilization of the business community as an influential voice for clean-tech advancement is also critical. Several clean-tech business advocacy groups came together in November 2011 to form Advanced Energy Economy (AEE), a coalition of state and regional chapters representing more than 700 companies (including nuclear energy companies as well as clean tech). Although efforts like this still have a long way to go to match the political muscle and money of long-established fossil-fuel advocates like the American Petroleum Institute, they demonstrate the industry's increasing clout to lobby state and federal legislators for clean-tech-friendly policies like renewable energy mandates. "Our idea is to get companies saying 'Don't tell us this is bad for the economy—we *are* the economy,'" says Jeff Anderson, former executive director of the Clean Economy Network, a group that merged into AEE. "That's a pretty powerful message."

This nascent movement's biggest victory came in California's statewide election in November 2010. Business groups helped raise more than $25 million to overwhelmingly defeat Proposition 23, an oil-industry-sponsored state ballot measure that would have suspended and likely killed off the state's landmark AB 32 law to reduce carbon emissions and expand its clean-energy economy. Leading the effort were billionaire San Francisco hedge fund manager Tom Steyer (profiled on page 224) and former secretary of state George P. Shultz; both are key principals at AEE.

The bottom line: Just about everyone's in favor of job creation and a growing economy. The more that clean tech is associated with those things in the minds of the American public and the business community, the more hope there is for a shift in the political mindset. The shift won't be easy. Even with the rapidly expanding political muscle of the clean-tech sector, the fossil-fuel industries have much more money to spend on campaign contributions. But as legendary Speaker of the House Tip O'Neill once said, "All politics is local." As officeholders, state and local chambers of commerce, and voters in places like Mississippi and Kansas start to see the positive economic impacts of clean-tech companies, we're confident that they'll start to share more the opinion of the nearly six million people (62 percent) who voted against California's Proposition 23 in 2010. The "No on 23" ballot choice actually received more votes than any proposition—or candidate—in the entire country in the 2010 midterm election.

THE TRANSFORMERS: 20 LEADERS SPURRING THE U.S. TRANSITION TO CLEAN TECH

No historic shift occurs without leadership. Fortunately, the U.S. has been blessed with a diverse and stellar lineup of clean-tech leaders in business, finance, science, advocacy, and government. In a book about the transformation of our economy, the following 20 profiles spotlight some of the top U.S. clean-tech leaders who have, in effect, transformed themselves. Most of them achieved success in other fields first but have transitioned themselves, and in some cases their organizations, into prominent and influential clean-tech leaders. To us, people like these—and thousands more like them—offer the best reason for confidence that the U.S. truly can succeed as a world-leading clean-tech nation.

THE EXECUTIVES
Cynthia "C. J." Warner
CEO and chairman, Sapphire Energy

As group vice president of global refining at BP, Cynthia "C. J." Warner was one of the oil industry's highest-ranking female executives. She entered the industry right out of college in the 1980s, spending time in refineries and field operations, where women were typically less than welcome. "I wanted to know how to throw a wrench around a pipe and be able to crack a valve," she said in a 2010 *Fast Company* interview. She worked on alternative-fuel projects at BP as early as 2000 but was frustrated by their slow progress and lack of corporate attention. When biofuels startup Sapphire came courting in 2008, Warner was ready to listen, and she moved her family from London to San Diego early the next year.

Sapphire's technology creates what it calls green crude—oil derived from algae that it grows in industrial-scale ponds in New Mexico—that can "drop in" to the existing petroleum infrastructure for refining into gasoline and other products. Well-funded with more than $200 million from investors, including Bill Gates, Sapphire employs about 150 people—quite a change from the 11,000 on five continents in Warner's purview at BP. But she's pursuing a different form of success. "What I want to do is leave a legacy for my kids where energy is secure," she told *Fast Company*. "I don't want to leave them a world where we're fighting for the last slice of the pie, but one where we're baking new pies."

Andrew Liveris
Chairman, CEO, and president, Dow Chemical

In recent years, Dow Chemical has undergone a marked transformation after a dark environmental history that included the manufacture of toxins like Agent Orange and dioxin, and responsibility for nearly 100 Superfund cleanup sites in the U.S. The company's transformation was already under way when Andrew Liveris became the company's top executive in 2004, but he has shifted it into a higher gear. Dow is now considered a global leader in clean-tech products, ranging from bio-based plastics to Dow Powerhouse Solar Shingles, which allow a residential roof to generate electricity without mounted PV panels. Since 1994, Dow has invested $2 billion in energy efficiency in its own operations—and saved a resulting $9 billion in energy costs through the end of 2010.

The Australia-born Liveris, a 36-year Dow veteran, has been an outspoken advocate for overhauling America's manufacturing base to compete in the 21st century. His book, *Make It in America: The Case for Re-Inventing the Economy*, calls for a comprehensive advanced manufacturing policy at the federal level, including support for makers of wind turbines, solar cells, electric vehicle batteries, and other key clean-tech components. "The world has changed," Liveris says, "and unless our economic policies change with it, this country will experience a massive long-term economic crisis." The nation's clean-tech future will clearly need century-old corporate giants like Dow as well as entrepreneurial startups, and CEOs like Liveris will be critical to making that happen.

Jim Imbler
President and CEO, ZeaChem
Like Sapphire Energy's C. J. Warner, Jim Imbler followed a long career path that didn't look as if it would lead to clean tech. After earning a chemical engineering degree and an M.B.A. from the University of Kansas, Imbler spent nearly two decades in the fossil-fuels industry, with stints in petrochemicals, coal, and oil and gas trading. In the 1990s he was president of the petroleum group of Koch Industries, the privately held conglomerate whose principals, Charles and David Koch, are among the leading opponents of policies that support clean tech.

In 2007, Imbler took the helm of ZeaChem, a Lakewood, Colorado–based startup developing fuels and chemicals made from the cellulose of woody biomass (such as waste from the forest products industry). ZeaChem's enzymes actually mimic the process of one of nature's most powerful and efficient wood cellulose converters: termites. The company is backed by top clean-tech venture capital firms, received a $40 million grant from the U.S. Department of Agriculture in 2011, and has a strategic-partner roster that includes Chrysler and Procter & Gamble. "As a chemical engineer out of the refining industry," says Imbler, "I like efficiency—and I like having a sustainable competitive advantage."

THE SCIENTISTS

J. Craig Venter
Cofounder and chairman, Synthetic Genomics

The first scientist to sequence and analyze the human genome, J. Craig Venter has brought clean tech into his wide range of pursuits. In a well-funded ($600 million) joint venture with ExxonMobil's R&D arm, Synthetic Genomics is applying genetic engineering research to develop the most productive ways to grow and harvest algae for biofuels. And working with Mexican investment firm Plenus, it has spun out a venture called Agradis to develop higher yields in biofuel crops such as sorghum and castor beans. The focus is on crops that don't need ideal growing conditions and therefore won't compete with food crops for prime land, Venter says.

A Vietnam War veteran in the U.S. Navy Medical Corps, Venter began working in neurochemistry research in the late 1970s and moved to the National Institutes of Health in 1984. His breakthroughs in gene identification led him to found the Institute for Genomic Research in 1992, and through a later company, Celera Genomics, he began sequencing the human genome in 1998. But he thinks that deriving fuel from algae—cheaply enough and at a large enough scale to displace fossil fuels—is even more daunting. "I did [the human genome] in nine months. . . . Algae is definitely a bigger challenge,"

Venter has said. "It also has a lot bigger implications for the world if we're successful."

Janine Benyus
President, the Biomimicry Institute

Biomimicry is the fascinating field of design based on structures and processes found in nature, and biologist Janine Benyus almost single-handedly brought the concept into wide public view in 1997 with her landmark book *Biomimicry: Innovation Inspired by Nature.* A summa cum laude graduate of Rutgers University with degrees in both natural resource management and writing, Benyus is considered the world's foremost biomimicry authority.

Benyus founded the Biomimicry Institute in Missoula, Montana, in 2006, and works as both an educator and consultant. The institute has taken teams of aerospace engineers from Boeing to the Costa Rican rain forests to study avian aerodynamics. Another client, British architecture firm Arup, used self-cooling termite mounds as a model for an office tower in Harare, Zimbabwe, that uses 90 percent less energy for air-conditioning than comparable conventional buildings. Other high-profile clients include GE, Herman Miller, Nike, and Procter & Gamble. Examples of such innovation abound. Japanese engineers redesigned the nose of the fabled 200-mile-per-hour Shinkansen bullet train based on the structure of a kingfisher's beak; the trains are now much quieter and consume 15 percent less energy. "One thing we've learned about organisms," says Benyus, "is that they never stop innovating."

THE ADVOCATES
Reed Hundt
CEO and founder, the Coalition for Green Capital

An attorney, business consultant, and technology policy consultant, Reed Hundt is a true Washington, D.C., insider. Hundt is best known as President Bill Clinton's first Federal Communications Commission (FCC) chairman, from 1993 to 1997. After that he was an adviser to McKinsey and the Blackstone Group, served on the board of Intel and other technology firms, and advised Barack Obama on communications and technology issues during the 2008 presidential campaign. After serving on Obama's transition team, Hundt began devoting himself to the advancement of clean tech, spearheading a campaign for "green banks"—government financing schemes that leverage both public and private capital to grow U.S. clean-tech companies and initiatives with low-cost financing. In addition to technology breakthroughs in clean tech, Hundt says, "the other way to lower the cost is to have a continuous, long-term, low cost of money. Any study of past industry buildout has shown that the lower cost of capital, the larger the buildout."

The Coalition for Green Capital (CGC, originally the Coalition for a Green Bank), founded by Hundt in early 2009, advocates for green banks at the federal and state levels. The concept is a key pillar in the Seven-Point Action Plan to Repower America that we present in chapter 6. The CGC has achieved two notable victories so far: Connecticut's establishment of the nation's first green bank, in 2011, and the U.S. House's passage of a federal green bank as part of the Waxman-Markey clean-energy bill in 2009. The bill died in the Senate, but Hundt continues his campaign in full force. More than ten states have contacted CGC about setting up their own green banks.

Bob Epstein and Nicole Lederer
Cofounders, Environmental Entrepreneurs

Very few people have been extolling the business benefits of a cleantech economy longer than Bob Epstein and Nicole Lederer, who founded Environmental Entrepreneurs (E2) back in 2000. (E2's first "EcoSalon" that year featured notable activist Robert F. Kennedy Jr.

speaking to Silicon Valley executives.) Epstein was a successful high-tech "serial entrepreneur" himself, founding five companies, including Sybase, a database management software powerhouse acquired by SAP in 2010 for $5.8 billion. He and Lederer, a former medical researcher at Stanford University Hospital, founded E2 to mobilize the independent business community in support of environmentally sustainable economic growth.

Started in the San Francisco Bay Area, E2 has grown to seven regional chapters nationwide and nearly 900 members (paying at least $1,000 annually to join). E2 sends regular delegations of business leaders to Capitol Hill, Sacramento, and Albany, New York, to make the economic case for environmental and clean-energy legislation. Among E2's successful campaigns are California's landmark AB 32 greenhouse-gas-reduction law, the Regional Greenhouse Gas Initiative among northeastern states, and increased statewide renewable energy mandates in California and Colorado.

Denise Bode
CEO, American Wind Energy Association

Denise Bode heads one of the most influential clean-energy trade groups, the American Wind Energy Association (AWEA). But she quite literally grew up in the oil industry, in Bartlesville, Oklahoma, as the daughter of a Phillips Petroleum executive. Bode would go on to become the first female president of an oil industry trade group, the Independent Petroleum Association of America, in the 1990s. She returned to Oklahoma to hold a seat on the Corporation Commission, the regulatory agency for the state's electricity, natural gas, and telecommunications markets. Although originally appointed to fill an open seat in 1997, Bode was elected the following year with the largest majority in state history (60 percent) for a first-time statewide Republican candidate. She didn't fare as well in unsuccessful runs for attorney general in 2002 and Congress in 2006, and headed back to Washington, D.C., in 2007 to head the natural-gas-promoting American Clean Skies Foundation. She took the helm of AWEA in 2009.

AWEA represents more than 2,500 members from all parts of the wind industry supply chain and hosts more than 20,000 attendees at the annual Windpower convention and trade show, one of clean tech's largest regular events. As for her transformation from a fossil-fuels advocate to a leading voice for clean energy, Bode has called herself "a poster child for change." "As I see it," Bode says, "I've moved from the finite energy sources to the infinite."

Tom Steyer
Senior managing member, Farallon Capital Management
Clean-tech champion and benefactor

Tom Steyer's San Francisco–based Farallon Capital Management is one of the nation's ten most profitable hedge funds, according to *Forbes*, and he makes that magazine's fabled *Forbes* 400 list of richest Americans, with an estimated net worth of $1.3 billion. Steyer has been a generous philanthropist to health and education causes and a major Democratic Party donor for years, but in 2010 he decided to take up another cause. Out-of-state oil industry interests had placed Proposition 23, a measure to suspend state carbon-reduction laws, on the California ballot, and Steyer wasn't happy about it. He recruited former secretary of state George P. Shultz to co-lead a campaign against it, contributed $5 million of his own fortune, and helped defeat the measure in a landslide. Steyer's leadership helped the measure's foes outspend their oil-interest adversaries, $31.3 million to $10.6 million.

Steyer's own investment business doesn't focus on clean tech; he's jumped to the forefront of influential advocates because of his certainty that clean-tech leadership is critical to America's future. A clean-tech center like California "must prove that it works from a business perspective," he said at the 2011 Clean-Tech Investor Summit conference. "We're under the microscope here." Steyer is cochair of Californians for Clean Energy and Jobs and a cofounder of Advanced Energy Economy, and has made a huge mark on clean-tech education and research. Along with his wife, Kat Taylor, Steyer donated $40 million to Stanford (he's a Stanford Business School grad) for the TomKat Center for Sustainable Energy, another $7 million to Stanford's Steyer-Taylor Center for Energy Policy and Finance, and $25 million to the Energy Sciences Institute at Yale, his undergraduate alma mater.

Jennifer Granholm
Senior adviser, the Pew Charitable Trusts' Clean Energy Program

The former two-term Democratic governor of Michigan, Jennifer Granholm presided over one of the hardest-hit states during the U.S. economic crash of 2008–9. Attracting clean-tech companies to the state played a part in Michigan's gradual recovery from the economic depths, and Granholm is bringing those lessons to the national stage as a clean-energy adviser to the nonprofit Pew Charitable Trusts.

"As a result of just some small policy changes, we got 47 companies to come to Michigan, creating [thousands of] jobs over the next few years," says Granholm. "If we can do that in Michigan, think of what the nation can do with smart, pragmatic energy policies." With some help from federal stimulus grants, Granholm's administration was able to lure firms like electric-vehicle battery maker A123 Systems, which brought production back from China. A123's Livonia factory employs 700 production workers and 400 engineers and managers; of the first 300 people hired, half had been laid off from their previous jobs. A Harvard Law School graduate, onetime federal prosecutor, and Michigan attorney general, Granholm was elected Michigan's first female governor in 2002 and served until she was term-limited in 2010. Many politicos considered Granholm a strong possible vice-presidential candidate in 2008, until they learned of one constitutional glitch: She was born in Canada. But she did play the role of Sarah Palin in Joe Biden's practice sessions before the campaign's vice-presidential debate. Granholm now hosts the nightly news program *The War Room with Jennifer Granholm* on Current TV.

THE SOLDIERS
Ray Mabus
Secretary of the Navy

The military is crucial to the advancement of clean tech in the U.S., and Navy Secretary Ray Mabus has been at the forefront of the armed forces' drive to energy efficiency and clean energy. Mabus's ambitious goals for the Navy include 50 percent of all energy from non-fossil-fuel sources by 2020, half of all worldwide bases to be net-zero energy by the same year, and half of nontactical vehicles to be alternatively fueled by 2015. "Since the 1850s, the Navy has moved from wind power to coal to oil to nuclear," says Mabus. "And every time we changed, plenty of people said the new energy source was too expensive, too hard, and too unproven. But every time, we made a better Navy."

Big goals and bold words, but boldness has marked the career of a man whose bio reads like an American dream cliché. The son of a hardware store owner in Ackerman, Mississippi (population 1,500), Mabus graduated summa cum laude from Ole Miss and magna cum laude from Harvard Law School, with a Johns Hopkins master's degree in between. After two years in the Navy, he began a career in law and politics. He was elected Mississippi state auditor in 1983, at age 35, and governor just four years later, becoming the nation's youngest governor at the time. Mabus later served as ambassador to Saudi Arabia in the Clinton administration and was appointed Navy secretary by President Obama in 2009. Mabus says the Navy is pursuing clean-energy goals "for one reason: to be better fighters. There are lots of ancillary things that flow from it—more jobs, cleaner environment, better stewards of the earth—but those are all side effects. We are a military organization, and we're doing this so we can fight better and perform duties and missions given to us by this country."

Major General Anthony Jackson
Commanding general, Marine Corps Installations West

The official bio of Major General Anthony Jackson's 37-year Marine Corps career runs for five long paragraphs, one devoted solely to some 15 military medals and commendations, without a word about clean tech. Yet few people, military or civilian, are as charismatic or passionate about the imperative for the U.S. to reduce its use of petroleum. And as commander in charge of the Marines' seven bases in Southern California and Arizona, he is doing plenty about it.

Clean-energy achievements on Jackson's watch include a 37 percent reduction in fossil-fuel use at 125,000-acre Camp Pendleton from 2009 to 2011, mainly from simply metering base residences for the first time; earning the Marines' first LEED Platinum building rating for the Wounded Warrior Barracks at Camp Pendleton; installing a 1.3-megawatt ground-mounted PV solar system at the Air Ground Combat Center, in Twentynine Palms, California; and opening a 3-megawatt landfill-gas-to-energy plant that will make the air station in Miramar, California, the Marines' first net-zero-energy base. The Marines are doing all this, Jackson says, for a simple and powerful reason: "So I don't have to order a 19-year-old Marine to clear a road to secure our access to oil."

THE ENTREPRENEURS
Shai Agassi
Founder and CEO, Better Place

There's a long list of people who have moved from successful high-tech careers to start high-impact ventures in clean tech, and Shai Agassi has to rank near the top. Born in Israel but a Silicon Valley resident since the 1990s, Agassi founded his first company, Quicksoft Development (later renamed TopTier Software Solutions) at age 24 and sold it to SAP for $400 million in 2001. Agassi joined the top management ranks of SAP after the German software giant acquired another of his startups, TopManage, the following year. His "aha" moment came at a 2005 World Economic Forum (WEF) meeting of its Young Global Leaders when WEF founder Klaus Schwab asked, "How do you make the world a better place by 2020?"

That gave Agassi both the impetus and the name for his next venture—a bold plan for a network of stations where electric vehicles could swap a drained battery for a fully charged one in less time than filling a gas tank. He left SAP in 2007 to lead Better Place, which had raised an eye-popping $750 million in funding through 2011; investors include GE and global financiers HSBC, Morgan Stanley, and UBS. (The company enjoyed the world's largest VC funding round in 2010, a $350 million infusion that easily bested Twitter's $200 million.) Palo Alto–based Better Place was slated to launch operational nationwide charging networks in Denmark and Israel in 2012, and is building regional networks in the San Francisco Bay Area, Hawaii, Australia, Canada, Japan, and China. Battery swapping is a huge bet that still meets with skepticism among EV industry analysts, but Agassi won't be swayed. Better Place "doesn't mean that oil is not necessary," he said at WEF in Davos in 2011, "but we're starting the way out."

Scott Lang
Chairman, president, and founding CEO, Silver Spring
Networks

Scott Lang learned the entrepreneurial game from one of its grand masters: H. Ross Perot. As a senior at the University of Mississippi, Lang met Perot at a college job fair and was immediately hooked. He joined Perot's Electronic Data Systems in 1985 and would work for him for the next two decades. Lang, who grew up on a farm in southern Illinois, followed the iconoclastic businessman and presidential candidate to his new company, Perot Systems, in 1988 and would eventually head the company's Strategic Markets Group. In 2004, he took the helm of Silver Spring Networks, a new startup in the then nascent realm of the smart grid. It was a logical transition, as smart-grid products and services are built on software and networking technologies, and Lang has grown Redwood City, California–based Silver Spring into one of the sector's top companies. "I really wanted to do something about how we use global energy more intelligently and more efficiently," Lang says of his clean-tech transition. Silver Spring's top management includes several executives who followed a similar path from high tech, leaving positions at companies like IBM, Cisco, and Metricom.

Silver Spring's IP-based Smart Energy Platform is a large suite of applications that enable electric utilities to better manage electricity distribution, detect problems and outages, and integrate distributed generation such as rooftop solar. Its users include some of America's largest electric utilities, among them American Electric Power, Florida Power & Light, and PG&E. Lang was named Ernst & Young's Entrepreneur of the Year in clean tech in 2009, and the company filed for an IPO in July 2011.

Elon Musk
Chairman, product architect, and CEO, Tesla Motors;
chairman, SolarCity

Sometimes, founding a tech company actually *is* rocket science. That's the case with one of Elon Musk's startups, SpaceX, whose *Falcon 1* and *Falcon 9* launch vehicles and *Dragon* spacecraft have all had successful NASA test flights. Before founding SpaceX in 2002, Musk had already flown high in the Internet business with online payment provider PayPal, which he sold to eBay for $1.5 billion. Musk is aiming for similar revolutionary success with his two (so far) clean-tech companies: electric-vehicle pioneer Tesla Motors and fast-growing nationwide solar installer and financier SolarCity.

A South Africa native who came to Silicon Valley for doctoral work in applied physics at Stanford, Musk is most closely associated with Tesla. The first new U.S. auto company to launch an IPO since Ford in 1956, Tesla has been one of clean tech's most high-profile companies, for both its jazzy $100,000 electric sports car and its bumpy history. Tesla has endured management disputes, financial struggles, and layoffs but seems to have found its footing as it ramps up manufacturing of the more affordable Model S sedan. Tesla has already sold out its 2012 production run of 6,500 of the roughly $49,000 cars. Musk was named one of the world's most influential people by *Time* magazine in 2010 and won *WSJ. Magazine*'s inaugural Innovator of the Year award in 2011.

THE FINANCIERS

Vinod Khosla
Founder, Khosla Ventures

Arguably the most high-profile venture capitalist funding clean tech—and certainly the most outspoken—Khosla founded his company in 2004 and manages about $2 billion in venture investments. Born in Delhi, India, Khosla became one of Silicon Valley's most successful figures in high tech's early heyday, cofounding Sun Microsystems (now part of Oracle) in 1982 and becoming its first chairman and CEO two years later. He then spent 18 years at the Valley's premier VC firm, Kleiner Perkins Caufield & Byers, with highlight-reel investments like Compaq, Genentech, Google, and Amazon.com, before making the high-tech-to-clean-tech transition like so many others. Khosla is still heavily invested in IT as well, and in other areas, such as Indian microfinance.

Known for his strong opinions on specific clean-tech sectors (hot on next-generation biofuels and LED lighting, cold on solar PV and EVs), Khosla was one of clean tech's staunchest defenders during the autumn 2011 political fallout from the Solyndra bankruptcy. Khosla backed up his words with the formation of a new $1.05 billion fund devoted mainly to clean technologies. "For those people who said clean-tech investing is a disaster," Khosla has said, "I can say we have generated huge profits."

Nancy Floyd
Founder and managing director, Nth Power
Other clean-tech venture capitalists may have bigger investment portfolios or higher profiles, but no one can lay claim to the handle of "clean-tech investment pioneer" more than Nancy Floyd—dating back to before the phrase was invented. She founded Nth Power in 1997, and the San Francisco–based venture firm has focused exclusively on clean tech ever since, investing in nearly 60 companies in renewable energy, energy efficiency, smart grid, clean transportation, and green building. Floyd's career in energy dates back to 1977, when she began working for Vermont's public utilities commission. She founded, managed, and sold an energy company and a telecommunications firm in the 1980s. Nth Power's current $425 million portfolio includes smart-grid tech providers BPL Global and SmartSynch, utility-scale project manager Tioga Energy, and energy-efficiency pioneer Comverge (now public).

In recent years, Floyd has emerged as one of the most prominent and active voices in advocacy of clean-tech-supporting public policy through groups like the American Council on Renewable Energy. Holder of both a bachelor's and a master's degree in political science, Floyd addressed the 2008 Democratic Convention in Denver on behalf of the clean-tech industry.

THE GURUS
Amory Lovins
Chairman and chief scientist, Rocky Mountain Institute

Amory Lovins knew he was a thinker ahead of his time as a 23-year-old junior research fellow at Oxford in 1971. Lovins wanted to pursue a doctorate in energy, but the university had no such program (energy wasn't yet considered an academic subject), so he left—and has been shaking up the world of energy ever since.

Considered one of the world's foremost experts on energy-efficient design, Lovins has advised clients from Ford and Walmart to the Pentagon to 20 heads of state. In 1982, he and first wife L. Hunter Lovins (they divorced amicably in 1999) founded the Snowmass, Colorado–based nonprofit Rocky Mountain Institute, which has spun off five for-profit companies in clean tech. Among other influential ideas too numerous to list, Lovins originated the concept of the "negawatt" as a measure for energy saved by efficiency technologies and practices. He fervently believes that an energy-efficient world can be powered by clean, renewable energy sources without the need for new oil, coal, or nuclear power. He once said that trying to revive the U.S. nuclear energy industry was akin to "defibrillating a corpse."

Colorful and contrarian, Lovins continues to travel the world spreading the gospel of new thinking about energy—and new thinking in general. "I subversively advise students that if their studies are so disparate their advisers can't discern a pattern, they're probably on the right track," he wrote in 2011. "Wonder in the bewilderness. Go wild. Mix thermodynamics with Chinese art history with cultural anthropology with naval architecture and you'll learn how to learn."

William McDonough
Founding principal, William McDonough + Partners;
cofounder, McDonough Braungart Design Chemistry

One of the world's foremost green architects, William McDonough traces his clean-tech roots back to his design of the first solar-heated house in Ireland as a Yale graduate student in 1973. But his big break-through in thinking would come 11 years later, when his young New York City architecture firm was commissioned to design the new Environmental Defense Fund headquarters. When EDF warned him of legal consequences if the building experienced poor air quality or toxic fumes, McDonough learned that his building material suppliers considered the chemical content of their products to be proprietary information. That put McDonough on a lifelong path to transform design of all kinds, not just buildings, to a cleaner, greener, and healthier undertaking.

McDonough's book coauthored with German chemist Michael Braungart, *Cradle to Cradle: Remaking the Way We Make Things*, pioneered much of the philosophy behind current net-zero-waste design. McDonough and Braungart's design firm created cradle-to-cradle (C2C) certification for products with components and materials that are fully reusable. In architecture, notable projects of McDonough's firm (based in Charlottesville, Virginia, since 1994) include Nike's European headquarters, outside Amsterdam; the San Bruno, California, office complex that houses YouTube; and Ford Motors' historic Rouge Complex, in Dearborn, Michigan, which features the world's largest green roof—1.1 million square feet.

Art Rosenfeld
Retired commissioner, California Energy Commission

No one has worked on innovations in energy efficiency longer than Art Rosenfeld. After 20 years as an award-winning particle physi-cist, in 1974 Rosenfeld—spurred by the 1973 energy crisis after the

Arab oil embargo—changed his research focus to energy efficiency. He formed the Center for Building Science at Lawrence Berkeley National Laboratory, which he would run for the next two decades. Rosenfeld advised state regulators (he'd later become one himself) on efficiency standards for appliances (notably refrigerators) that would make Californians the nation's stingiest energy users. Despite the explosion of personal computers, Wii gaming systems, wide-screen televisions, home espresso machines, and untold other electronics, per capita electricity use in California has remained nearly flat for some 35 years—a phenomenon dubbed the Rosenfeld Effect.

Rosenfeld retired from the California Energy Commission in 2010 at age 83, but he is still an in-demand conference speaker and one of clean tech's most revered figures. When Rosenfeld received the DOE's highest honor, the Enrico Fermi Award, in 2006, it carried a special significance. Rosenfeld was the legendary Nobel laureate's last graduate student at the University of Chicago before he died in 1954. Fermi's Manhattan Project and other work changed the course of history in the 20th century; Rosenfeld's legacy continues to have a major impact on the world of clean tech in the 21st.

Diverse and inspiring, these Transformers, along with many others leading the charge, give us a good deal of optimism that the U.S. has the creativity and innovative capacity to overcome naysayers and inertia and meet the challenges of building a clean-tech economy. The economic, national-security, and climate imperatives are clear. We have met monumental global and technological challenges throughout our history as a nation, transforming our lives and the course of world history in the process. With the clean-tech imperative, we are confident that our nation's deep talent and leadership in business, science, finance, and entrepreneurship can meet this 21st-century challenge.

Now let's get to work.

6

A SEVEN-POINT ACTION PLAN FOR REPOWERING AMERICA

The United States stands at a critical crossroads, where it faces a clear choice. It can successfully wean itself off volatile foreign sources of fossil fuels; end its reliance on polluting oil and coal and waste-riddled nuclear power; innovate and build the lighter, faster, cheaper technologies of the 21st century; create competitive, well-paying jobs across the employment spectrum; and deploy a modern, emboldened infrastructure that meets the environmental and resource constraints of our day. Or it can pursue a business-as-usual pathway and lose out to a host of other nations, including Germany, Japan, and China.

We think the case for an advanced-energy, clean-tech buildout is so clear, and the need to move forward so obvious, that not meeting this imperative is both negligent and foolhardy. The advancement of clean-tech initiatives in governments large and small across the globe has proved that clean tech can garner strong bipartisan support. Governors from both the Republican and Democratic sides have supported clean-tech buildouts in the U.S., as have both progressive and conservative leaders around the world at the city, regional, and national levels.

And the American public is solidly behind a clean-tech buildout. In poll after poll, by large majorities of usually more than 80 percent, Americans support the development and deployment of wind, solar, and other clean-energy and efficiency technologies. But in order to succeed, we need a pathway to leadership that includes sustained and clearly defined programs and commitments.

"It's a travesty that the U.S. doesn't have a long-term strategic energy plan," says Ira Ehrenpreis, general partner at Technology Partners, in Palo Alto, one of the leading clean-tech venture capital investors. "Instead, the country has a hodgepodge of policies, a balkanized assemblage of legislation, and nothing close to a strategic plan. It's as ridiculous as an entrepreneur walking into our office and saying, 'We want to raise money for our company, but we don't have a business plan and we don't have any long-range plan.'"

So how can the U.S. ensure that it doesn't get left behind? That, like Germany, it can create hundreds of thousands of new jobs in clean-tech industries? That, like China, it can be more than just a service economy and manufacture the best electric streetcars, advanced lithium-ion batteries, and solar PV on the planet? How can the U.S. continue to be a beacon of innovation, as it has for so many other industries over the past two centuries, and create new advanced water filtration, energy storage and distribution, and renewable-energy and efficiency technologies? How can we move past entrenched partisan politics and pursue a long-term strategy that serves our nation and our world?

At our company, Clean Edge, we've been analyzing the clean-tech economy for more than a decade. Our focus on technology, policy, and capital trends has provided us with a unique perspective. The following represents our collective experience benchmarking, indexing, and analyzing the most dynamic and important industrial shift in a century.

THE FIVE LAWS OF CLEAN TECH

1. CLEAN TECH CAN SCALE

There's a misconception that clean energy and clean tech can't scale up to provide massive amounts of energy like coal, oil, natural gas, and nuclear power can. At a recent conference put on by a major oil company, for example, most people in the audience didn't know or believe that in 2010, utility-scale renewables (solar, wind, and geo-thermal) provided more than 10 percent of total generation in three states (Iowa, North Dakota, and California) and 5 percent or more in ten others. People assumed we were talking about total peak capacity, not the amount of megawatts actually generated, until we showed them the data.

Such common misconceptions, even among industry participants, are nothing new. But the depth of this perception problem is considerable. Commercially viable wind and solar energy, hybrid vehicles, smart meters, and other clean technologies are relative newcomers, but they are beginning to carve out an increasingly large portion of the energy technology pie. This law, the first on our list, is a critical one to grasp and comprehend: Clean technologies can scale, in some cases quite dramatically.

This increasing penetration shouldn't be too surprising to avid technology watchers. Most clean technologies are more akin to such high-tech sectors as computer chips, the Internet, and cell phones than to the extractive fossil-fuel energy industries that they are replacing. The companies that are gaining traction, and the countries that are pursuing mass adoption, are those with deep high-technology roots: GE, Siemens, ABB, and Toyota; the U.S., Japan, Germany, and China.

Ten Years in Clean Tech: At a Glance		
	2000	2010
Combined Global Market for Solar PV and Wind	$6.5 billion	$131.6 billion
Average Cost to Install a Solar PV System (Per Peak Watt)	$9	$4.82
Number of Hybrid Electric Vehicles on the Road in U.S.	Fewer than 10,000	More than 1.4 million
Number of Hybrid Electric Vehicle Models Available Globally	2	30
LEED–Certified Commercial Green Buildings in the World	3	8,138
Number of U.S. States with RPS	4	29
Percentage of Total U.S. Venture Capital Invested in Clean Tech	Less than 1%	More than 23%

Source: Clean Edge, Inc., 2011.

For example, since Clean Edge began tracking the solar and wind industries more than a decade ago, these two markets have expanded by more than 30 percent annually. During the same period, Iowa significantly ramped up its wind industry, and in 2011 more than 20 percent of the state's generation came from wind turbines. In the same time frame, Germany moved from around 6 percent renewables (of total electricity supply) to more than 20 percent in 2011, creating more than 300,000 jobs in the process. General Electric's clean-tech revenues have expanded from $5 billion in 2005 to more than $20 billion in 2011. Toyota's best-selling car in Japan is now the hybrid Prius, and it has been for more than two years running. And in perhaps the most telling and eye-opening statistic, renewables—hydro, solar, biomass/biofuels, geothermal, and wind, combined—now produce more energy in the U.S. than nuclear reactors do.

The speed of such transitions, and their related cost reductions, can be stunning. In the past three years, for example, the cost of solar PV modules has dropped by more than half. Many startup companies, most notably Solyndra, have been left unable to compete in this new low-cost environment, ceding the solar market to large multinationals, Chinese producers, and more established players like First Solar and SunPower. But while the marketplace isn't very forgiving, and has led some once-promising solar companies into bankruptcy, it also points to a new low-cost solar future. The Holy Grail of solar systems with installed costs as low as $2 per peak watt—where solar power becomes cost-competitive at the retail level in many U.S. and global electricity markets—is upon us, mostly due to this hypercompetitive landscape. And that, we believe, is good news for market growth.

The increasing size of manufacturing and deployment projects also demonstrates how solar, wind, and other advanced-energy technologies are leveraging new economies of scale. Solar Frontier, a subsidiary of Showa Shell Sekiyu, began operating a solar manufacturing facility in Miyazaki, Japan, in 2011, in what will be one of the world's largest thin-film solar PV plants when brought fully online. It has a targeted capacity of 900 megawatts' worth of solar modules annually, roughly equivalent in size to the *total amount of solar PV installed globally* in 2004. In the wind power industry, GE, Siemens, Vestas, and others are now developing and/or testing mammoth offshore turbines, in the 5-to-8-megawatt range—about three to five times larger than average onshore wind turbines. Across the globe, these types of utility-scale projects are bringing down costs and dramatically reshaping the renewables landscape.

Moving forward, as the sector matures, we believe that clean technologies will become increasingly ubiquitous and will scale up much like their high-tech brethren before them. The stakes are considerable. Existing and newly emerging energy companies that follow a 21st-century tech-driven energy pathway, instead of an extractive, 20th-century-entrenched strategy, will lead the way. They will continue to drive down costs and improve output and efficiencies for solar, wind, biomass conversion, energy storage, and other clean technologies.

2. THE DEVELOPED WORLD DOES NOT NEED
   NEW NUCLEAR OR COAL

Of all of our laws, this one is perhaps the most controversial, especially among incumbent players seeking to ensure their ongoing dominance in traditional energy fields. But we firmly believe that most developed countries, with already well-established and diverse energy infrastructures, can move forward without bringing on new coal-fired and nuclear power plants.

Instead, most developed countries can meet their increased energy demands by focusing on the buildout of renewables combined with smart-grid infrastructure, efficiency deployment, and the use of current and next-generation natural-gas-fired power plants. Contrary to those who say that all technologies must be on the table, we believe that developed countries do not need to use an "all of the above" approach to meet their future energy requirements. While China and India might be in such a predicament, more developed nations are not.

As we noted in chapter 1, on the global landscape, since the 2011 Fukushima disaster a number of nations are shifting away from nuclear power. Germany, in an about-face for the Merkel government, announced plans in 2011 to shutter all of the country's nuclear power plants and move to renewables, energy efficiency, and natural gas. Switzerland announced it would build no new nuclear power plants and would not replace its five existing nuclear plants at the end of their life spans. Similarly, new nuclear power is no longer tenable in Japan, and there's a renewed push there on clean-energy deployment. Even in the U.S., nuclear use as a percentage of total is dwindling rapidly, and new coal-fired plants are being canceled at a rapid clip—a total of more than 150 coal plants in the past decade—as state governments and utilities decide that the risks for new coal plants are just too great.

Our law states that most developed countries can pursue a future with no new nuclear and coal, and instead build out a secure energy future with the following strategies:

- **Large-scale deployment of both centralized and distributed renewables, including solar, wind, and geothermal.** Most of the 34 industrialized nations in the Organization for Economic Cooperation and Development (OECD) can reach 30 percent or more renewables by 2030, depending on overall investment and need, and far larger amounts by 2050 as advanced grid infrastructure and energy storage technology is put in place.

- **Targeted use of current and next-generation natural gas power plants.** A number of manufacturers, including GE, have launched advanced natural-gas-fired power plants that can be powered up and down quickly and efficiently. This means that next-generation gas-fired plants can act as perfect partners with intermittent renewables, offering an easy on-and-off backup to wind and solar power sources. States, utilities, and governing bodies, rather than pitting natural gas against renewables, can use these new plants, along with current low-emissions gas plants, in their arsenal of technologies to reduce emissions and reliance on more carbon-intensive fossil fuels, especially coal. The natural gas will have to come from environmentally benign sources, and the very serious issues related to hydraulic fracturing (commonly known as fracking) will have to be comprehensively addressed, monitored, and regulated. But if extracted properly and efficiently, natural gas is our fossil fuel of choice as a bridge to an expanded renewables- and efficiency-driven future.

- **Aggressive investment in a smart, two-way grid.** The electrification of automotive transportation and the growing requirements for reliable energy storage and backup for a data-driven economy will be the underpinning of a new smart grid. Nations that invest in smart meters, reliable networks that can accommodate the two-way flow of electrons, and resilient networks that do not result in cascading blackouts will be in a better position to accommodate the advanced generation technologies of the future.

- **Exploit the cost-effective and low-hanging fruit of energy efficiency.** Lightbulbs that use significantly less electricity, windows that insulate much better than their predecessors, and data centers optimized for squeezing the most out of every watt provide great hoards of untapped "negawatt" power, reducing the need for new generation plants and enabling renewables to increase their overall share of the energy pie.

3. "SMALL TECH" WILL PLAY A CENTRAL ROLE

Around the same time that we launched Clean Edge in 2000 and began working with industry and investment stakeholders to develop a new energy and environmental lexicon, others were focused on the advent and growth of nanotechnology—the development of new materials, devices, and structures at the molecular level, between 1 and 100 nanometers in size. Although nanotech hasn't reached the same level of mass awareness and popularity as clean tech, it has nonetheless been central to the advancement of new technologies and industries since the beginning of the millennium.

Indeed, nanotech lies at the core of many clean-tech advancements. Whereas microtechnology fueled the last wave of high-tech innovations, nanotech, which occurs at an even smaller scale, is at the center of today's innovation. By ordering molecules down to a billionth of a meter, scientists and engineers are redefining the concept of *small*. From porous membranes for water filtration and purification to advanced lithium-ion batteries and solar PV cell materials, nanotech is enabling a new class of technologies. These breakthroughs, as microtechnology initially did for computers, will enable the long-sought embedded energy systems of building-integrated solar PV, improved battery technologies for low-cost EVs, and much more.

4. IT'S A DISPERSED REVOLUTION

The very nature of energy consumption and resource usage means that they are often local affairs, highly influenced by regional geography, resource availability, and local regulations and commitments. Add in the fact that many clean technologies are distributed—located at the point of use, like rooftop solar, instead of centralized, like a power plant—and it becomes clear why clean tech is experiencing such a dispersed revolution.

The distributed nature of clean tech offers economic developers and businesses a silver lining. No single city, state, region, or nation will lead in any single clean-tech sector, but instead clean tech will bloom in a thousand places. Already, centers of manufacturing leadership for a host of clean-technology sectors span the globe. And the deployment of clean tech relies heavily on regional supply chains and installation skills that cannot be outsourced or exported. For these reasons, Toledo and Detroit can compete against Phoenix and San Francisco, and Denmark and India can have a go at it against South Korea and Brazil. The clean-tech sector, born in the age of highly advanced communication and well-honed technology incubation networks, enables rapid prototyping and growth across the globe.

But against this backdrop, companies and places will certainly specialize and focus their efforts in order to compete effectively. The distributed nature of clean tech is a double-edged sword, and requires that cities, states, and nations focus on their strong suits or risk spreading themselves too thin. For this reason, a place like Oregon can lead in solar PV manufacturing but will not likely be an EV-manufacturing powerhouse like Tennessee or Michigan. Any city, state, or national economic development plan for clean tech should include a full assessment of a region's clean-tech strengths and weaknesses to determine the best area of focus, future investment, and likely success.

5. ENERGY TRANSITIONS TAKE DECADES

As noted in law number 1, clean tech is already scaling, and in some sectors quite aggressively. But this isn't like the Internet. In clean tech, you can't quickly set up a new Web service like Groupon that offers half-off restaurant coupons or create a medium like Twitter that offers people a new form of media expression and almost instantly eliminate or bypass the incumbents. While the transition to a clean and efficiency-oriented energy system is well under way, it will still take an additional two to four decades for it to reach dominant market share. The decarbonization of our energy system, moving from carbon-intensive sources like the burning of coal and oil to lower-carbon sources like natural gas, and then to near-zero or zero-carbon resources such as renewables and efficiency, is a long-term proposition.

"It was interesting being at Google," says Dan Reicher, executive director of the Steyer-Taylor Center for Energy Policy and Finance at Stanford University and former director of climate change and energy initiatives at Google. "They'd create a new software code, spend six months perfecting it, then push a button and take it live. Months later they'd have five million users. For clean energy, we're decades into it, and solar still represents just a quarter of 1 percent of total electricity generation in the U.S. You need to think in decades, not months."

Our Five Laws of Clean Tech provide a strong grounding in the new marketplace that is emerging all around us. From the Toyota Prius in your neighbor's driveway to the solar PV systems being installed on U.S. Army barracks, the Five Laws offer an important frame for understanding this dynamic market. But how can the U.S. solidify its clean-tech leadership and garner the fruits of this monumental shift around the world? We have identified seven important steps that the nation can take to ensure its dominance in the biggest economic, environmental, and energy shift of our time.

THE ACTION PLAN

The following Seven-Point Action Plan represents our ideas on how the U.S. can best remain a viable and competitive clean-tech leader in the face of significant global competition. Other nations such as China, Japan, South Korea, Germany, and the U.K. are certain to play central roles, but we believe that the U.S., as one of the world's most innovation-oriented nations, has a unique role to fill.

The clean-tech actions outlined below are based on feedback and insights from the latest research; conversations with leading industry, government, and financial experts; polling of Clean Edge subscribers; and our more than a decade of experience running Clean Edge. The Action Plan is designed for the broadest bipartisan support—we've avoided highly controversial, polarizing actions such as a nationwide carbon tax, which has little likelihood of passage. While the devil will be in the details, we believe the actions and programs outlined below, if implemented, would ensure U.S. clean-tech leadership well into the 21st century. Here are the Action Plan details.

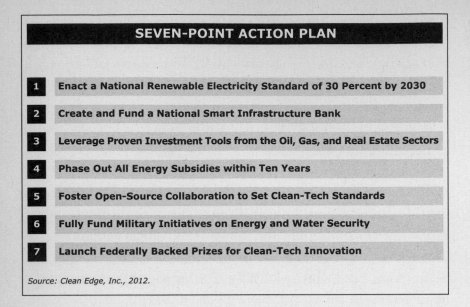

SEVEN-POINT ACTION PLAN

1. Enact a National Renewable Electricity Standard of 30 Percent by 2030

2. Create and Fund a National Smart Infrastructure Bank

3. Leverage Proven Investment Tools from the Oil, Gas, and Real Estate Sectors

4. Phase Out All Energy Subsidies within Ten Years

5. Foster Open-Source Collaboration to Set Clean-Tech Standards

6. Fully Fund Military Initiatives on Energy and Water Security

7. Launch Federally Backed Prizes for Clean-Tech Innovation

Source: Clean Edge, Inc., 2012.

1. ENACT A NATIONAL RENEWABLE ELECTRICITY STANDARD OF 30 PERCENT BY 2030

As outlined in chapter 2, on states' leadership, one of the most effective clean-energy deployment tools in the U.S. over the past decade has been renewable portfolio standards (RPS). Also known as renewable energy standards, these programs call for a certain percentage of a state's electrons to come from renewable sources by a specified date. Twenty-nine states and the District of Columbia had enacted an RPS by the end of 2011, and they are driving much of the clean-energy development in the U.S.

California, for example, recently upped its target from 20 percent to 33 percent of its electricity from renewables by 2020 for its investor-owned utilities (IOUs). The new law, signed by Governor Jerry Brown in early 2011, has some budget safeguards in it as well. It requires the state utility commission to place limits on how much utilities can spend on renewable power—a critical cost-curbing detail in today's budget-constrained environment.

With the right policies and a federal RPS mandate in place, we believe the U.S. can generate 20 percent of its electricity from wind by 2030. The DOE, during the Bush administration, reached the same conclusion in a 2008 report. And our projections show that solar power, along with geothermal energy, small-scale hydro, and sustainable waste-to-energy and biomass could easily provide another 10 percent. In other words, renewables could combine to account for 30 percent of the nation's total electricity supply by 2030.

A well-structured national RPS can help create a vibrant market for clean-tech products and services across the U.S. and would be a cornerstone of a national security initiative that greatly reduces America's reliance on imported fossil fuels. Historically, at the state level at least, RPS initiatives have received strong bipartisan support. Republican George W. Bush, as governor of Texas, enacted an RPS and other policies that helped make his state the nation's largest generator of wind power by a wide margin. Both Republican and Democratic governors have carried the torch forward on California's RPS, now the most aggressive in the nation. Political leaders on both sides of the aisle have seen the RPS as an effective and reliable tool for growing a region's clean-energy contributions. And in three states—Colorado, Washington, and Missouri—the RPS was enacted by voters through a ballot initiative.

We believe that a strong federal RPS should be enacted as soon as possible, with a binding target of 30 percent by 2030, including a large mix of zero-emissions solar power, wind power, geothermal, and small-scale hydro, along with a mix of energy-efficiency efforts and some power from sustainably harvested biomass.

One key provision of any national RPS must be the right for states to exceed the federal mandate. The last thing the federal government should do is penalize or disincentivize states like California and Hawaii from reaching bigger goals. In addition, any national-level RPS must allow regions to leverage their best in-state or neighboring-state resources—some regions have strong wind but weak solar resources, others have strong geothermal but not biomass, and so on. The RPS must also provide states with the ability to import out-of-state resources efficiently and effectively via an enhanced and updated electric grid.

It's critical that any federal plan avoid a more generic, watered-down clean-energy standard, which often includes nuclear power and so-called clean coal. A national target should be focused on new renewables and efficiency measures and not allow states to claim old and existing sources of hydropower or nuclear power. Of the 29 states with an RPS, only one, Ohio, currently includes nuclear power, and we believe the federal government should take the lead from the states on this count. As we noted earlier, some nations, like Germany and Switzerland, are moving away from nuclear power entirely.

Of all the recommendations in our Action Plan, a well-structured national RPS could best leverage the lessons learned from states that currently have such standards—and provide a critical target and benchmarking tool for the entire nation. A national policy would ensure that states that currently lack a renewables target would have one, and the mandate would ensure that different regions could tap the most appropriate resources for their requirements. In the end, it could be one of the most effective tools for ensuring that the U.S. reach 30 percent renewables by 2030, a goal that we, and many others, believe is in reach.

2. CREATE AND FUND A NATIONAL SMART INFRASTRUCTURE BANK

America is crumbling—literally. The nation's electric grid is burdened by decades-old infrastructure that is woefully inadequate for a 21st-century digital economy. Nearly a third of the pipes in the nation's largest water systems—those that deliver water to 100,000 or more people—are now between 40 and 80 years old, and every day the nation experiences an average of 700 water-main breaks and more than 7 billion gallons of leaked water. The U.S. Department of Transportation estimates that of the nation's more than 600,000 bridges, at least 12 percent are structurally deficient and 15 percent are now functionally obsolete. That's more than one in four bridges that need major repairs or total replacement. In its *2009 Report Card for America's Infrastructure*, the American Society of Civil Engineers gave U.S. infrastructure an overall grade of D and estimated that the nation needs to spend $2.2 trillion over five years to bring its infrastructure into good condition.

"As recently as 2005, the World Economic Forum ranked the U.S. No. 1 [among the world's nations] in infrastructure economic competitiveness," noted former Democratic governor Ed Rendell of Pennsylvania and Republican mayor Scott Smith of Mesa, Arizona, in an August 2011 opinion piece in the *Wall Street Journal*. "Today, the U.S. is ranked 15th. This is not a surprise considering that the U.S. spends only 1.7 percent of its gross domestic product on transportation infrastructure while Canada spends 4 percent and China spends 9 percent."

While private industry can and will fund some infrastructure, historically the government has played a central role in supporting public infrastructure investment and buildout. Without government backing, private industry is simply unwilling to fill the void. But there is a solution: a smart infrastructure bank that leverages both public and private capital. "Smart infrastructure" refers to the deployment of lighter, faster, cheaper, cleaner, and more efficient systems for transportation, green buildings, water filtration and delivery, and the production, storage, transmission, and distribution of energy.

"We probably have the most well-developed environmental regulations of any nation in the world, and we have a tremendous investment infrastructure, from VC to late stage to public markets," says former FCC chairman and current Coalition for Green Capital CEO

Reed Hundt, whose group has spearheaded efforts to develop green-focused infrastructure banks at the state and national levels. "As a public company, you'd still rather be listed on the American stock markets than anywhere else in the world. So these are all strong points. But right now, we do not have the necessary financial infrastructure to support the deployment of new clean electrons."

In order to address this shortcoming, we are proposing a smart infrastructure bank that would open up investments and leverage private capital with public dollars. We believe there's a great, long-standing model for such an investment vehicle that could super-charge the nation's ailing infrastructure: the Export-Import Bank of the United States (Ex-Im Bank). Ex-Im Bank, established as part of the New Deal in 1934, provides low-cost, public- and private-backed loans to American companies looking to export their products abroad. By focusing on gaps in private financing, the bank can support projects that would not likely get done otherwise and still provide a decent return on investment. And it's been very successful. Since its inception during the Great Depression, the bank has supported more than $450 billion of U.S. exports, including more than $30 billion in financing in 2011 alone. And it has a strong history of loan repayment.

Much like Ex-Im, a federal smart infrastructure bank could help overcome significant hurdles by providing financing to U.S.-based manufacturing and deployment projects that need extra investment that the private sector isn't able or willing to offer. A properly structured smart infrastructure bank would be a winning proposition for developers, investors, and the public. Other nations certainly think so. Brazil, China, and some European countries have successfully used similar bank structures to fund development in their nations. Such a vehicle in the U.S. would help bring money that's currently sitting on the sidelines, from pension, private equity, and other institutional investors, into much-needed projects.

The idea has strong bipartisan support. The U.S. Chamber of Commerce and the AFL-CIO, two groups that agree on little else, both support the push for more federal investments in public works. Such a bank "could leverage the government's outlay to lend more," touted a column by Bloomberg editors in August 2011. "An initial $5 billion a year for five years could result in $50 billion or more in loans. And because these loans would be paid back with interest, the institution could become self-sustaining. Financing for such a bank should be seen as an investment, not 'spending.'"

It's not just the federal government that can leverage the power of public-private infrastructure banks. In 2011, the state of Connecticut, with the backing of both Democrats and Republicans, became the first state in the nation to initiate a green bank. The bank's aim is to fund clean-energy and energy-efficiency investments in the state by using public dollars to encourage private equity and debt investments in Connecticut-based projects and companies.

"By not picking winners, leveraging private capital, and focusing on stuff that's market ready, we've been able to reframe the debate," explains Connecticut Department of Energy and Environmental Protection commissioner Daniel Esty, a former professor of environmental law and policy at Yale University and coauthor of the highly acclaimed environmental business book *Green to Gold*. With his unique background, Esty knows better than most how the environment and the economy are intricately linked, and he's aiming to take the best practices from across the country and around the world to spearhead Connecticut's efforts.

But it won't be easy. Esty is the first to admit that there's a fine balance in getting the details just right. He invokes the "Goldilocks principle" of clean tech. "If you pay too much, it's not sustainable and you invite backlash. Instead, you have to have the policies [and financing] just right, not too hot and not too cold."

We believe that a well-structured national smart infrastructure bank, with active public-private participation and oversight, would go a long way in ensuring America's future competitiveness. Such a public-private partnership would need to avoid pork-barrel projects like "bridges to nowhere," limit taxpayers' liability, and focus on efficient and smart infrastructure investments. Fortunately, clean energy, electric utility, water delivery, and efficiency projects all offer the added benefit of recurring revenue streams (sales of water delivered, electricity generated, and energy saved, for example). If designed properly, the smart infrastructure bank would provide both job creation and mission-critical investments in a budget-constrained world. And it could be partially funded by the American people, via repatriated corporate dollars that are now sitting overseas, or via smart infrastructure bonds sold to the public. Now, that's a win-win-win.

3. LEVERAGE PROVEN INVESTMENT TOOLS FROM THE OIL, GAS, AND REAL ESTATE SECTORS

As Google goes, so goes the nation? If that's the case, then investments in revenue-producing clean-energy projects may soon become increasingly commonplace. In recent years, Google has made a business out of investing in renewables projects, backing such initiatives as a $280 million solar fund to support thousands of SolarCity residential rooftop PV system installations nationwide; a $100 million infusion into the massive Shepherds Flat Wind Farm, in Oregon; and $168 million into BrightSource Energy's Ivanpah utility-scale solar project, in California's Mojave Desert. Although Google has pulled back from energy R&D activities better suited to clean-energy-focused companies, the firm continues to invest in renewable-energy projects, totaling more than $900 million through the end of 2011. Our projections show that Google can rack up impressive returns that reach into the double digits annually, plus reap the added benefits of federal and state tax credits. "Google has made a series of investments in renewable energy because they make business sense," says Rick Needham, the company's director of energy and sustainability.

How can such relatively low-risk, high-yield investment opportunities become more widely available not only to large corporate and institutional investors like Google, but to the average retail investor? And how can renewables and efficiency projects begin to tap the proven investment vehicles and business structures historically used in the fossil-fuel and real estate industries to gain access to an expanded pool of much-needed capital?

We believe there are at least two such business structures and investment tools that could be adapted to meet these goals: master limited partnerships (MLPs) and real estate investment trusts (REITs). Both of these vehicles have proved successful for traditional oil, gas, and real estate investments but are not currently structured to cover most clean-tech investments. Simple tax code changes could enable these investment structures to leverage the built-in annuity streams of clean-energy, energy-efficiency, and green infrastructure projects and could expand such investment opportunities to a broader market.

"Oil and gas investments through MLP offer an important source of development capital for the traditional energy sector," explain John Joshi and Malay Bansal, managing directors at CapitalFusion Partners, an advisory firm focused on renewable energy and infrastructure projects, in an insightful article published on *AOL Energy* in July 2011. "Following the energy crisis of the 1970s, Congress looked to spur investment in the energy sector for oil and gas exploration and created the MLP structure that provided specific tax advantages to investors. . . . The time has come for Congress to level the investment field for energy production and investment by allowing MLPs for renewable energy investments."

A tax code change by Congress or the IRS could change the equation by adding renewables to the current list of covered activities. MLPs, which offer a business structure that is taxed as a partnership but whose ownership interests are traded on financial markets like corporate stock (providing benefits over being taxed as a corporation), are currently limited to certain types of carefully—and, we'd argue, arbitrarily—defined businesses. In 2010, for example, approximately 90 percent of market capital in MLPs was attributable to energy and natural resources, with the bulk focused on oil and gas operations, representing a whopping $220 billion. Historical government definitions of qualifying industries and operations bear much of the blame for this inequity, as they "allowed oil and gas extraction and transportation activities access to the MLP structure, while renewable-energy resources were generally excluded," explains a June 2011 report by the nonpartisan Congressional Research Service.

This special treatment for fossil fuels, we believe, puts clean energy at a significant disadvantage. Renewables and energy-efficiency developers and financiers should be able to use this same business structure to tap investment opportunities. Leveling the playing field by allowing access to clean-energy sectors, just as oil and gas are currently covered, seems like a critical next step.

An additional option would be a new breed of real estate investment trust (REIT) that is optimized for clean-energy generation and/or transmission projects. As with MLPs, this would require a tax code change that would allow REITs to cover renewables and/or energy infrastructure as they currently do for other real-estate-based assets. In 2010, five major institutional and corporate investors, including Hunt Power, Marubeni Corporation, John Hancock Life Insurance, and Teachers Insurance and Annuity Association–College Retirement Equities Fund (TIAA-CREF), received approval to invest $2.1 billion in electric-transmission and gas-distribution REITs, the first such trusts ever used for U.S. energy-infrastructure investments. An IRS ruling opened the way for this new trust by allowing income from transmission networks (not generation) to count as real estate income.

REITs, as historically defined, invest in real estate and make money for investors from collected rental fees. They can be either privately held or publicly traded. Like MLPs, REITs pay less tax than corporations, by avoiding paying both a corporate and a dividend tax. Historically, REITs must have at least 75 percent of their total assets in, and revenue from, real estate holdings. But with changes in such requirements, such as those noted above, Congress and the IRS could start to allow energy-infrastructure and renewable-generation investments to qualify.

"Over the last several years, favorable IRS private-letter rulings sanctioning the use of REITs to own electric and gas distribution systems have increased interest in their role in infrastructure investments," says Lou Weller, a principal at Deloitte Tax. "I think that the REIT is a familiar model to people, especially to smaller investors. One of the hopes of a REIT structure is to open investment in infrastructure to a larger group of people."

And as prices for renewables drop significantly in the coming years, these types of business models and investment vehicles would make even more sense. The majority of new wind projects in the U.S., for example, produce electricity at around 7 cents per kilowatt-hour, comparable to current and expected near-term pricing for natural gas power. In some places, like Texas, wind can come in at less than 4 cents per kilowatt-hour. And solar power is on a steep price-reduction curve, enabling PV to compete not only for peak generation but increasingly at the retail level (the customer side of the meter) in markets across the nation.

These new breeds of MLPs and REITs would need to be carefully structured, with standards and safeguards in place to ensure that project developers, financial managers, and investors have the tools and resources to structure and evaluate deals effectively. The participation of large trusted banks and developers, backed by insurance companies and nonprofit, industry, and public watchdog groups, should go a long way in helping retail investors feel increasingly confident in these types of vehicles.

As we move forward, it's clear that financing innovations, whether MLPs, REITs, or others, will be critical to the growth of clean-energy solutions. "There's been a mini-meltdown in the bond markets," says Matt Cheney, CEO of solar-energy developer and financier Clean-Path. "CDs don't offer much more than 1 or 2 percent. So the question is 'Where do I hide my money?' There's a big appetite for a product that would get 5 percent return right now. But how do you package this opportunity so that it can be wrapped and sold into the financial marketplace?" Whoever can answer that question in the clean-tech arena, we believe, has much to gain.

4. PHASE OUT ALL ENERGY SUBSIDIES WITHIN TEN YEARS

Energy is one of the most subsidized and regulated industries on the planet. An intricate and complex web of programs and incentives has been used by governments for decades to offset the price of energy to consumers (direct consumption subsidies) and to lower the cost to energy producers (indirect production subsidies). The impact of such subsidies, in many cases, has been to prop up certain energy sectors and modes of transportation at the expense of others.

According to a November 2010 report by the International Energy Agency, the OECD, and the World Bank, direct-consumption subsidies for fossil fuels amounted to more than $300 billion globally in 2009. In 2010, due in part to increased costs of energy, these same subsidies expanded 36 percent, to $409 billion. Add in indirect subsidies, such as below-market-rate access to government lands and low-cost, government-backed insurance programs or guarantees (which are harder to track), and the number balloons much further.

The time to end such wasteful and distorting subsidies is long over-due. Historically, subsidies have been touted as serving the growth of emerging and nationally critical industries and to support the poor, but more often than not they serve to prop up mature industries and, perversely, support the wealthy. As the IEA, OECD, and World Bank report: "Phasing out fossil-fuel subsidies represents a triple-win solution. It would enhance energy security, reduce emissions of greenhouse gases, and bring immediate economic gains . . . as in many cases [subsidies] are creating market distortions, imposing unsupportable fiscal burden on government budgets, and are weakening trade balances."

The IEA projects that, if left unchecked, this free-for-all subsidy spending on mature fossil-fuel industries is likely to reach nearly $600 billion globally by 2015. No matter your political views, it's becoming increasingly clear that such advanced industries, operated by multibillion-dollar behemoths, should be able to operate without further government subsidies.

And against the backdrop of a budget-constrained world, such government largesse for mature industries, we believe, no longer makes sense. We propose that energy subsidies should be phased out, starting with fossil-fuel subsidies right away, followed by renewable energy and nuclear power subsidies over the next ten years.

Yes, you read that right—as part of our plan to ensure U.S. leadership as a clean-tech nation, we're calling for an end to government subsidies for clean tech—but ten years out. This would end the most wasteful and distorting subsidies immediately and provide renewables with breathing room to catch up with approximately 100 years of fossil-fuel subsidy largesse. By the early 2020s, we believe that wind, solar, geothermal, and other clean energy sources will be able to compete head-to-head with fossil fuels on a subsidy-free level playing field. For nuclear power, we propose ending subsidies for all *new* facilities now, including loan guarantees, and remove subsidy supports for existing nuclear plants within a decade as the industry prepares for an orderly transition.

While this is still admittedly a minority view, support for all-encompassing energy-subsidy reform is growing and increasingly crossing political and ideological boundaries. Groups as diverse as the right-wing Heritage Foundation, the libertarian Heartland Institute, and the progressive Public Citizen have all called for varying degrees of energy subsidy slashing. The latter two, along with environmental nonprofit Friends of the Earth and nonpartisan watchdog Taxpayers for Common Sense, published the 2011 version of the annual *Green Scissors* report together. The report identified, over a five-year period, more than $380 billion in federal spending that the group considers "subsidies and programs that both harm the environment and waste taxpayer dollars." Proposed cuts spare no one, and cover many fossil-fuel, nuclear, and clean-energy subsidies, along with cuts to agriculture, transportation, land, and water subsidies.

As the report notes: "From the more than a century old 1872 Mining Law that gives away precious metals—like gold and copper—on federal lands for free, to $53 billion in lost oil and gas revenues from royalty-free leases in federal waters granted in the late 1990s, to the $6 billion per year ethanol tax credit, there are dozens of reforms that can return hundreds of billions to taxpayers while helping to address our nation's top environmental priorities."

George P. Shultz, President Ronald Reagan's secretary of state, President Richard Nixon's secretary of the Treasury, and now a distinguished fellow at the Hoover Institution at Stanford University, is another influential voice for major reform. "What we need to do [on energy policy] is so blindingly obvious," Shultz said at an October 2011 energy conference at Stanford. "We need a permanent national energy policy that is simple and clear . . . [and we must] end energy tax breaks and subsidies. It's just a morass that leads to regulatory activity that holds things back."

A September 2011 report titled *What Would Jefferson Do? The Historical Role of Federal Subsidies in Shaping America's Energy Future*, by Nancy Pfund and Ben Healey, of venture capital firm DBL Investors, highlights just how skewed investments in fossil fuels and nuclear energy have been, compared with renewables. Pfund and Healey found that "in an apples-to-apples comparison, the federal commitment to oil and gas was five times greater than the federal commitment to renewables during the first 15 years of each subsidy's life, and it was more than 10 times greater for nuclear."

Current global-subsidy supports paint a similar picture, with fossil-fuel subsidies averaging six times those of renewables in 2010, according to IEA data and analysis.

Jeffrey Leonard, CEO of the Global Environment Fund, an investment firm with significant holdings in environmental and energy technologies, said it well: "To set us on a path to a sustainable-energy future—and a green one, too—[the president] should propose a very simple solution to the current mess: eliminate all energy subsidies." He went on: "Yes, eliminate them all—for oil, coal, gas, nuclear, ethanol, even for wind and solar. It will be better for national security, the balance of payments, the budget deficit, and even, believe it or not, the environment. Indeed, because wind, solar, and other green energy sources get only the tiniest sliver of the overall subsidy pie, they'll have a competitive advantage in the long term if all subsidies, including the huge ones for fossil fuels, are eliminated."

It's time that the U.S. end supports for all energy industries, starting with the long-established coal, oil, and gas industries, and followed by nuclear and renewables, and once and for all level the playing field so that energy technologies can compete on their own merits. The government should not be protecting incumbent players at the expense of emerging sectors.

Congress must show political backbone and come to an agreement on ending wasteful oil, gas, and coal subsidies now. The public overwhelmingly supports the idea of ending taxpayer subsidies for mature and wealthy energy players. In the October 2011 ORC International poll for the Civil Society Institute that we cited in chapter 5, Americans said they supported clean-energy subsidies over those for fossil fuels by a three-to-one margin. The voice of the voters should be heard over those of Washington lobbyists. Subsidies to the nuclear and renewables industries should also be abolished, but after a ten-year catch-up period. In the case of nuclear, we believe that an orderly transition is the most prudent course in light of remaining waste-disposal issues, the need for the industry to line up private accident insurance after years of government-backed support via the Price-Anderson Act, and not so insignificant security concerns. But it's critical that, after ten years, the industry be prepared to exist without government cash. For the much newer technologies of renewable energy, we believe a modicum of subsidy support for the next ten years, after decades of heavy fossil-fuel and nuclear-power subsidies, just makes sense and represents fiscal fairness. With a history of disproportionate support for coal, oil, gas, and nuclear, we believe that renewables should receive a final incubatory boost in their journey to cost parity.

5. FOSTER OPEN-SOURCE COLLABORATION TO SET CLEAN-TECH STANDARDS

Open-source networks provide a number of unique and critical advantages over private, command-and-control, solo efforts. These include the ability to openly and broadly share insights, quickly and efficiently leverage the skills of a diverse set of contributors, and build competitive markets based on a set of commonly agreed-upon standards. It doesn't mean that intellectual property shouldn't be aggressively protected; quite the contrary. Agreed-upon standards provide the infrastructure, in many industries, to enable competition and creative breakthroughs, including patented ones, to flourish.

Why are open standards becoming so important in a hypercompetitive and rapidly changing world? The battle between Google's

Android device and Apple's iPhone offers an interesting lesson about the power of shared standards. Android, which had just 4 percent of the global market share for smart phones in 2009, had expanded by an order of magnitude to more than 40 percent by the second quarter of 2011. Apple, during the same period, only slightly grew its market share, expanding from 14.4 percent to 18.2 percent. The former is based on open standards; the latter, for all its brilliant design and intuitiveness, is built on a private Apple-dictated environment. In today's world, "open" increasingly leads to market dominance.

Indeed, for nearly two decades, open-source collaboration has played an increasingly important role in the expansion of key industries. Imagine the Internet, for example, without open protocols and standards. In the mid-1990s, the World Wide Web Consortium (W3C) began to harvest the intelligence and knowledge of a broad group of stakeholders to ensure the growth of the Web via a shared learning environment and commonly agreed-upon standards. Founded in October 1994 by Tim Berners-Lee, the inventor of the World Wide Web, W3C's mission was to develop "open standards to ensure the long-term growth of the Web." The organization has been very successful in its mission and continues to work to establish open standards for systems architecture, privacy rights, and other core Internet issues.

Earlier technology revolutions, although lacking the instant online collaboration tools of today, have followed a similar path. "Go back to Society of Automotive Engineers, IEEE, and SEMATECH—there's no secret that standards drive industry," says Doug Payne, cofounder and executive director of SolarTech, a Silicon Valley–based nonprofit consortium focused on building next-generation solar systems via breakthroughs in finance, installations, and operations. "In the semiconductor industry, the SEMATECH consortium [formed in 1988] played a significant role in enabling Moore's Law to actually occur. They brought together industry stakeholders to embrace a common set of technology standards, plug-and-play intercompatibility rules, and device architectures to make cheaper, faster, and better chips."

And if ever there was a market that could use common standards and public and private collaboration, clean tech is it. From EV-charging stations to smart meters to distributed solar power deployment, the clean-tech marketplace, much like the semiconductor, Internet, and cell phone industries before it, requires a significant level of standards-setting agreement.

In the past we've written that "standards, standards, standards" will play a central role in clean-tech growth. And we believe that public-private consortiums that leverage open-source networks for standards setting and information sharing are the best route to industry growth. Fortunately, the U.S. is uniquely positioned, due to technical and organizational strengths, historical successes, and an existing political and social framework for democratic cooperation, to support such open and transparent dialogue and collaboration. In clean tech, groups like the GridWise Alliance, National Institute of Standards and Technology, and SolarTech are just beginning to play an active role in such endeavors.

SolarTech, along with 16 other partners, including such stalwarts as Underwriters Laboratories and the Rocky Mountain Institute, has been awarded $2.5 million by the DOE to deploy what it calls "Solar 3.0—a national platform for process innovation to deliver PV." The goal is to help bring standardization to the financing, permitting, installation, and interconnection of solar PV systems, thereby reducing overall costs throughout the industry.

"Our endgame is to come up with a standardized set of agreement forms and contracts akin to the rental car industry and the mortgage industry," says SolarTech's Payne. "No such standards currently exist for the solar industry."

From smart-grid networking, EV charging, and renewables integration with the existing grid to new financing models for clean energy and energy efficiency, there's clearly a vast need for open-source communities to help inform and enable industry growth. As highlighted above, the U.S. government and U.S.-based organizations have a long and rich history playing a central role in such standards-setting efforts. We encourage American enterprise, government, nonprofits, and other domestic stakeholders to continue playing a leadership role in the buildout of clean technologies via international open standards setting. We believe that nothing less than the future of clean-tech systems interoperability—and the determination of which nations' and companies' products and services flourish—relies on it.

6. FULLY FUND MILITARY INITIATIVES ON ENERGY AND WATER SECURITY

Of all the public and private agencies on the planet, the U.S. military is perhaps in the best position to forward the buildout of clean technology. Since the military makes decisions based on security issues first and foremost, clean tech—which minimizes resource use, provides both distributed and centralized power free of imported fossil fuels, and enables net-zero energy and water use—is a natural fit.

Just think about what it takes to keep a battalion supplied with fuel, water, food, ammunition, and other necessities in the theater of war, and the military's need for secure and independent energy, water, and transport becomes obvious. And the needs aren't just on the battlefield in remote locations. The U.S. Air Force alone is the nation's largest user of energy, spending approximately $8 billion on fuel and electricity every year, a sum that can rise dramatically whenever there's a spike in energy prices. Add in the military's long-term planning approach (unlike private industry, the military tends to think in decades, not quarters) and the clean-tech/military connection becomes all the more compelling.

Because of their unique mission and mandate, U.S. military leaders clearly see the risks of our current energy policy—one that places an inordinate dependence on foreign oil supplies, which they are often on the front lines defending. Congress must encourage and fully fund the military's efforts in its transition to a more secure and energy-independent future, like it has in past transitions. The U.S., for example, which has only an estimated 3 percent of the world's proven oil reserves, currently uses more than 20 percent of the world's oil production each year. This puts the nation and military in an untenable situation. "We simply do not have enough oil to keep our country and our military operating without continuing to pay higher and higher prices, and at greatly increased risk to the lives of our service men and women," retired senior military officers Steven Anderson, John Castellaw, Dennis McGinn, and Norman Seip, representing all four branches of the military, wrote in an October 2011 op-ed piece in the *Tampa Tribune*. "Without changing our energy mix, we will continue to undermine our economic stability—and with it, our stature in the world."

To meet this challenge, the military is increasingly working to reduce its own reliance on volatile energy supplies and meet rigorous security requirements. The Army, Air Force, Navy, Marines, and Coast Guard are all embracing actions that would have once seemed radical. The Navy and Air Force, for example, have a target to get half of their fuel from non-petroleum sources by 2020. The Army has embraced a "net zero" strategy to have entire bases that consume only as much energy and water as they produce. The Marines aim to cut their battlefield requirement for energy in half by 2025. Troops in the field are increasingly using portable solar PV arrays, LED lighting systems, and other clean-tech measures to power their missions and reduce the need for the delivery of fuels by enemy-vulnerable convoys.

From an operational and tactical perspective, clean-tech solutions are as much about hedging price volatility as ensuring human survival. Most patrols on the front lines in Afghanistan and elsewhere require enough batteries to last three or four days, which represents

20 to 35 pounds of batteries per soldier. Solar panels and highly efficient lighting and communication devices like those mentioned above can dramatically change the equation—enabling troops to shed weight and stay in the field for weeks, not days, without the need for dangerous resupplies.

"Marines in Afghanistan use about 200,000 gallons of fuel a day to power our war fighting capabilities and sustain our forces," explains the U.S. Marine Corps Expeditionary Energy Strategy and Implementation Plan, "Bases-to-Battlefield." "While we have proven lethal fighting in rugged environments for nearly a decade now, we've dramatically increased our energy consumption. Because of our thirst for liquid fuel, we're not as light and agile as we once were, putting both our Marines and our expeditionary capabilities at risk. [We must change] the way we think about energy—that our warrior ethos equates the efficient use of energy and water resources with increased combat effectiveness."

Off the battlefield, it is estimated that the Department of Defense is currently reliant on civilian utility companies for 99 percent of its domestic electricity requirements, putting some operations at risk during power outages. Breakthroughs that enable both combat soldiers and personnel at domestic bases to operate independently of expensive and volatile conventional energy sources has become mission-critical.

And make no mistake—climate change is also of great concern to the military. Everything from rising sea levels and depleted water tables to extreme heat, drought, and food shortages impacts the military's ability to do its job. In many ways, it's an Armageddon scenario straight out of a Hollywood thriller. And as in a good summer near-end-of-the-world blockbuster, who better than the U.S. military to play a leading role?

But the military can't be the lone savior. If private industry can be incentivized by our government leaders to support the buildout of the military's green ambitions, they can provide many of the technical breakthroughs and much of the financing required. "We have the land, we have the energy requirements, so how can we work with third parties to get private capital?" asks the aptly named Jonathan Powers, special adviser on energy in the Office of the Assistant Secretary of the Army.

Powers, who's been closely tracking and advising on the role of clean tech in the military, is part of an Energy Initiatives Office Task Force established in 2011 to help the Army meet its goal of 25 percent energy from renewable sources by 2025. The task force is in charge of finding and creating models for involving private-sector investors in meeting this goal—a target that could require an estimated $7 billion in investments over the next decade. "We've done this in the military before with privately constructed, managed, and leased buildings," explains Powers. "Over the last ten years the Army has put in about $2 billion in equity and gotten around $12 billion in privately backed building and operations investments (for a total of $14 billion) from such efforts." Now the question is, can it do the same with renewables, energy efficiency, micro-grids, and other clean-tech deployments?

A recent example of such public-private collaboration was announced in November 2011, when SolarCity inked a deal with Bank of America–Merrill Lynch to install up to 300 megawatts of solar generation capacity on privatized military housing communities across the country. Dubbed SolarStrong, the five-year plan aims to build more than $1 billion worth of solar power projects for privately developed and managed U.S. military housing, providing solar electricity at a lower cost than utility power. SolarStrong represents the largest residential solar PV project in U.S. history and would effectively double the nation's current total residential solar installations.

The Pentagon "has established ambitious and far-reaching goals that would transform military energy use, from platforms to practices," states a 2011 report by the Pew Charitable Trusts, *From Bar-*

racks to the Battlefield. "But these lofty goals are unlikely to be met unless DOD's rhetoric is matched by sustained policies and resources. Energy innovation must be a budgetary priority, a focus of cooperation between the department and Congress, and part of the reward structure and culture of the department."

It's clear that long-term national security interests, along with the need for strong, reliable, and resilient tactical operations, form the bedrock of U.S. military planning. Day-to-day operations require reliable, inexhaustible, lightweight forms of energy, transportation, and water delivery to meet the needs of a 21st-century military. Given how critical these clean-energy and water investments are to the U.S. military's future, such initiatives must be supported by our elected officials. We recommend that the military be fully supported and funded in its pursuit of cleaner, leaner, and more secure operations, facilities, and forces. The different branches of the military, from the Navy to the Army to the Air Force, all seem to be gunning to outgreen one another. We should provide them with the fiscal arsenal to do so.

7. LAUNCH FEDERALLY BACKED PRIZES
FOR CLEAN-TECH INNOVATION

The history of offering prizes to spur competition spans centuries, from military competitions in ancient Greece to perhaps the most famous award of all: the Orteig Prize of $25,000 to the first solo flier across the Atlantic, won by Charles Lindbergh (eight years after it was announced) in 1927. Such awards have captured the imaginations of entire nations, pushed the boundaries of human creativity, innovation, and achievement, and helped to create entirely new industries.

In 1990, for example, several major U.S. utilities and the Environmental Protection Agency launched the Super Efficient Refrigerator Program, also known as the "Golden Carrot" award. The award challenged refrigerator manufacturers to make a super-efficient refrigerator that would change home food refrigeration from a major energy hog to an energy sipper. The winner's payment depended not only on reaching technical milestones but, equally important, on the number of units manufactured and deployed, thereby rewarding incremental success and commercialization. Other, more recent government-backed awards include the L Prize, launched in 2008 by the DOE to challenge the lighting industry "to develop super high-performance, energy-saving replacements for conventional light bulbs." The first prize of $10 million went to Philips Lighting North America in August 2011 for developing an LED 60-watt replacement bulb. The bulbs were expected to be on store shelves in 2012.

We believe that government-backed prizes let the government do what it does best (provide frameworks, incentives, and supports) and then get out of the way to let private industry and public-private collaborative efforts come up with innovative solutions. It offers the added benefit of providing a multiplier effect on the government's expenditures and, depending on the prize structure, can provide unique guarantees—e.g., no one gets paid until milestones and deliverables are reached.

Based on the historical success of such programs, and recent innovation in program design, we are calling on the federal government to support ten clean-tech challenges with appropriately sized purses to garner significant applicants and open competition. Awards in the $100 million to $1 billion range, including deployment awards (for example, payment for the first million units shipped or systems installed), shouldn't be out of the question. The ten challenges could be decided by a panel consisting of public and private representatives well versed in clean-tech challenges, and/or opened up to nominations and online votes by the general public.

Potential awards could include the first all-electric passenger vehicle to travel 300 miles on a single charge, and cost-competitive biofuels from nonfood feedstock. As noted above, these awards should include cash for both developing new technology or systems and for reaching deployment milestones. We estimate that an approximate $5 billion budget (equivalent to less than one-tenth the total dollars earmarked for clean energy as part of the American Recovery and Reinvestment Act) over the next decade would unleash $50 billion or more in innovation.

Among the most well-known present-day awards are the philanthropically funded X Prizes, founded in 1995 by Peter Diamandis. The first one, the Ansari X Prize, promised $10 million to the first privately funded firm whose aircraft could carry a pilot and the weight of two passengers 100 kilometers into space twice in two weeks. An aviation-design firm led by Burt Rutan, with investment from Paul Allen of Microsoft, won the prize in 2004. The firm and its funders spent more than twice the value of the prize to win it, and the combined spending of all contestants was estimated at about $100 million. "These investment-to-prize ratios are roughly similar to those elicited by the Orteig Prize in the 1920s," wrote William A. Masters and Benoit Delbecq in a paper titled *Accelerating Innovation with Prize Rewards*.

While patents, intellectual property rights, traditional R&D support, and other incentives and protections have been used effectively to spur innovation, prizes offer another avenue of encouraging advancements and broad participation. By leveraging private capital, such prizes offer significant benefits to cash-strapped governments. While they aren't a replacement for traditional R&D and funding efforts and well-established patent protections, they do provide a unique and very effective complementary option.

There are many types of awards, but not all are well suited to innovation. For example, the Nobel Prize recognizes a person's past accomplishments. This type of "exemplar" prize focuses not on future advancement but on past achievements. We believe that "inducement," "point solution," and/or "market stimulation" prizes, which award technology breakthroughs, are the ones best suited to the current clean-tech landscape and ecosystem. Such market-oriented prizes provide incentives to companies, inventors, startups, and others to solve difficult problems and create products and solutions that don't yet exist.

Governments aren't the only ones using such prizes to leverage innovation. As noted, the X Prize is a philanthropic organization that has played a central role, with six innovation prizes to date and more in the works. And corporations have increasingly begun to use awards to expand their innovation capacities. GE, which oversees five global research centers on four continents, sees considerable value in such open innovation programs and awards. In 2010, it launched the Ecomagination Challenge, along with major venture firms such as RockPort Capital and Kleiner Perkins Caufield & Byers, to garner breakthroughs in home energy and power-grid technologies from innovators around the world. "It's very dangerous to believe that all great ideas are created within our four walls," says Mark Vachon, VP of GE Ecomagination. "This is not a cute exercise. We saw a real opportunity here. And opportunity, at our scale, generally starts with a '$B.'"

Our action item calls for a government commitment to ten major clean-tech innovation prizes, with a ten-year budget of approximately $5 billion. It would go a long way in cost-effectively spurring innovation while effectively leveraging private capital and working in conjunction with other government clean-tech R&D efforts. With a historical multiplier that is often greater than 10x, such a prize-oriented program could provide some of the most impactful "bangs for the buck" and unleash considerable value to U.S. companies and U.S.-based operations.

"Some say that we can't afford it, that we're too strapped for cash," said President Ronald Reagan in a national address in 1988, talking about the need for government R&D investments and echoing very similar debates raging in the U.S. today. "Well, leadership means making hard choices, even in an election year. We've put our research budget under a microscope and looked for quality and cost-effectiveness. We've put together the best program for the taxpayers' dollars. After all, the American tradition of hope is one we can't afford to forget."

As it did then, we believe the U.S. government must now play an active role in R&D and help spark innovation and enable massive scale-up and deployment. The U.S. has never shirked its role in such endeavors in the past, and should be resilient and steadfast now against calls to abandon government support for early-stage development and market deployment.

WHAT IT'S ALL ABOUT: CLAIMING THE FUTURE

The U.S. faces a stark choice. It can help lead the world in clean-tech development and reap the resulting benefits, or it can drag its feet and lose its global economic competitive edge. As firm believers in the nation's pioneering spirit, entrepreneurial creativity, and competitive fortitude, we believe the country will opt for the former. Throughout this book, we have profiled the states, cities, business leaders, and other pioneers clearly committed to making the shift and moving the nation forward. We trust that many additional business titans, entrepreneurs, educators, and policymakers will join the leaders profiled in this book and seize the clean-tech opportunity.

Admittedly, it will not be easy. Major transformations never are. And with a realistic understanding of the harsh economic and polarized political realities of our time, our Seven-Point Action Plan has been carefully designed to:

- **Be technology-agnostic.** The recommendations avoid picking or anointing new technology winners, but instead provide guidance and parameters. Beyond that, the cleanest, smartest, cheapest technologies will rise to the top on their own merits.

- **Focus on real-world infrastructure deployment.** The bulk of the recommendations focus on putting shovel-ready clean technologies in the ground to fix and upgrade America's ailing infrastructure, create jobs, and repay loans from ongoing revenue streams.

- **Leverage private capital and keep public funding for the "edges."** The plans are not about government largesse. Instead of overly rich and unsustainable subsidies, the programs work to maximize private investment flow and limit public capital to the "edges," where subsidies or low-cost capital make all the difference. Over the next ten years, our goal is to end all energy subsidies for mature sectors—starting with oil and gas, then nuclear—and finally phasing them out for solar PV, wind, and other clean technologies.

- **Inspire and exploit American innovation.** The U.S. is a global leader in patent activity, university research, and venture-backed creation. The programs outlined above aim to leverage this unique American resource and ensure the creation of the Googles and Apples of clean tech.

We will not get a top-down energy plan like China's; that's not the American model. "We don't typically write broad plans that dictate very specifically how we proceed as a country in big, broad areas," says Stanford's Dan Reicher. "It tends to be more of a bottom-up process that comes out of government, banks, Silicon Valley, and elsewhere. And given the complexity of energy, the broad range of technologies, the extraordinary range of financing needs, and the various venues for policy at the local, state, and national level, I'm not very hopeful that we can get a comprehensive plan—or that we need one."

This is a sage observance of the U.S. market, and a key differentiator of the U.S. compared with China's far more top-down control. It's the contrast between a western-frontier mentality that can sometimes seem lawless and unruly compared with a more regimented, toe-the-line autocracy.

But at the same time, the market abhors nothing more than uncertainty. If the U.S. is to succeed, we'll need an amalgam of innovative public and private actions that work in concert and provide market certainty. We'll need dedicated commitments like we've had for past industrial shifts.

The drivers for action are clear and multifold. They span from the macro down to the personal, and will determine everything from the types of vehicles we drive to how we generate, store, and transmit energy to how we construct our buildings and guarantee fresh water supplies. The coming decade will determine what types of clean-tech products, services, and models the U.S. develops and innovates for its own consumption and—even more important for global economic competitiveness—exports to the rest of the world.

Make no mistake: Like past industrial shifts, from railroads and telephony to airplanes and computers, U.S. leadership in clean tech is not a fait accompli. It will require carefully orchestrated business, investment, social, and political actions, with great and far-reaching implications. The choice is clearly ours. The steps we take in the next decade will define who we are as a people and determine whether we are able to ensure our status as a robust and competitive Clean Tech Nation.

POLICY CHECKLIST (1–25)

State columns (ranked 1–25): MA, NY, CA, WA, OR, NM, NH, MN, CT, IL, DE, ME, MT, RI, CO, NJ, MI, NC, WI, HI, MD, VT, FL, TX, NV

REGULATIONS & MANDATES

Qualifying States	Policy Category Rank
29	Renewable Portfolio Standard
16	Strong RPS: At least 20% by 2020 or 25% by 2025
26	Smart RPS: No Clean Coal
28	Smart RPS: No Nuclear
9	Smart RPS: No Large Hydro
27	Energy Efficiency Resource Standard
11	State Renewable Fuel Standard
37	Climate Action Plan
18	GHG Reduction Target
10	Membership in Active Regional Climate Initiative
14	Low Carbon Fuel Standard
36	State Fleet High Efficiency Vehicle Requirement
8	Mandated Green Power Purchasing Option
42	Interconnection Law/Policy
46	Net Metering Law/Policy
n/a	Commercial Building Energy Policy
n/a	Residential Building Energy Policy

INCENTIVES

Qualifying States	Policy Category Rank
25	Grants - Renewable Energy
24	Grants - Energy Efficiency
48	Loans - Renewable Energy
48	Loans - Energy Efficiency
46	Rebates - Renewable Energy
50	Rebates - Energy Efficiency
3	Bonds - Renewable Energy
3	Bonds - Energy Efficiency
20	Clean-Tech Vehicle Purchasing Incentive
27	Utility Revenue Decoupling - Electricity
27	Utility Revenue Decoupling - Natural Gas
31	Utility Performance Incentives - Electricity
19	Utility Performance Incentives - Natural Gas
29	Utility On-Bill Financing

Source: Clean Edge, Inc., 2011.

POLICY CHECKLIST (26–50)

Policy Category	Rank	IA	IN	PA	KY	KS	AZ	VA	UT	MO	OH	GA	ID	SC	TN	LA	OK	AR	SD	AL	WY	NE	AK	MS	ND	WV
		26	27	28	29	30	31	32	33	34	34	36	37	38	39	40	41	42	43	44	44	46	47	48	48	50
REGULATIONS & MANDATES																										
Renewable Portfolio Standard		—	—	—			—	—	—	—	—															
Strong RPS: At least 20% by 2020 or 25% by 2025																										
Smart RPS: No Clean Coal																										
Smart RPS: No Nuclear		—	—							—																
Smart RPS: No Large Hydro																										
Energy Efficiency Resource Standard		—	—	—						—																
State Renewable Fuel Standard																										
Climate Action Plan				—					—																	
GHG Reduction Target																										
Membership in Active Regional Climate Initiative																										
Low Carbon Fuel Standard																										
State Fleet High Efficiency Vehicle Requirement																										
Mandated Green Power Purchasing Option																										
Interconnection Law/Policy		—	—	—	—	—	—	—	—	—	—	—	—	—	—	—	—	—	—	—	—	—	—	—	—	—
Net Metering Law/Policy		—	—	—	—	—	—	—	—	—	—	—	—	—	—	—	—	—	—	—	—	—	—	—	—	—
Commercial Building Energy Policy		●	●	●	●	○	○	●	●	●	○	○	○	●	●	○	○	○	○	○	○	○	●	○	○	○
Residential Building Energy Policy		●	○	●	●	○	○	●	●	●	○	○	○	●	●	●	○	○	○	○	○	○	○	○	○	○
INCENTIVES																										
Grants - Renewable Energy		—	—	—						—																
Grants - Energy Efficiency		—	—	—						—																
Loans - Renewable Energy		—	—	—						—																
Loans - Energy Efficiency		—	—	—						—																
Rebates - Renewable Energy		—	—	—						—																
Rebates - Energy Efficiency		—	—	—						—																
Bonds - Renewable Energy		—	—							—																
Bonds - Energy Efficiency		—	—							—																
Clean-Tech Vehicle Purchasing Incentive		—	—							—																
Utility Revenue Decoupling - Electricity				—						—																
Utility Revenue Decoupling - Natural Gas				—						—																
Utility Performance Incentives - Electricity																										
Utility Performance Incentives - Natural Gas																										
Utility On-Bill Financing																										

Source: Clean Edge, Inc., 2011.

ACKNOWLEDGMENTS

Many people were instrumental in the conception and writing of *Clean Tech Nation*. We would like to thank particularly our colleague at Clean Edge, senior research analyst Trevor Winnie, whose tireless contributions in both research and writing made him a true partner in the completion of this book (his first, but we feel certain, not his last). Our agent, Leah Spiro of Riverside Creative Management, has inspired and motivated us with her passion and enthusiasm for this book from day one. Colleen Lawrie, our editor at HarperCollins, has been a pleasure to work with—a consummate professional with a keen eye for readability. And the other members of our Clean Edge team, including Bryce Yonker and Sean Sosnovec, have been great supporters and made sure to keep the company engines running throughout the book-writing process. We also owe deep thanks to Clean Edge designers Kelly Perso and Tanya Nelson for helping to visualize our data so clearly and effectively.

Ron Pernick would like to first and foremost thank his wife, Dena Shehab, and his children, Jonah and Sanaa, who supported and inspired him throughout the book-writing process. Professionally, I would like to recognize the many people who have influenced my career for nearly three decades, including Clean Edge strategic advisers Joel Makower, Nick Rothenberg, and Alan Caplan; past managers who taught me how to be my best, including Melody Haller, Bruce Katz, Ed Niehaus, Ken Orton, Danica Remy, and Bill Ryan; and the countless colleagues and clients who have inspired, pushed, and educated me in such far-flung places as Detroit, Kobe, and San Francisco. Many clean-tech and sustainable-business luminaries have contributed to my ongoing education, development, and inspiration, including the more than 150 thought leaders who have spoken at our annual Clean-Tech Investor Summit in Palm Springs, among them Ray Anderson, Janine Benyus, Majora Carter, Ralph Cavanagh, Stuart Hart, Amory Lovins, Hunter Lovins, Elon Musk, T. Boone Pickens, Carl Pope, Bill Ritter, and Tom Steyer. And of course I owe the deepest debt of gratitude to my colleague, friend, and coauthor, Clint Wilder, without whom this book and our earlier collaboration, *The Clean Tech Revolution*, would not have been possible.

Clint Wilder would like to thank his sister, Rachel, and brother, Rob, and their families—and his extended family of in-laws, the Barretts, Lokitzes, and Knapps—for being such great fans and supporters. Thanks also to many friends and colleagues who contributed ideas, inspiration, and support in countless ways: Hunter Lovins, Joe Khirallah, Diane Rezendes, Sean Monahan, Justin Bean, Bret Mueller, John Mejia, Joel Makower, Nadine Weil, Brad and Kim Fisher, Pete Pedersen, Nancy Bargar, Bob and Pam Bowers, Holly Egan, Steven Herrmann, Julie Mahony, Gina Catania, Edyta Saltsman, Harvey Bartnof, JoAnn Scordino, Kelly Fitzgerald, Alison Hotchkiss, Kelsey Sheofsky, Alyssa Brown, Susie Papadin, Esin Karliova, Rafi Kushick,

Sarah Glicken, Lucinda Jewell, Bas van der Veen, Bunny and Dick Blattner, Steve Abt, Bob Howe, Sam Teeple, Allen Rivers, Mike Bradley, Noreen Doyle, Chab Betz, Karen Jackson, Chloe Byruck, Peter Schmale, Kristen Steck, and too many others to name here. To my coauthor and friend, Ron Pernick, for our decade of partnership and two books, helping steer the nation and the world toward a cleantech future. And thanks finally to my wife, Ellie, for all your patience, advice, support, and love.

NOTES

INTRODUCTION

Data and analysis for this chapter came from a range of research reports, in-person interviews, and our ongoing research and outreach activities at Clean Edge. As noted in the text, the original presentation of the "Six C's," the global forces moving clean tech forward, appeared in our first book, *The Clean Tech Revolution* (HarperCollins, 2007). Reports from Clean Edge included *Clean Energy Trends 2011*, the *2011 State Clean Energy Leadership Index*, and a March 2011 report on clean-energy pricing. Other reports cited and researched included Cleantech Group's annual tracking of clean-tech venture capital investments, January 2011; the U.S. Energy Information Administration's *Monthly Energy Review*, July 2011; annual tracking of global clean-energy investments by Bloomberg New Energy Finance, January 2011; *Powering Autos to 2020: The Era of the Electric Car?*, Boston Consulting Group, July 2011; and the *Carbon Disclosure Project Global 500 Report 2011*, September 2011. Interviews included Bill Watkins and Steve Lester of Bridgelux and Alan Salzman of VantagePoint Venture Partners. Other sources cited were articles from Bloomberg and *The Atlantic*, and L. Hunter Lovins and Boyd Cohen's *Climate Capitalism: Capitalism in the Age of Climate Change* (Hill and Wang, 2011).

CHAPTER 1: THE GLOBAL LANDSCAPE

A range of public reports were used for this chapter, including *Renewables 2011 Global Status Report*, by REN21, July 2011; *Market Report 2011*, by the European Photovoltaic Industry Association; *Renewable Energy Country Attractiveness Indices*, by

Ernst & Young; and *Who's Winning the Clean Energy Race?* by the Pew Charitable Trusts and Bloomberg New Energy Finance, March 2011. Media and online research included references from Bloomberg, *Clean Edge News, China Daily, The Economist, Financial Times, The Guardian, The New York Times,* and *Reuters.* Interviews for this chapter included talks with a range of clean-tech venture capital, political, and corporate stakeholders, including Andrew Beebe, Suntech Power; Andrew Wilson, New England Clean Energy Foundation; David Yeh, clean-tech angel and entrepreneur; Jesse Pichel, Jefferies; Ron Kenedi, solar-industry veteran and consultant; Holmes Hummel, U.S. Department of Energy; and Nancy Floyd, Nth Power. Additional research was culled from Clean Edge's annual *Clean Energy Trends* and *State Clean Energy Leadership Index* reports and from a survey of Clean Edge's more than 30,000 newsletter subscribers.

CHAPTER 2: VYING FOR LEADERSHIP

Much of this chapter's material—including the state data, rankings, and performance scores—is derived from the 2011 edition of Clean Edge's *State Clean Energy Leadership Index,* a subscription service that aggregates state-level industry data to provide a comprehensive view of clean tech in the U.S. *State Clean Energy Leadership Index* data sources include the American Council for an Energy-Efficient Economy; American Wind Energy Association; the Aspen Institute; Brookings Institution; Building Codes Assistance Project; the Center for Measuring University Performance; Cleantech Group; Clean Energy Alliance; Consortium for Energy Efficiency; Database of State Incentives for Renewable Energy (DSIRE); Energy Star; Federal Energy Regulatory Commission; Geothermal Energy Association; Heslin Rothenberg Farley & Mesiti P.C.; Interstate Renewable Energy Council; National Renewable Energy Laboratory; Renewable Fuels Association; R. L. Polk & Co.; Solar Energy Industries Association; U.S. Bureau of Economic Analysis; U.S. Department of Energy; U.S. Energy Information Administration; U.S. Environmental Protection Agency; and the U.S. Green Building Council. Other important sources for this chapter include *20% Wind Energy by 2030: Increasing Wind Energy's Contribution to U.S. Electricity Supply,* U.S. Department of Energy, July 2008; Lester R. Brown, *World on the Edge* (Norton & Company, 2011); "How Biomass Energy Works," Union of Concerned Scientists, October 29, 2010; Kathie Bassett, "Net-Zero Energy Development Nearly Done in Jerseyville," *The Alton Telegraph,* July 19, 2011; Iain Carson and Vijay V. Vaitheeswaran, *ZOOM: The Global Race to Fuel the Car of the Future* (Twelve, 2007); Richard Florida, *Who's Your City?* (Basic Books, 2008); *Sizing the Clean Economy: A National and Regional Green Jobs Assessment,* the Brookings Institution, 2011; Christian Gaston, "State Tax Break Aids SolarWorld, Walmart," *Portland Tribune,* April 9, 2009; *A Future of Innovation and Growth: Advancing Massachusetts' Clean-Energy Leadership,* Clean Edge, April 2010; Amanda Little, *Power Trip* (HarperCollins, 2009); *Assessing the Electric Productivity Gap and the U.S. Efficiency Opportunity,* Rocky Mountain Institute, January 2009; *California Green Innovation Index 2009,* Next10, 2009.

CHAPTER 3: CENTERS OF INNOVATION

This chapter's list of the top 15 U.S. clean-tech cities, and the underlying data, were drawn from *Clean Tech Job Trends 2010*, a report from Clean Edge and our research partners, Hobbs and Towne, Bloomberg New Energy Finance, PayScale, and Heslin Roth Farley & Mesiti P.C. Other Clean Edge reports cited were the *2011 State Clean Energy Leadership Index* and *Carbon-Free Prosperity 2025*. The July 2011 report from the Brookings Institution and Battelle Memorial Institute, *Sizing the Clean Economy: A National and Regional Green Jobs Assessment*, was a useful source of clean-tech employment data and notable employers in the industry. Additional key research sources were the U.S. Conference of Mayors' June 2011 report, *Clean Energy Solutions for America's Cities;* the U.S. Environmental Protection Agency Green Power Partnership "National Top 50" web page; Richard Florida, *Who's Your City?* (Basic Books, 2008); Michael E. Porter, *The Competitive Advantage of Nations* (Free Press, 1998); and *Scientific American*'s special issue "Cities: Smarter, Greener, Better," September 2011. The chapter also drew heavily from in-person interviews with David Allen, McKinstry; Michael Butler, Cascadia Capital; Jacques Chirazi, City of San Diego; Tom Ranken, Washington Clean Technology Alliance; Susan Leeds, New York City Energy Efficiency Corporation; Ross Macfarlane, Climate Solutions; Matt Maloney, Silicon Valley Bank; and Marc Cummings, Pacific Northwest National Laboratory. The 2011 Clinton Global Initiative Annual Meeting in New York was the source of quotes and information from People's Republic of China minister of foreign affairs Yang Jiechi, California lieutenant governor Gavin Newsom, and Ford Foundation president Luis Ubiñas.

CHAPTER 4: THE BIGGEST CLEAN-TECH DEVELOPMENTS RESHAPING THE WORLD

Material for this chapter drew on a large number of reports and articles from market researchers, industry experts and participants, government organizations, and primary Clean Edge research. For the section titled "Smart Grids and the Utility of the Future," valuable sources included: Om Malik, "For OPower, Cloud, Big Data & Digital Energy Equal Magic," *GigaOM*, April 5, 2011; *China: Rise of the Smart Grid*, ZPryme Research & Consulting, January, 2011; Jesse Berst, "Undeterred by Wall Street Critics, Itron Pursues Ambitious Growth Plan," *Smart Grid News*, June 7, 2011; *The Old Model Isn't Working: Creating the Energy Utility for the 21st Century*, American Council for an Energy-Efficient Economy, September 2011.

For the section titled "The Fast Lane to Vehicle Electrification," key sources were *Will Electric Cars Transform the U.S. Vehicle Market?*, Harvard Kennedy School, July 2011; *Plug-In Electric Vehicles Market: State of Play*, Pew Center on Global Climate Change, July 2011; *Wells-to-Wheels Energy Use and Greenhouse Gas Emissions*, Argonne National Laboratory, February 2009; *Transportation Electrification: A Technology Overview*, Electric Power Research Institute, 2011; Keith Barry, "Croatian Supercar Is Electric for a Reason," *Wired*, September 14, 2011; "Nissan's Carlos Ghosn Seeks Revenge for the Electric Car," *Yale Environment 360*, May 4, 2011; "Making Stuff: Cleaner," *NOVA*, PBS, February 2, 2011; *Plug-In Electric Vehicles: A Practical Plan for Progress*, Indiana University, February 2011.

For the section titled "Green Buildings: Deep Retrofits and Net-Zero Ambitions," sources included: Carolyn Said, "Ford Point Bringing New Life to Richmond," *San Francisco Chronicle*, November 14, 2010; *Weatherization Assistance Program: Program Overview*, U.S. Department of Energy, June 2006; *Building R&D Breakthroughs: Technologies and Products Supported by the Building Technologies Program*, U.S. Department of Energy, May 2011; *Ground-Source Heat Pumps: Overview of Market Status, Barriers to Adoption, and Options for Overcoming Barriers*, Navigant Consulting, February 2009.

For the section titled "One Person's Trash, Another Person's Treasure: The Vast Potential of Waste-to-Resource," important sources were: Jackie Noblett, "Purpose Energy Turns Beer Byproducts into Brewery Power," *Mass High Tech*, February 26, 2010; *Reconsidering Municipal Solid Waste as a Renewable Energy Feedstock*, Environmental and Energy Study Institute, July 2009; *Waste-to-Energy Technology Markets*, Pike Research, December 2010; "Turning French Fries Green and Growing Profitable, Too," *The Huffington Post*, February 4, 2011; "Innovation Awards: Polymers Put CO_2 to Use," *ICIS Chemical Business*, October 17, 2011; *Combined Heat and Power: Effective Energy Solutions for a Sustainable Future*, Oak Ridge National Laboratory, December 2008; Nick Leiber, "Innovator: Matt Scullin, Power Recycler," *Bloomberg Businessweek*, September 29, 2011.

CHAPTER 5: THE CLEAN-TECH IMPERATIVE

This chapter used data and quotes from a variety of interviews, conference presentations, reports, and print and online articles. In-person interviews included Cathy Zoi, Silver Lake Kraftwerk; Matthew Lewis, ClimateWorks Foundation; and Jeff Anderson, Clean Economy Network. Conference presentations included U.S. Marine Corps Major General Anthony Jackson at the Pew Charitable Trusts' Accelerating Clean Energy Conference, at Stanford University, and Mark Vachon of GE Ecomagination at the GreenBiz Innovation Forum, in San Francisco, both in October 2011. Quoted publications included *The Economist*, November 6, 2011; *Science*, November 17, 2011; *Outside*, November 9, 2011; *Computerworld*, July 20, 2009; and the *Wichita Eagle*, September 11, 2011. Articles on the New Energy World Network's *NewNet* were the source of most of the international clean-tech news from September 22, 2011. Research data came from reports including *Getting Back in the Game: U.S. Job Growth Potential from Expanding Clean Technology Markets in Developing Countries*, World Wildlife Fund, 2010; *U.S. Solar Energy Trade Assessment 2011*, GTM Research; and 2011 opinion polls by ORC International (for the Civil Society Institute), Public Opinion Strategies, Kelton Research (for SCHOTT Solar), and the University of Texas.

Sources of U.S. historical references included *The American Economy during World War II*, EH.net, February 2010; Wikipedia.org; *Government as a Catalyst for Innovation*, a 2011 report provided by Cathy Zoi; and Walter Isaacson's *Steve Jobs* (Simon & Schuster, 2011). For the Transformers profiles, sources of quotes and information included company, nonprofit-organization, and government websites; *Fast Company*; *Denver Business Journal*; *Forbes*; *LiveScience*; *Grist*; *Harvard* magazine; conference presentations or speeches by Tom Steyer, Major General Anthony Jackson, Ray Mabus, Scott Lang, and Vinod Khosla; and interviews with Reed Hundt and Nancy Floyd.

CHAPTER 6: A SEVEN-POINT ACTION PLAN FOR REPOWERING AMERICA

In-depth interviews for this chapter included Ira Ehrenpreis, Technology Partners; Daniel Esty, Connecticut Department of Energy and Environmental Protection; Matt Cheney, CleanPath; Jeffrey Leonard, Global Environment Fund; Jonathan Powers, U.S. Army; Doug Payne, SolarTech; Nicole Lederer, Environmental Entrepreneurs (E2); Alisa Gravitz, Green America; Scott Jacobs, McKinsey; Denis Hayes, Bullit Foundation; Tim Woodward, Nth Power; Dan Reicher, Steyer-Taylor Center for Energy Policy and Finance at Stanford University; and Andrew Shapiro, GO Ventures. In addition to the above interviews, our "Seven-Point Action Plan" ideas were pulled from a survey of Clean Edge's more than 30,000 newsletter subscribers. Respondents to the survey provided invaluable ideas and concepts that helped in selecting and forming our final Seven-Point Action Plan recommendations. Additional research came from reports and commentary in a range of publications, including *Report Card for America's Infrastructure*, the American Society of Civil Engineers; "A Bank That Can Get Americans on the Road and on the Job: View," *Bloomberg* editorial, August 2011; "The Case for Master Limited Partnerships" *AOL Energy*, July 2011; *Master Limited Partnerships: A Policy Option for the Renewable Energy Industry*, Congressional Research Service, June 2011; *The Scope of Fossil Fuel Subsidies in 2009 and a Roadmap for Phasing Out Fossil Fuel Subsidies*, International Energy Agency, the Organization for Economic Cooperation and Development, and the World Bank, November 2010; *Green Scissors: Cutting Wasteful and Environmentally Harmful Spending*, Friends of the Earth International, Taxpayers for Common Sense, Public Citizen, and Heartland Institute, August 2011; William A. Masters and Benoit Delbecq, *Accelerating Innovation with Prize Rewards*, International Food Policy Research Institute, December 2008; *What Would Jefferson Do? The Historical Role of Federal Subsidies in Shaping America's Energy Future*, DBL Investors, September 2011; and *From Barracks to the Battlefield*, the Pew Charitable Trusts, September 2011. Additional sources for this chapter included Gartner Group; the U.S. Marine Corps Expeditionary Energy Strategy and Implementation Plan, "Bases-to-Battlefield"; *Washington Monthly*; and the *Tampa Tribune*.

INDEX

Page numbers in *italics* refer to charts and tables.

A123 Systems, 80, 85, 93, 125, 168, 172, 225
ABB Group, 4, 28, 160, 237
Abound Solar, 84, 97, 98
Abu Dhabi, 30
Accelerating Innovation with Prize Rewards (Masters and Delbecq), 269
Accel Partners, 149
Acciona Energy, 134
Adobe, 181
Advanced Energy Economy (AEE), 130, 216, 225
advanced metering infrastructure (AMI), 153
Advanced Research Projects Agency (ARPA), 211
   -Energy (ARPA-E), 196
AeroVironment, 139
AFL-CIO, 251
Afval Energie Bedrijf (AEB), 188
Agassi, Shai, 169, 228
Agilyx, 191

Agradis, 220
agricultural waste, 164, 191
Agriculture, U.S. Department of, 220
air conditioning, 98, 155, 177–79, 183
Air Ground Combat Center, 227
Alaska, 70, 82
Alaska Airlines, 192
Albany, New York, 121, 144–45
Albeo Technologies, 98
Aldrin, Buzz, 212
algae, 131, 164, 193–94, 198, 218, 220–21
AllEarth Renewables, 107
Allen, David, 112
Allen, Paul, 269
Allen, Scott, 194
Allison Transmission, 143
Alphabet Energy, 195–96, 199
Altairnano, 143–44
Alta Wind Energy Center, 63–64
American Clean Skies Foundation, 224
American Council for an Energy-Efficient Economy (ACEEE), 157, 158

American Council on Renewable Energy, 130, 232
American Electric Power, 229
American Petroleum Institute, 216
American Recovery and Reinvestment Act (2009), 74, 171, 178, 269
American Society of Civil Engineers, 249
American Wind Energy Association, 223–24
Ames, Bob, 192
Ames Research Center, 213
Amsterdam, 188–89
Amyris, 88
Anderson, Jeff, 216
Anderson, Ray, 138
Anderson, Steven, 264
Andreessen, Marc, 211
Ansari X Prize, 269
AOL Energy, 253
Apollo Alliance, 212
Apollo moon program, 212–13
Apollo Solar, 105
Apple, 31, 85, 261, 272
  iPhones/iPads, 18, 31, 261
Applied Materials, 122
Aptera Motors, 124
AQUS system, 196–97
Architecture for Humanity, 18
AREVA, 48
Argonne National Laboratory, 51, 135
Arizona, 13, 29, 67, *68*, 75, 79–80, 150–51, 153, 175
Armstrong, Neil, 212
ARPANET, 21, 210–12
Array Technologies, 101
Arup, 221
Aspen Aerogels, 93
Assessing the Electric Productivity Gap, 109
Atlanta, *120*, 121, 137–38
Ausra, 48
Austin, Texas, 79, *120*, 132, 135–36
Austin Energy, 135–36
Austin Technology Incubator, 135–36
Australia, 30, 207, 228
Autodesk Freewheel, 18

automobiles, 6, 7, 10, 14–15, 19, 23, 76–78, 80–83, 117, 124, 143, 163, 162–74. *See also* clean transportation; *and specific manufacturers and vehicle types*

Baker, Brent, 192
Bank of America, 266
  Tower, 118
Bansal, Malay, 253
Barbour, Haley, 215
Bath Iron Works, 210
Battelle Memorial Institute, 123, 127, 128
batteries, *26*, 50–51, 80–81, 95, 103, 108, 125, 128, 138, 143, 165–72, 225, 243, 264–65
  lithium-ion, 12, 51, 80, 93, 96, 135, 143, 168–69, 242
Beebe, Andrew, 24
Bell Labs, 3, 36
Bently Biofuels, 144
Benyus, Janine, 221
Berkeley Earth Surface Temperature Study, 207
Berlusconi, Silvio, 42
Berners-Lee, Tim, 261
Berst, Jesse, 155
Better Place, 84, 169, 172, 228
bicycling, 89, 117
Biden, Joe, 226
biobutanol, 98
biodiesel, 38, 48, 76, 117, 137, 144, 191–92, 198
biodigester, 186
biofuels, 3–5, 39, 49, 102–3, 108, 113, 122, 130–32, 137, 141, 144, 164–65, 171–72, 191–94, 198, 206, 218, 220–21, 231, 268
biogas, 186, 190–91
biomass, 43, 70–71, 90, 108–9, 134, 137, 141, 175, 189, 191, 220, 247
biomimicry, 131, 221
bioplastics, 103–4, 125, 219
biopolymers, 50
biotech, 25, 92, 130
Birmingham, Alabama, 116

Blackstone Group, 222
Bloomberg, Michael, 118, 126–27
Bloomberg Businessweek, 196
Bloomberg New Energy Finance (BNEF), 11, 36, 38, 49
Bloomberg News, 10, 251
Bloom Energy, 181, 184
Bluefire Ethanol, 108
BMW, 167, 171
Bode, Denise, 223
Boeing, 112, 192, 211, 221
Bonneville Power Administration, 64
Boston, 59, 113, 120–21, 125–26, 135, 162
Boston Consulting Group (BCG), 14, 15
Boston Power, 85, 93
Boulder, Colorado, 75–76
Boulder Wind Power, 128–29
BP, 7, 218
BPL Global, 231
Brammo Motorsports, 91
Branstad, Terry, 215
Braungart, Michael, 233
Brazil, 8, 14, 20, 24, 27, 30, 49–50, 250
Bridgelux, 1, 10, 184
Bright Automotive, 143–44
BrightSource Energy, 10, 84, 88, 252
Brightworks, 140
British Gas, 47
Bronicki, Lucien and Dita, 144
Brookings Institution, 82, 123, 127–28
Brown, Jerry, 88, 246
Brown, Lester, 69
Brownback, Sam, 215
Buffett, Warren, 124
building codes, 55, 73, 176
building materials, 193–94. *See also* green building
Bureau of Energy Resources, 205–6
Bush, George H. W., 133
Bush, George W., 53, 62, 213, 247
business advocacy groups, 216–17
Business Energy Tax Credit (BETC) program, 90
Butler, Michael, 115
Butterfield, Sandy, 129
BYD Auto, 124, 173

CAFE standards, 163
Calera, 194, 199
California, 5, 13, 28, 29, 35, 59–64, 66–67, 69–73, 83–90, 106, 109–10, 211, 237
companies, 88–89
California Assembly Bill 1890 (1996), 88
California Energy Commission, 233–34
California Global Warming Solutions Act (AB 32, 2006), 88, 141, 216, 223
Californians for Clean Energy and Jobs, 225
California Preservation Foundation Design Award, 174
California Proposition 23, 216, 217, 224
Caltech, 124
Cameron, David, 47
Canada, 15, 30, 50, 228
Canadian Solar, *32*
cap-and-trade, 15, 94, 141, 213
capital, 11, 118. *See also* financial capital and investment; human capital; venture capital
CapitalFusion Partners, 253
Carbon Disclosure Project (CDP), 16, 192
carbon emissions (CO_2), 15–17, *26*, 46, 95, 109, 118, 126, 141, 163, 176, 181, 207–8, 213, 215–16, 241, 244–45
low- and zero- sources, 7–8, 90, 94, 98–99, 244
taxes on, 207, 245
waste-to-resource and, 189–90, 193–94, 198
Carbon-Free Prosperity 2025, 136
Carson, Iain, 81
Carter, Jimmy, 204–5
Cascade Investment, 131
Cascadia Capital, 115
Castellaw, John, 264
Catchlight Energy, 137
cement, 193–94
Center for Building Science, 234
Center for Market Innovation, 118
Center for Sustainable Energy Systems, 126

Center for the New Energy Economy, 54–55

Central Intelligence Agency (CIA), 130, 205

CFLs (compact fluorescent light-bulbs), 7, 13, 179, 184, 213

C40 Cities Climate Leadership Group, 126

CH2M Hill, 140, 185

Changzhou, China, 23

Charette, Bob "Brutus," 206

chemicals, 23, 88, 104, 193–94

Chernobyl disaster, 42

Chevrolet, 173
  Volt, 51, 76–77, 79, 80, 117, 135, 162, 166, 167

Chevron, 7, 137

Chicago, 120–21, 134–35, 162

Chicago Infrastructure Trust, 134

China, 8, 11–15, 20, 22–24, 27–36, 70, 139, 201, 203–4, 225, 228, 235–37, 240, 245, 272–73
  batteries, 168
  companies, 31, 35
  green building, 175, 181, 183
  India vs., 44–45
  infrastructure banks, 250
  IP, 24, 34–35
  Japan vs., 40
  jobs, 32
  smart grid, 151–52
  solar, 9, 23, 27, 41–42, 65, 181, 238
  transportation, 27, 163, 170
  urbanization, 113
  waste-to-resource, 195

Chirazi, Jacques, 131

Chrysler, 220

Cisco, 17, 122

Citibank, 134

cities, 12, 21, 36, 55, 80–82, 89, 111–46, 243–44
  leading large, 111, 117–42
  leading smaller, 121, 142–45
  three pillars and, 118–19

Civil Society Institute, 214, 260

Claremont Creek Ventures, 195–96

Clark, Wesley, 205

Clean Economy Network, 216

Clean Edge, 10, 20–21, 24, 25, 31, 52, 54, 56, 68, 92, 108, 119–20, 136, 209, 236, 238, 245

Clean Energy Patent Growth Index, 101

clean energy sector, 22, 25. See also renewable energy; and specific types
  taxonomy, 26, 117

Clean Energy Works Oregon, 141

Clean Line Energy, 133

CleanStart initiative, 141

Clean Tech Corridor, 125

Cleantech Group, 4, 35, 92

Clean-Tech Investor Summit, 225

Clean Tech Job Trends 2010, 120, 128

Clean Tech Revolution, The, 8, 12, 15, 147, 150

CleanTECH San Diego, 132

clean transportation, 21–22, 25–27, 78, 127, 148, 162–74. See also electric vehicles; hybrid vehicles; mass transit
  cities and, 117
  companies, 172–74
  states and, 57, 76–81, 87, 89, 99, 123, 125
  taxonomy, 26

ClearEdge Power, 185

climate, 15–17, 39, 90, 163, 193, 206–8, 265

Climate Capitalism (Lovins and Cohen), 16

Climate Solutions, 112, 136

ClimateWorks Foundation, 215

Clinton, Bill, 222, 227

Clinton, Hillary, 206

Clinton Climate Initiative, 123–24

clustering, 91, 113–14, 116–18, 140–41, 144–45, 172

coal-fired plants, 34, 39, 46, 99, 108, 123, 213, 191, 240–41, 248, 259

Coalition for Green Capital (CGC), 130, 221–22, 249–50

Coates, Geoff, 194

Coca-Cola, 138

Cochran, Tom, 114

CODA Automotive, 124
cogeneration, 182, 195–96
Cohen, Boyd, 16
collaboration, 18–20, 24, 119, 204
Colorado, 35, 53–54, 59, 68, 72–76, 80, 85, 96–98, 110, 120, 128–29, 223, 247
　companies, 91, 98
Colorado Clean Air Jobs Act, 54
Colorado Climate Action Plan, 54
Colorado State University, 54–55, 74, 129
Columbia Ridge landfill, 137
combined heat and power (CHP) 182, 195
Commerce, U.S. Department of, 136
Commonwealth Edison, 149
Commuter Cars, 145
companies to watch, 15–16, 216–17
　California, 88–89
　China, 12
　clean transportation, 172–74
　Colorado, 98
　Connecticut, 105–6
　France and, 48–49
　green building, 184–86
　Japan, 41
　Massachusetts, 93–94
　Minnesota, 103–4
　New Mexico, 101–2
　New York, 96
　Oregon, 90–92
　smart grid, 160–61
　South Korea, 50
　three pillars and, 28–29
　Vermont, 107
　Washington, 99–100
　waste-to-resource, 199–200
competition, 11–13, 20, 24, 204, 235, 249
Competitive Advantage of Nations, The (Porter), 117
composting, 190, 197–98
computers, 25, 122, 177, 212
Comverge, 17, 138, 155–56, 160, 231
concentrating solar power (CSP), 36, 65, 84, 88, 101, 124
Congressional Research Service, 254

Connecticut, 59, 68, 78, 83, 83, 104–6, 109, 222, 251
　companies, 105–6
Connecticut Clean Energy Finance and Investment Authority (CEFIA), 104
Connecticut Department of Energy and Environmental Protection, 104, 251
Connecticut Green Loan Guaranty Fund, 104
connectivity, 17–20, 116
ConocoPhillips, 7
Conservation Services Group, 93
Consortium for Energy Efficiency, 93
consumers, 13–15
Conto Energia (Italy), 43
cooking oil, 191–92
Cornell University, 127, 194
Costa Rica, 221
costs, 8–10, 68, 76, 106, 152–53, 157–59, 162, 168, 180–81, 184, 238–39, 255–56
Covanta, 199
Cradle to Cradle (McDonough and Braungart), 233
Credit Suisse, 14
Cree, 185
crowdsourcing, 18–19
crystalline-silicon solar modules, 23
Cummings, Marc, 133
Cymbet, 103
Czech Republic, 27, 30

Daley, Richard M., 134
Dallas–Fort Worth, 120, 138–39
DARPA, 211
DBL Investors, 259
decoupling, 158–59
Defense, U.S. Department of (DOD, Pentagon), 130, 205–6, 211–12, 265–67
Delaware, 83
Delbecq, Benoit, 269
demand-response services, 155–56, 159
Democratic Party, 37, 213, 224, 232, 235, 247, 251
Deng, Xunming, 143

Denmark, 6, 30, *32*, 35, 46, 169, 195, 228, 243
Denver, 97, *120*, 128–29, 133
deployment pillar, 28–29, 108–9, 118
deregulation, 157
desalination, *26*
Detroit, 117, 124, 243
Deutsche Bank, 118–19
Diamandis, Peter, 269
Dillinger Hütte, 201
direct-consumption subsidies, 256–57
distributed energy, 153, 158–59, 243–44
Dow Chemical, 35, 50, 218–19
DSM, 194
Dynamic Fuels, 192
Dynapower, 107

Eaton, 80
Echelon, 155, 160
EcoFab, 112
economic recession, 2–3, 11, 114–16, 153, 202–4
Economist, The, 81
EcoSalon, 222
ECOtality, 139, 173
Ecova, 145
Edison, Thomas, 147, 195
Efficiency Vermont, 106, 107
Ehrenpreis, Ira, 236
electric cars. *See* EVs; hybrid vehicles
electricity. *See also* specific types
    costs, 10, 67–68, 104
    demand, 71–72, 75, 87, 106, 152, 175, 178–79
    generation, 5, 6, 23, 37–38, 47, 49, 53, *57*, 90, 98–99, 102, 110, 114, 234
    infrastructure, 28
    productivity gap, 109
    types, 59–65, 70–71
Electrovaya, 145
Element Partners, 138
Emanuel, Rahm, 134
Emcore, 101
Emissions Technology, 132
Empire State Building, 127–28, 178
Enel Green Power, 43–44
Enercon, 38

EnerDel, 143
EnerG2, 100
Energias de Portugal, 133
EnergyConnect, 28
Energy Control, 102
Energy, U.S. Department of (DOE), 60, 63, 68, 80, 97, 128–29, 131, 133, 136, 138, 144, 176–77, 195–96, 206, 234, 247, 262, 268
energy efficiency, 8, 17, 22, 72, 142, 148, 167, 176–80, 195, 233–34, 240, 242, 252
    cities and, 117, 122, 125–27, 132, 134, 141
    companies, 28, 93
    RPS, 247
    sector taxonomy, *26*
    states and, *57*, 87, 92–93, 95, 99, 103–4, 106–7, 109, 233–34
    utilities and, 158–59
EnergyHub, 96
Energy Independence and Security Act (2007), 213
Energy Innovations, 124
Energy Initiatives Office Task Force (U.S. Army), 266
energy management, 93, 96, 102, 138, 149–50, 159
Energy Sciences Institute (Yale University), 225
energy security, 12–13, 17, 19–20, 204–6, 263–67
Energy Star buildings, 73, 106
energy storage, 36, 85, 91, 92, 93, 98, 100, 131, 136, 144, 153, 156, 159, 156, 160, 179, 241
    taxonomy, *26*
energy subsidies, 256–60
energy transitions, 244–45
EnerKem, 108, 191
EnerNOC, 93–94, 126, 155–56, 160
Enerpulse, 102
Enrico Fermi Award, 234
Entrepreneur, 186
Environmental Defense Fund, 233
Environmental Entrepreneurs (E2), 222–23

Environmental Protection Agency (EPA), 62, 73, 133, 189, 267
Epstein, Bob, 222–23
eSolar, 124
Esty, Daniel, 104, 251
ethanol, 27, 48, 49–50, 76, 103, 137, 191–92, 198, 258
e2e Materials, 96
eVgo Freedom Stations, 139
EV Project, 79–80, 131
EVs (all-electric vehicles), 6, 10, 12–15, 25–27, 29, 48, 76–81, 87, 99, 108, 122, 124, 128, 131, 137, 139, 141–45, 148, 160, 162–74; 225, 231, 243
    battery swaps, 84, 169, 228
    charging stations, 14, 26, 79–80, 87, 89–90, 124, 131, 134, 139, 163, 169, 171–72
    companies, 16, 89, 91, 172–74
    prizes, 268
Exelon, 56
Exergonix, 108
Exide Technologies, 138
Export-Import Bank, 250
ExxonMobil, 7, 131, 220

Facebook, 18, 149
Farallon Capital Management, 224–25
Fast Company, 218
Federal Communications Commission (FCC), 222
Federal Energy Regulatory Commission (FERC), 64
federal policy, 21–22, 55, 60, 64–65, 115, 163, 171, 176, 201–13, 222. See also taxes
    funding, 36, 128, 136, 141, 143, 151, 194
    history of, 208–13
    incentives, 64–65, 80, 83
    infrastructure bank, 222, 249–52
    loan guarantees, 123, 144, 201
    national energy plan, 35
    need for, 201–6
    prizes, 267–71
    purchases, 80, 130
    RPS, 246–48
    smart grid, 151–52

subsidies, 256–60
tax credits, 10, 74, 252
feed-in tariffs (FITs), 38, 43, 47
Fen Farm installation, 47
Fermi, Enrico, 234
Fernandez, John, 8
Ferrari, Enzo, 167
financial capital and investment, 11, 16, 35–37, 208–10. See also venture capital
    Brazil, 49–50
    China, 30–31, 36, 113
    cities and, 95, 113, 119, 125, 131, 135, 141
    Germany, 38
    green banks, 222, 248–42
    India, 45
    Japan, 40
    leveraging tools for, 252–56
    states and, 57, 83–85, 97, 95, 104, 108–10
Finland, 195
Firefly, 136
First Solar, 28, 67, 143, 238
First Utility, 149
Fisker Automotive, 80, 124
Fisker Karma, 143
Fitch, Eric, 186–87
5 Channel Center, 126
FloDesign, 85, 94
Florida, 71, 79, 82, 83
Florida, Richard, 81–82
Florida Power & LIght, 154, 229
Floyd, Nancy, 37, 231–32
FMC-Tech, 19
Forbes, 224
Ford, Gerald, 115
Ford, Henry, 162
Ford Motor, 6, 80, 117, 167, 174–75, 210, 233
Fort Collins, Colorado, 74, 129
FortZED project, 74, 129
fossil fuels, 10, 34, 54, 106, 108–9, 132–33, 189, 216–17, 237, 241
    subsidies, 256–60, 259
Fox News, 206
France, 30, 35, 48–49, 153, 176

Frank, Andrew, 142
Fraunhofer Institute, 126
Friends of the Earth, 258
Frito-Lay Casa Grande facility, 175, 176
From Barracks to the Battlefield, 266–67
Fuel-Cell Energy, 10405
Fuel Cells 2000, 105
fuel cells, 83, 103–6, 109, 122, 145, 156,
    181, 184
  vehicles, 103, 164–65
fuel efficiency, 163–65, 172
Fukushima disaster, 37, 41, 240
Future of Innovation and Growth, A, 92

Gamesa, 130
gasoline taxes, 170
Gates, Bill, 131, 194, 203, 218
Gates Foundation, 112
General Compression, 93
General Electric (GE), 4, 8, 10, 35, 50,
    129, 152, 153, 160–61, 221, 228,
    237–39, 241
  Capital, 119
  Ecomagination, 18, 50, 144, 208, 270
  Energy, 145
  Global Research, 95, 96, 144
  Open Innovation Challenge, 18–19
  prizes, 270
General Motors (GM), 51, 77, 80, 166,
    210
Generation Investment Management, 27
Genomatica, 191
Georgia, *75*, 80, 121
geothermal energy, 5, 39, 41, 43, 55, 60,
    61, 69–70, 90, 127, 130, 144, 182,
    237, 247–48
Geothermal Energy Association, 69
Gerding Edlen, 91, 140
German, Jacob, 162
Germany, 8, 11, 13, 20, 22, 24, 27, 29,
    34–35, 37–43, 47, 65, 176, 201–3,
    204, 235–38, 245
  nuclear phase-out, 37–40, 240, 248
Getaround, 18
Getting Back in the Game, 203–4
Gevo, 98
Geysers complex, 69

Ghosn, Carlos, 77, 167
GigaOM, 149
Gillard, Julia, 207
global competition, 11–12, 20–21,
    23–52, 113, 116, 163, 170–71, 182–
    83, 203, 235, *238*, 245. *See also*
    specific countries
Global Environment Fund, 259
Goldman Sachs, 133, 181
Goldwind, 134
Google, 4, 17, 63–64, 85, 122, 149, 154,
    244, 252–53, 260–61, 272
Google Ventures, 18
Go Solar California campaign, 66
government policy, 17. *See also* cities;
    federal policy; politics; states; *and*
    specific policies
  Brazil, 49
  business advocacy, 216–17, 231–32
  China, 32–33, 203
  cities, 115–18, 121–22, 124–25, 127,
    130, 136–37, 139, 140–41
  climate, 206–8
  Germany, 37–40, 203
  incentives, 85, 87–88, 90, 94–95, 99,
    108, 116, 171
  Italy, 43
  Japan, 40
  loan guarantees, 97, 123, 144, 201, 257
  loans, 104, 118–19, 201
  national energy plans, 35
  pillar, 118
  purchasing, 117, 130, 133, 135, 139
  South Korea, 50
  states, 53–54, *57*, 59–60, 62, 66,
    86–88, 90, 94–95, 100–105, 108–9,
    145, 215–16, 222
  transportation, 80, 171
  UK, 46–47, 202
Governors' Wind Energy Coalition, 215
Granholm, Jennifer, 225–26
Great Depression, 250
green banks, 36, 104, 105, 222, 251, 250
green building, 3, 21–22, 25, *26*, 28,
    36, 118–19, 148, 174–86, 202, 221,
    233, *238*, 249
  cities and, 114, 127–28, 136–40

companies, 184–86
states and, *57*, 71–74, 89, 91, 100, 102, 106
green chemistry, *26*, 191, 194
GreenChoice option, 135
greenhouse-gas (GHG) emissions, 14–16, 88, 175, 189, 193–94, 206–7, 223. *See also* carbon emissions
Green New Deal (South Korea), 50
Green Power Partnership, 133
green power purchases, 130, 133, 139
Greenprint Denver program, 129
green roofs, 134, 233
Green Scissors, 258
Green to Gold (Esty and Winston), 104, 251
Greenwise Initiative, 141
GridWise Alliance, 130, 262
groSolar, 107
Gross, Bill, 124
GTM Research, 204

Hagman, Larry, 13
Hanwha Solarfun, *32*
Hanwha SolarOne, 201
Harrisburg, Pennsylvania, 116
Hawaii, 67, *68*, *70*, *78*, *79*, 80, 228, 247
Healey, Ben, 259
Heartland Institute, 258
heat-and-power facilities, 191
heating and cooling, 177–78, 180, 182–83, 195
heat pumps, 74, 182
Heritage Foundation, 258
Herman Miller, 221
Hickenlooper, John, 129
Hickory Ridge Landfill, 138
high tech, 4, 17–18, 23, 25, 92, 117, 122, 237
Himin Solar Energy Group, 181, 185
HKS Architects, 139
Hobbs & Towne, 119
Home Depot, 6, 13
Honda, 6, 40, 124
Honeywell, 149
Hoosier Heavy Hybrid, 143
Hoover Institution, 258

Horizon Wind Energy, 133
Houston, *120*, 132–33
HRFM, 101
HSBC, 228
Hubbard, G. Scott, 212
human capital, 45, *57*, 81–82, 90, 109, 112–13, 125, 129–30, 134–35, 137
Humvee, 143
Hundt, Reed, 221–22, 250
Hunt Power, 254
hybrid vehicles, 3, 6, 13, 15, *26*, 40, 50, 77–80, 87, 89–90, 99, 102, 106, 124, 138, 141, 143, 165–66, 169, 171–72, 238
plug-in (PHEV), *26*, 76–77, 117, 142, 166, 169, 171–72
hydroelectricity, 5, 6, 41, 43–44, 49, 64, 70–71, 90, 112, 247–48
hydrogen fuel, 76, 103, 130, 164–65
Hydrovolts, 100, 112

Iberdrola Renewables, 91
IBM, 4, 17, 35
Ice Energy, 98, 178–79, 185
Iceland, 30
ICIS Chemical Business, 194
Idaho, 70, 75, 153
Idealab, 124
IEEE, 261
IHS Global Insight, 31
IKEA, 13
Illinois, 59, *72*, 73–74, 80, 82–83, 134–35
Imbler, Jim, 219–20
Immelt, Jeffrey, 8
Independent Petroleum Association of America, 223
India, 14–15, 18, 24, 27, 29, 44–46, 163, 170, 183, 240, 243
Indianapolis, 121, 143–44
Indonesia, 14
infrastructure, 34, 44–45, 71–76, 95, 110, 115, 249, 272
national bank for, 248–42
U.S. history and, 208–13
Inner Mongolia, 24
Innovation and Entrepreneurship Center, 128

insulation (weatherization), 93, 176–78, 183. *See also* green building
integrated resource planning, 99
Intel, 4, 29, 85, 122, 133, 222
intellectual property (IP, patents), 24, 29, 34–35, 40, *57*, 82–83, 101, 104–5, 109, 113, 120, 144, 269
  pillar, 28
Interface Engineering, 140
internal combustion engines (ICEs), 164, 165, 167, 169
International Energy Agency (IEA), 31, 204, 256, 257, 259
International Living Building Institute, 176
Internet, 17–21, 210–12, 244, 261
Iosil Energy, 102
Iowa, 5, 59, 60, 62, 102, 215–16, 237, 238
Iowa Wind Energy Association, 63
Iran, 13, 19
Ireland, 19
Isaacson, Walter, 213
Isofoton, 143
Israel, 18, 30, 169, 228
Issa, Darrell, 201
Italy, 27, 29, 38, 42–44, 47, 65
Itron, *32*, 100, 145, 154–55, 161
Ivanpah project, 252

Jackson, Anthony, 205, 227
Japan, 20, 24, 27–29, 34–35, 37, 40–42, 44, 78, 151, 165–67, 168–69, 204, 209, 221, 228, 235, 237, 239–40, 245
JA Solar, *32*
jet fuel, 137, 192, 198
Jiangsu Province, china, 23
jobs, 2, 17, 21, 68–69, 82, 97, 102, 108, 110, 112–13, 117, 119–20, 127–29, 134–36, 138, 140, 143, 145, 201–4, 252
  China, 31–32
  Germany, 37–38, 236, 238
  India, 45
  UK, 46
Jobs, Steve, 213
John Hancock Life Insurance, 254
Johnson, Kevin, 141

Johnson Controls, 28, 128, 185
Joshi, John, 253
Joy, Bill, 193–94

Kansas, 215, 217
Kennedy, Robert F., Jr., 222
Kennedy, John F., 212
Khosla, Vinod, 230–31
Khosla Ventures, 194, 230–31
King, Steve, 216
KiOR, 108
Kleiner Perkins Caufield & Byers, 149, 193, 231, 270
KMC Constructions, 202
Koch, Charles and David, 207, 219
Kohl's Department Stores, 133
Konarka, 93
Korea Development Bank, 201
Korea Electric Power, 51
Kuiper, Duane, 13
Kyocera, 41
Kyoto Protocol, 15, 115, 207

LA Cleantech Incubator, 125
landfills, 197
  gas generators, 71, 137, 190, 191, 227
  solar power, 138
Landis+Gyr, 155, 161
Lang, Scott, 229
Lauckner, Jon, 166
Lawrence Berkeley National Laboratory, 234
LDK Solar, *32*
Lederer, Nicole, 222–23
LEDs (light-emitting diode), 1–2, 7, 13, *32*, 50, 98, 114, 124, 136, 179–80, 183, 184, 213–14, 231, 268
LEED (Leadership in Energy and Environmental Design), 7, 72–74, 89, 106, 118, 127–28, 136, 140, 176, 227, *238*
Leeds, Susan, 119, 127
Leffingwell, Lee, 135
Lemnis Lighting, 179
Leno, Jay, 168
Leonard, Jeffrey, 259
LePage, Paul, 215

Leppert, Tom, 139
Lester, Steve, 2
Lewis, Matthew, 214–15
Lexington Farm Estates, 73–74
LG Chem, 51, 80, 168, 173
Libya, 13
lighting, 1–3, 36, 74, 85, 114, 177, 179–80, 184, 213–14, 268. *See also* specific types
Lincoln, Abraham, 208–9
Lindbergh, Charles, 267
Linde, 194
Little, Amanda, 95
Little, Mark, 10, 144–45
Liveris, Andrew, 218–19
Lone Star Wind Farm, 133
Los Alamos National Laboratory, 101
Los Angeles, 84, 115, *120*, 123–25
Los Angeles Department of Water and Power (LADWP), 123, 125
Louisiana, 80
Lovins, Amory, 232–33
Lovins, L. Hunter, 16, 232
Lowe's, 6, 13
L Prize, 268
Luminous (India), 48
Luminus Devices (Massachusetts), 85

Mabus, Ray, 226–27
Macfarlane, Ross, 112
Magic Hat Brewing, 186–87
Magma Energy, 144
Mahindra Reva, 15
Maine, 71, *72*, 215
Majumdar, Arun, 196
Make It in America (Liveris), 219
Malik, Om, 149
Maloney, Matt, 122
Manhattan Project, 209, 234
manufacturing, 3. *See also* specific products
China, 31, 204
closed-loop, 198
pillar, defined, 28
states, 80–81, 90–91, 97, 102, 104, 108, 129, 243–44
WW II and, 209–10

MARTIN, 188, 199
Marubeni Corporation, 254
Maryland, *72*, *78*, 80, *85*, 130
Massachusetts, 29, 35, 59, *68*, *72*, 83, 85, 92–94, 110, 120, 125–26
companies, 93–94
Massachusetts Clean Energy Center, 92
Massachusetts Institute of Technology (MIT), 18, 92, 125–26, 194
Mass High Tech, 186
mass transit, 89, 116–17, 126, 127
master limited partnerships (MLPs), 253–56
Masters, William A., 269
materials, advanced, 25, *26*
biomaterials, 96, 122, 131
captured-carbon, 193–94, 198
McDonough, William, 233
McDonough Braungart Design Chemistry, 233
McFarlane, Robert, 205
McGinn, Dennis, 264
McGraw-Hill, 16
McKinstry, 100, 111–12, 137, 222
MEMC Electronic Materials, 91, 140
Merkel, Angela, 8, 37, 240
Metabolix, 125
metal-organic chemical vapor deposition (MOCVD), 1–2
methane digesters, 190
Mexico, 30, 150
Michigan, 59, 79–83, 135, 225, 243
microgrids, 153, 160
micro-hydro power turbines, 100
Microsoft, 4, 112, 137, 149, 154, 203, 269
microtechnology, 212, 243
MidAmerican Energy, 149
Middle East, 17, 205
Midwest Energy Forum, 134
Million Solar Roofs, 66
Mingyang, 139
Mining Law (1872), 258
Minnesota, 59, 102–4
companies, 103–4
Mississippi, 108, 137, 215, 217

Missouri, *75*, 108, 247
Mitsubishi, 10, 41, 167
Mitsui, 50
mobile power stations, 130, 145
MoneyTree Report, 84
Montalto di Castro solar plant, 43
Montana, 82, 108
Montgomery County Clean Energy Buyers Group, 130
Moore's Law, 261
Morgan Stanley, 228
Morocco, 30
Morris, Jeff, 99
Morrissey, Michael, 74
Moser Baer, 45
Muller, Richard, 207
municipal solid waste (MSW), 188–90, 198
Musk, Elon, 230

nanotechnology, 100, 242–43
National Aeronautics and Space Administration (NASA), 212–13, 230
National Geographic, 183
National Highway Transportation Safety Agency, 77
National Institute of Standards and Technology, 262
National Renewable Energy Laboratory (NREL), 97, 108–9, 128–29
natural gas, 54, 76, 99, 224, 155, 175, 241, 244
    plants, 39, 155–56, 240, 241
    vehicles, 164–65, 171
    waste-to-resource, 186, 190
Natural Resources Defense Council (NRDC), 118, 149
NatureWorks, 103
Navistar, 80, 117
Nebraska, 108
Needham, Rick, 253
"negawatts," 156, 158, 232, 242
Nelson, Donald, 209
Neo-Neon Holdings, *32*
Netscape Navigator, 211

net-zero buildings, 73–74, 129, 148, 175–76, 180–82, 184, 226–27, 264
Nevada, 67–69, *70*
Nevada Geothermal Power, 144
Nevada Wind, 144
New Belgium Brewery, 194
New Enterprise Associates, 149
New Flyer, 103
New Hampshire, *78*, *79*, *85*
New Jersey, 66–67, *68*, 80, 87, 109
New Mexico, 14, 59, *68*, *70*, *72*, *83*, *85*, 100–102
    companies, 101–2
Newsom, Gavin, 114
New York City, 21, 79, 95, 113, 115, 117–21, 126–28, 162
    Greener, Greater Buildings laws, 127
New York City Energy Efficiency Corporation (NYCEEC), 118–19, 127, 134
New York State, 5, 59, *79*, 82–83, 94–96, 110, 120, 144–45
    companies, 96
New York State Energy Research and Development Authority (NYSERDA), 94, 145
New Zealand, 30
Nigeria, 205
Nike, 221, 233
Nissan, 173
    LEAF, 10, 48, 77, 79–80, 162, 167
Nixon, Richard, 258
Norcross, Georgia, 138, 155
Nordex, 134
North Carolina, 73
North Dakota, 5, 13, 60, 63, *79*, 108, 237
Northern Power Systems, 107
Novacem, 194
Novomer, 194
NRG Energy, 139
Nth Power, 37, 231–32
nuclear power, 5, 6, 10, 34, 37–42, 46–48, 56, 108, 213, 232, 238, 240–42, 248
    subsidies, 257, 259–60
NUMMI plant, 210

Obama, Barack, 20, 37, 64, 77, 163, 171, 201, 207, 213, 222, 227
Office of Energy Efficiency and Renewable Energy (DOE), 97
Office of War Mobilization, 209
Ohio, 82, 143, 248
oil and gas industry, 7, 12, 48, 54, 53, 76, 81, 162, 163, 164, 204–5, 207, 213, 216–17, 223, 237, 264
  investment tools for, 253–54
  subsidies, 257–60
oil crises of 1970s, 162, 234, 253
Oklahoma, 75, 79
Oklahoma Corporation Commission, 223
Oklahoma Gas & Electric, 75
Old Model Isn't Working, The, 157
Oncor, 139
One Block Off the Grid, 67
O'Neill, Tip, 217
on-site energy systems, 153, 156–60, 176, 180–82, 184
Ontario, Canada, 50–51
Open Architecture Network, 18
open-source standards, 260–63
Opower, 149–50, 161
OptiSolar, 28
Optiwind, 105
Orbital Traction, 132
ORC International, 214, 259–60
Oregon, 29, 35, 59, 63, 70, 72, 75, 78–80, 82, 83, 85, 89–93, 106, 110, 120, 139–41, 153, 243, 252
  companies, 91–93
Organization for Economic Coopera-tion and Development (OECD), 241, 256–57
Ormat Industries, 144
Ormat Technologies, 144
Orteig Prize, 267, 269

Pacific Gas and Electric (PG&E), 149, 154, 229
Pacific Northwest National Labora-tory (DOE), 133
Pacific Railroad Act (1862), 208
Parsons Brinckerhoff, 127

Patent and Trademark Office (U.S.), 101
Payne, Doug, 261–62
PayPal, 230
PayScale, 128, 135, 140
peak demand, 155, 159, 179
Pennsylvania, 71, 75, 82, 133, 153
Perot, H. Ross, 229
Perry, Rick, 62–63
Petrobras, 49–50
Pew Charitable Trusts, 36, 225–26, 266
Pfund, Nancy, 259
Philadelphia, 115
Philippines, 30
Philips, Warner, 179–80
Philips Lighting North America, 268
Phillips Petroleum, 223
Phoenix, 243
Pike Research, 190
PlaNYC initiative, 118, 127
Plenus, 220
Plug-In Hybrid & Electric Vehicle Research Center (UC-Davis), 141
politics, 16–17, 21, 39–42, 115–16, 201–2, 206, 213–17, 236, 245, 251
pollution, 33, 123, 162–63, 189–90
polysilicon feedstock, 204
population growth, 45, 113, 116, 183
Porter, Michael, 8, 116
Portland, Oregon, 21, 89, 90–91, 120, 132, 136, 139–41, 190
Portland General Electric, 89
Portugal, 6, 30, 44, 133
power-conversion equipment, 107
power outages, 150–51
power purchase agreements (PPAs), 36, 156–57
Powers, Jonathan, 266
Power Trip (Little), 95
Premium Power, 93
Price-Anderson Act, 260
prizes, 267–71
Procter & Gamble, 220, 221
production tax credit (PTC), 64–65
Project Plug-IN, 143
Propel Fuels, 137
Proton OnSite, 104

Prudential Securities, 119
Public Citizen, 258
public-private partnerships, 125, 251–52, 266
Puralytics, 91
PurposeEnergy, 186–87, 199

Quicksoft Development, 228

Radiant Store, 145
Radio Corporation of America, 210–11
railroads
  high-speed, 33–34, 221
  transcontinental, 208–9
Ram Power, 144
Rancho Seco nuclear plant, 142
Ranken, Tom, 137
Reagan, Ronald, 258, 270
real estate investment trusts (REITs), 253–56
REC Solar, 91
Recurrent Energy, 28
Recyclebank, 96
recycling, 26, 96, 117, 187, 190, 197
refrigerators, 177, 267–68
Regional Greenhouse Gas Initiative (RGGI), 94, 223
regions, 12, 55, 59, 99, 243–44, 247–48
regulations, 49, 85, 87, 95, 99, 137, 150, 157–59, 162, 234
Reicher, Dan, 244, 272
RelayRides, 18
Reliant Energy, 133
ReliOn, 145
Renault, 171
Rendell, Ed, 249
Renewable Energy Finance Forum
  China (2006), 11
  Wall Street (2011), 54–55
renewable energy. See also specific types
  federal incentives and, 64–65
  large-scale, 241
  MLPs and REITs for, 253–46
  risk analysis, 99, 137
  sector taxonomy, 26
  subsidies, 257, 259–60

renewable fuels sector taxonomy, 26. See also specific types
renewable portfolio standard (RPS), 47
  California, 88, 142, 246
  cities and, 130
  Colorado, 53–54, 247
  Minnesota, 103
  Missouri, 247
  national proposed, 246–48
  New Jersey, 67
  New Mexico, 101
  New York, 94
  Ohio, 248
  states and, 55, 238
  Texas, 247
  Washington, 247
Renewables Obligation (RO), 47
Reno, Nevada, 121, 144
Report Card for America's Infastructure (2009), 249
Republican Party, 201, 205, 213–15, 235, 247, 251
research and development (R&D), 2, 24, 83, 131
  China, 12, 35
  cities and, 113, 124–25, 128, 134–37, 140, 144–45
  federal funding, 201–13
  prizes, 267–71
  states and, 93, 95–97, 101, 174
  utilities and, 154, 157
retrofitting, 112–13, 118–19, 124, 126–28, 134, 141, 148, 177–78, 183
Rice Alliance for Technology and Entrepreneurship, 133
Richmond Tank Depot, 210
Rimac, Mate, 167
Riman, Richard, 193
Ritter, Bill, 53–55, 129
RockPort Capital Partners, 138, 270
Rocky Mountain Institute, 109, 232–33, 262
Roland Berger, 77
Roosevelt, Franklin D., 209, 210
Rosenfeld, Art, 233–34
Rosie the Riveter National Historical Park, 174, 210

Royal Philips Electronics, 179, 185
Russia, 195
Rutan, Burt, 269

S&P Global 500, 16
Sacramento, *120*, 141–42
Sacramento Municipal Utility District (SMUD), 142
SAGE Electrochromics, 48, 103
Saint-Gobain, 48
Salzman, Alan, 10
Sam's Club, 7
Samsung, 4, 50–51, 168
Sanders, Jerry, 131
Sand Hill Road, Menlo Park, 85, 122
Sandia National Laboratory, 101
San Diego, 84, 113, *120*, 124, 130–32, 151
San Diego Gas & Electric, 131
San Diego Zoo, 131
San Francisco Bay Area, 13, 59, 84, 117, 120–23, 135, 169, 174, 190, 197, 223, 228, 243
San Onofre nuclear plant, 151
Sanyo, 41, 91, 140, 168
Sapphire Energy, 131, 194, 199, 218
SAP, 228
Saratoga Technology + Energy Park, 145
scaling, 237–39, 244
Schneider Electric, 48, 154
Schott Solar, 38
Schwab, Klaus, 228
Schwarzenegger, Arnold, 66, 88
Scotland, 202
Scullin, Matt, 196
Seattle, 79, 99–100, 111–12, *120*, 132, 136–37
Seattle City Light, 137
Segetis, 104
Seip, Norman, 264
SEMATECH, 261
semiconductors 17, 29, 122, 196, 261
SERA Architects, 140
Serious Energy, 128, 178, 186
Seven-Point Action Plan, 21–22, 206, 210, 222, 235–36, 245–73

energy subsidies phase-outs, 256–60
innovation prizes, 267–71
investment tools, 252–56
military energy and water security, 263–67
national renewable electricity standard, 246–48
national smart infrastructure bank, 248–52
open-source standards, 260–64
Shanghai Automotive Industry Corporation, 80, 168, 173
Sharp, 28, 40–42, 44
Shell, 7
Shepherds Flat Wind Farm, 63, 90, 252
Showa Shell Sekiyu, 42, 239
Shultz, George P., 205, 216, 224, 258
Siemens, 4, 237, 239
Sierra Club, 190
silicon, 102, 196
Silicon Valley, 84, 117, 122, 230–31
Silver Lake Kraftwerk, 203
Silver Spring Networks, 17, 89, 161, 229
Sinclair, Cameron, 18
Singapore, 30
Six "C's," 11–20, 116
Sizing the Clean Economy (Brookings/Battelle), 123, 127–28
Skelly, Michael, 133
SkyBuilt Power, 130
Skylights, 180
Skype, 18
small tech, 242–43
Smart Energy Platform, 229
SmartGridCity project, 75–76
Smart Grid News, 155
smart grids, 4, 17–19, 22, *32*, 36, 84, 98, 148–61, 240–42, 248
  China, 151–52
  cities and, 122, 128, 131, 134–35, 137
  companies, 17, 89, 160–61
  defined, 74
  France, 48
  Italy, 44
  states and, 71, 74–76, 100, 145, 153
  taxonomy of, *26*

smart infrastructure bank, 210, 248–52

smart infrastructure bonds, 252

smart meters, 28, 44, 74–75, 90, 100, 124, 145, 153–55, 159

SmartSynch, 231

SMA Solar Technology, 97

Smith, Scott, 249

Smith Electric Vehicles, 108, 168

Society of Automotive Engineers, 261

SoCore Energy, 134

solar cells, 21, 33, 44, 50, 125, 138

solar cities, 23

SolarCity, 6, 10, 36, 139, 156, 158, 161, 181, 230, 252, 266

solar energy, 3, 5–6, 22, 36
    China, 12, 23, 30, 31–32, 33, 181, 201, 204, 238
    cities and, 114, 117, 122, 124–31, 134–35, 138–41, 143
    companies, 13, 54
    costs, 9–10, 67–68, 156–58, 180–81, 201–2, 255
    deployment, 36, 38
    federal RPS targets and, 247–48
    Germany, 22, 38, 39
    green building, 74, 174, 180–82
    ground-mounted, 227
    growth of, 238
    India, 45, 202
    IP, 28
    Italy, 27, 42–44, 47, 65
    Japan, 27–28, 40–42, 239
    jobs, 32
    leasing, 10, 181
    military, 206, 227, 265–66
    on-site, 156–57
    passive, 180
    rooftop, 43, 45, 47, 67, 124, 127, 131, 134, 139, 158, 180, 184, 219, 243, 252
    South Korea, 50
    Spain, 41, 47
    states and, 21, 54, 55, 60, 61, 65–69, 87–88, 90–93, 100–102, 105, 107, 109, 122, 143–44, 181
    time required for, 244

trade associations, 130

UK, 47, 202

utility-scale, 10, 114, 124, 237, 252

Solar Energy Industries Association (SEIA), 36, 66, 100, 204

Solar Frontier, 42, 239

solar inverters, 97

solar manufacturing, 27, 30, 40–41, 44, 90–92, 97, 102, 108, 137, 239, 140, 143, 243

solar photovoltaics (PV), 3, 4, 9–13, 17, 23, 25, 27–28, 36, 39–48, 54, 65–69, 74, 87–93, 102, 105, 117, 122, 124, 127, 129, 134, 137, 140, 143, 201, 204, 210, 231, 239, 242–44
    array, 16, 43, 47
    building-integrated, 180–81, 184, 243
    costs, 156, 159, 238–39
    distributed, 158
    green building, 175–76, 180, 184
    military, 266
    open-source standards, 262
    patents, 101
    portable arrays, 264
    thin-film, 28, 42, 84, 97–98, 129, 143, 239

solar power purchase agreements (PPAs), 156–57

solar renewable energy certificates (SRECs), 67

solar shingles, 219

SolarStrong, 266

SolarTech, 261, 262

"Solar 3.0," 262

solar water heaters, 24, 41, 127, 145, 181

SolarWorld, 13, 38, 90, 92, 140

Solidia Technologies, 193–94, 200

Solix Biofuels, 194, 200

Solo, Pam, 214

SolSource, 53

Solyndra, 123, 144, 201, 213–14, 231, 238

South Africa, 30

South Carolina, 13–14, 75, 137

South Dakota, 108

Southern California Edison (SCE), 63, 124
South Korea, 11, 30, 35, 50–51, 80, 151, 168, 243, 245
Soviet Union, 211
SpaceX, 230
Spain, 6, 27, 30, 41, 44, 47, 151, 153
Spokane, Washington, 121, 145
Spring Networks, 154
Standard Chartered Bank, 201
standards, 260–63
Stanford University, 18, 225, 244, 258
State Clean Energy Leadership Index, 20–21, 54, 56–59, 86, 108, 121, 125, 139
State Department, 205–6
State of the States: Fuel Cells in America, 105
states, 12, 53–110, 215–16, 222–23. *See also specific states*
   benchmarks, 56–59
   city leaders, 120–21
   financial capital, 36, 83–85
   green banks, 222
   human and intellectual capital, 81–83
   incentives, 80
   infrastructure banks, 251
   lagging, 107–9
   leading, 20–21, 35, 53–107, 109–10
   Policy Checklist, 85, 275–76
   RPS, 53–55, 67, 88, 94, 101, 103, 142, 246–48
   smart grids, 153
   tax credits, 252
Steiner, David, 191
Steyer, Tom, 216, 224–25
Steyer-Taylor Center for Energy Policy and Finance, 225, 244
stimulus funds, 11, 74, 143. *See also* American Recovery and Reinvestment Act
   China, 151
   South Korea, 50
Stion, 108
STMicroelectronics, 44
STR Holdings, 105

SunEdison, 181
Sungevity, 6, 36, 156
Suniva, 138
Sun Microsystems, 230–31
SunPower, 43, 48, 66–67, 89, 136, 174, 238
SunRay Renewable, 43
SunRun, 6, 36, 156, 181
Sunshine Program (Japan), 40
Suntech Power, 23, 24
Super Bowl, 152–53
Super Efficient Refrigerator Program, 267–68
Superfund sites, 218
Suzlon company, 45, 134
Sweden, 46, 153
Switzerland, 28, 38, 44, 155, 240, 248
Sybase, 223
SynapSense, 142
Synthetic Genomics, 131, 220–21
synthetic oil, 191
Syntroleum, 192

Taiwan, 30
Tango EV, 145
Targeted Growth, 137
targets, 87–88, 118, 142
Tata, 45
taxes, 49, 64–65, 90, 108, 117, 170, 207, 253–56
Taxpayers for Common Sense, 258
Taylor, Kat, 225
Teachers Insurance and Annuity Association–College Retirement Equities Fund (TIAA-CREF), 254
TechBridge, 126
Technology Partners, 236
Technology Review 50 Most Innovative Companies, 194
telecommunications, 154
Telvent, 48
Tendril, 17, 98
Tennessee, 79, 80, 167, 243
ten-year plans, 49
Terra-Gen Power, 144
Tesla Motors, 10, 29, 76, 80, 89, 168, 173, 210, 230

Texas, 14, 59, 62–63, *75*, 79–83, 102, 109, 121, 132–39, 215, 247, 255
Thanet Offshore Wind Farm, 46
thermoelectricity, 195–96, 198
1366 Technologies, 29, 93, 125
3Sun joint venture, 44
3TIER, 99, 137
Time, 230
Tioga Energy, 231
Toledo, Ohio, 121, 142–43, 210, 243
TomKat Center for Sustainable Energy, 225
TopManage, 228
TopTier Software Solutions, 228
Total oil company, 43, 48, 89
toxins, 189, 218
Toyota, 40, 80, 124, 174, 210, 237
  Prius, 6, 40, 77–78, 162, 165–66, 238, 244
TPG Biotech, 195
tradable-renewable-energy certificates, 45
trade deficit, 164, 204
transmission lines, 133, 139, 152–54, 157, 254
Transportation Department (DOT), 249
Treasury Department, 208
Trilliant, 84
Trina Solar, *32*
Tri-State Biodiesel (TSB), 191–92, 200
Turkey, 30, 41
Twin Creeks Technologies, 108
Twitter, 84, 244
TXU Energy, 139
Tyson Foods, 192

UBS, 228
Underwriters Laboratories, 262
Union of Concerned Scientists, 71
United Arab Emirates, 30
United Kingdom (UK), 29, 33, 35, 46–47, 149, 153, 176, 202, 245
  Department of Energy and Climate Change, 202
  Non-Fossil Fuel Obligation (NFFO), 46–47

United Nations
  international climate talks, 15, 17
  Intergovernmental Panel on Climate Change (IPCC), 189, 206
  World Intellectual Property Organization, 35
United States Advanced Battery Consortium, 168
U.S. Air Force, 263
U.S. Army, 130, 143, 244, 264, 266
U.S. Chamber of Commerce, 251
U.S. Coast Guard, 264
U.S. Conference of Mayors, 114
  Climate Protection Agreement, 115
U.S. Congress, 15, 129–30, 133, 201, 209, 213–14, 222, 253, 255, 259, 264, 267
U.S. Green Building Council (USGBC), 72, 176
U.S. Marine Corps, 205, 206, 227, 264
  Expeditionary Energy Strategy, 265
U.S. military, 205, 210–12, 226–27, 263–67
U.S. Navy, 192–93, 206, 210–11, 226–27, 264
University Center of Excellence for Photovoltaics (Georgia Tech), 138
University of California
  Berkeley, 196, 207
  Davis, 141, 142
  Los Angeles, 124
urbanization, 113–16
Utah, 14, 70, 211
UTC Power, 104, 106
utilities, 7, 19, 252. *See also* specific plants and plant types
  cities and, 95, 124, 139
  EVs and, 169
  green financing, 14, 94, 141
  investor-owned (IOUs), 88, 246
  management, 229
  municipal, 117, 123, 135, 137, 142
  national standards, 246–48
  smart grids and, 149–50 (*see also* smart grids)

states and, 66, 68–69, 89–90, 93, 99–100, 103, 106, 142
UK and, 47
utility-scale renewables
solar, 66, 68–69, 100, 124, 142, 237, 252
wind, 90, 237, 239

Vachon, Mark, 208, 270
Vaitheeswaran, Vijay, 81
VantagePoint Capital Partners, 10
Vattenfall, 46
vehicle-to-grid (V2G) services, 160
Venezuela, 13, 205
Venter, J. Craig, 131, 220–21
venture capital, 4, 5, 10–11, 27, 35, 37, 59, 83–86, 92, 97, 122, 130, 138, 149, 166, 228, 230–32, 236, 238
Ventyx, 28
Veolia Environnement, 48
Vermont, 59, 68, 72, 78, 79, 82, 83, 85, 93, 106–7
companies, 107
Vestas Wind Systems, 32, 35, 46, 91, 92, 97, 129, 140, 239
Vietnam, 14
Villaraigosa, Antonio, 123
Virginia, 13, 72, 73, 78, 85
Volkswagen, 171

Walgreens, 134
Wall Street Journal, 249
Top 10 Clean-Tech Companies, 131
Walmart, 7, 13, 16, 114
Walney Wind Farm, 46
Walt Whitman Bridge, 67
war bonds, 209
Waring, Jim, 132
Warner, Cynthia "C.J.," 218
Warner, John, 205
Warner-Lieberman bill, 213
War Production Board, 209
Washington, D.C., 79–80, 120, 121, 129–30
Washington Clean Technology Alliance, 137

Washington State, 59, 71–72, 78, 79, 80, 85, 99, 120, 136–37, 145–46, 247
companies, 99–100
Washington STEM, 112
Washington Suburban Sanitary Commission, 130
Waste Fired Power Plant (Amsterdam), 188
waste management and recovery, 26, 48, 137, 148, 186–200. See also composting; recycling
companies, 199–200
heat, 187–88, 195–98
waste-to-energy, 144, 188–91, 198, 247
water, 130, 190, 195–98
water, 17, 25, 33, 106, 130, 190, 195–98
cities and, 127–28, 130, 135, 138
companies, 48
filtration and delivery, 3, 25, 26, 91, 197, 242, 249, 252
green building and, 175
infrastructure, 248–49
recovery and capture, 26, 130, 175, 190, 195–98
smart meters and, 26, 155
security, 263–67
taxonomy, 26
water heaters, 24, 41, 127, 145, 177, 181, 195
WaterSaver Technologies, 196–97, 200
Watkins, Bill, 2
Waxman-Markey bill (2009), 222
Weatherization Assistance Program (WAP), 177–78
Weller, Lou, 255
West Coast Green Highway, 99
Weyerhaeuser, 137
What Would Jefferson Do? (Pfund and Healey), 258–59
Wheal Jane Solar Park (UK), 47
Wheelock, Clint, 190
Whole Foods, 133
Who's Winning the Clean Energy Race?, 36
Who's Your City? (Florida), 81–82

Wilson, Pete, 87–88
wind energy (turbines), 3–5, 24, 28, 30–34, 50, 85, 94, 97, 99, 102, 105, 107, 129–30, 134, 140
  Brazil, 49, 50
  China, 12, 24, 30, 32–34
  cities and, 128–30, 133–34, 139–40
  cost of, 10, 255
  Europe, 6
  federal incentives, 64–65, 97
  federal RPS, 247, 248
  FITs, 38
  garage-mounted, 74
  Germany, 38, 201
  global leaders, 27
  global market, 238
  green building, 181
  growth of, 238–39
  Italy, 43–44
  Japan, 41
  jobs, 32
  military, 206
  offshore, 39, 46, 64, 202, 239
  patents, 83
  small-scale, 144, 156, 181
  South Korea, 50
  Spain, 27
  states and, 54, 55, 60–65, 90–92, 94, 97, 101–2, 105, 107–9, 121, 129, 144, 215–16, 238, 247, 255
  targets, 247
  trade associations, 130
  utility scale, 237
wind farms, 24, 36, 133, 144
windows, 28, 48, 102, 103, 128, 176–78, 180, 184
Windpower convention, 224
Windspire energy, 144
Wired, 167

Wisconsin, 14, 59, 73, 75, 75, 153
wood waste, 137
Woolsey, James, 205
Worcester Polytechnic Institute, 126
World Bank, 33, 256, 257
Worldchanging network, 18
World Economic Forum, 228, 249
World Health Organization, 33
World on the Edge (Brown), 69
World War II, 21, 174, 209–10
World Wide Web consortium, 261
World Wildlife Fund, 203
WSJ Magazine, 230
Wuxi, China (solar city), 23
Wynn, Will, 135
Wyoming, 70, 83, 108

Xcel Energy, 53, 75–76, 103
X Prizes, 269, 270
Xtreme Power, 136
Xunlight, 143

Yale Environment 360, 167
Yang Jiechi, 113
Yeh, David, 27
Yingli Green Energy, 32
YouTube, 233

ZeaChem, 219–20
zero emissions, 244, 247
zero-energy buildings (ZEBs), 175, 182. See also negawatt; net-zero buildings
Zilkha, Selim, 133
Zilkha Renewable Energy, 133
Zoi, Cathy, 203
ZOOM (Carson and Vaitheeswaran), 81
Zpryme, 151–52

ABOUT THE AUTHORS

Ron Pernick is cofounder and managing director of Clean Edge, a leading clean-tech research and advisory firm, and co-author of two books on clean-tech trends, investment opportunities, and innovation. Pernick has worked actively within three major technology waves: telecommunications, the Internet, and clean technology. At Clean Edge he has coauthored more than two dozen reports on clean technologies, coproduces the annual Clean-Tech Investor Summit, manages the company's stock and leadership index products and services, and consults to governments, corporations, investors, and entrepreneurs. Pernick is widely cited in the media, lectures at industry events in the U.S. and abroad, and has taught MBA-level courses at New College and Portland State University. He lives with his wife and two children in Portland, Oregon.

Clint Wilder is senior editor at Clean Edge and has covered the high-tech and clean-tech industries as a business journalist since 1985. At Clean Edge for the past ten years, he has coauthored reports on clean energy trends and regional economic development, and is a regular contributor of the web site's CE Views columns on a range of topics. Wilder is coauthor of two books with Ron Pernick and has been a facilitator in the energy and climate change track of the Clinton Global Initiative. He is a frequent speaker at clean energy and green business events in the U.S. and overseas, and a regular blogger for the Huffington Post. As editor-at-large and columnist for *Information Week*, he won the 2002 American Society of Business Publication Editors gold award for best feature series. He lives with his wife in Sausalito, California.